Church and Stage

Church and Stage

*The Theatre as Target of
Religious Condemnation in
Nineteenth Century America*

CLAUDIA DURST JOHNSON

McFarland & Company, Inc., Publishers
Jefferson, North Carolina, and London

The groundwork for parts of the present study appeared in *American Actress: Perspective on the Nineteenth Century* (Nelson Hall, 1984), and articles in *Theatre Survey* (1980 and 1985); *Nineteenth Century Theatre Research* (1985); and *American Quarterly* (1976).

Unless otherwise stated all photographs are courtesy of the Library of Congress.

LIBRARY OF CONGRESS CATALOGUING-IN-PUBLICATION DATA

Johnson, Claudia D.
    Church and stage : the theatre as target of religious condemnation in nineteenth century America / Claudia Durst Johnson.
    p.   cm.
    Includes bibliographical references and index.

    ISBN-13: 978-0-7864-3080-2
    softcover : 50# alkaline paper ∞

    1. Theater — Moral and ethical aspects — United States. 2. Theater — Religious aspects — Christianity. 3. Theater — United States — History — 19th century. I. Title.
PN2049.J57   2008
792.0973'09034 — dc22   2007044158

British Library cataloguing data are available

©2008 Claudia Durst Johnson. All rights reserved

No part of this book may be reproduced or transmitted in any form or by any means, electronic or mechanical, including photocopying or recording, or by any information storage and retrieval system, without permission in writing from the publisher.

On the cover: Boston's Tremont Temple; Henry Ward Beecher, the most powerful minister in the nineteenth-century (both courtesy Library of Congress); background Sky ©2007 PhotoSpin

Manufactured in the United States of America

McFarland & Company, Inc., Publishers
  Box 611, Jefferson, North Carolina 28640
    www.mcfarlandpub.com

Table of Contents

Introduction — Church and Stage: The Two Temples	1
1. The English and Early American Beginnings	9
2. The Power and Values of the Church	28
3. Plays, Playgoers, and Actors	38
4. The Impact of Clerical Attacks on Actors and the Profession	49
5. The Church and the Actress	66
6. Trading Religious Approval for Work	77
7. Wearing the Pants, Making the Choices, Writing the Plays	92
8. Children in Industry: Children on Stage	103
9. Prostitutes and the Bar	120
10. Violence in the Audience, Irreverence on the Stage	135
11. The Winding Down of an Old War	159
Appendix 1: Cornelius Logan's Defense of the Stage	175
Appendix 2: Cincinnati Daily Enquirer *on the Third Tier*	182
Appendix 3: Mark Twain on the Reverend Sabine	185
Chapter Notes	187
Bibliography	199
Index	213

Introduction — Church and Stage: The Two Temples

One fine day in 1843, in the cradle of American Puritanism, clerical jubilation overflowed, as no less a luminary than the Reverend Henry Ward Beecher came up from Brooklyn to Boston to join in the dedication of that city's Tremont Temple. As the Reverend Beecher made clear, it was a moment of sheer typology, marking God's triumph over the devil himself, for the building, now being dedicated to the glory of God, had for sixteen years been the Tremont Theatre, one of Boston's most prominent theatres, drawing stars of the magnitude of Tyrone Power and Junius Brutus Booth, who was also its manager for a time. Now the building was in the hands of the Reverend Mr. Colver's Baptist Society. The charismatic Beecher was the ideal choice for the occasion, not only because he was, indisputably, the most prominent minister of his day but also because he was well-known for his fiery sermons and books against the theatre. As the conversion of the building began, Beecher led the devout participants in considering the similarities between church and theatre architecture and the theatre's inversion of the church's mission.

Physically the theatre was a parody and a mirror image of the church. If one found himself mysteriously plunked down inside a structure with aisles and seats facing forward, toward an elevated structure from which a man orated, he might have to take a second to figure out whether he was in a theatre or a church. Above the congregation was the church's choir loft, roughly paralleling the theatre's notorious galleries or balconies. The seats faced a raised structure, which had been the theatre's stage, but was now the church's pulpit and altar. Both were designed for performance. Behind

In the dedication of Boston's Tremont Temple, which had once been a theatre, the theatrical professional was excoriated by Henry Ward Beecher, enraging actors and heightening the animosity between church and stage.

Introduction

the church altar lay the holy sacristy or baptismal font. Behind the stage lay what were regarded as its scandalous features: dressing rooms and green rooms where actors and actresses mingled in careless proximity. A building could be a theatre one week and a church the next—and vice versa. Many theatres, like the Tremont in Boston, were converted into churches, and many churches were converted into theatres, for example, a Baptist Church in Washington, D.C., became Ford's Theatre, where President Lincoln was shot. Solomon Smith recalls such a conversion in Albany, New York.

> These were the last days of the Old Albany theatre previous to its being converted into a church, in which capacity it served for over thirty years; but I am happy to learn that it has recently resumed its theatrical character, and is now open as a temple of the Drama.[1]

For centuries, the clergy pointed to the theatre as the devil's sanctuary, an inversion of the house of God. The gallery was an "unholy *choir*." Its votaries were invariably called "the gallery *gods*." Actors were *ministers* of the devil. Herman Melville made the comparison in "The Two Temples." In Melville's tale, the narrator is barred from entering New York City's Grace Cathedral because he hasn't paid for a pew and looks disreputable, so he is forced to sneak in by a side door. Eventually he is arrested for being there. But, later, standing outside a London theatre—a counter temple—without a penny to his name, he is given a free ticket and enjoys the more welcoming, bright atmosphere.[2]

Those who gathered on this occasion in Boston looked forward to the glorious moment when a church choir would replace the obscene gallery, a holy man rather than a debased actor would speak from the stage, hymns rather than lewd songs would rise to its magnificent ceiling, and the Bible would replace the promptbook. The Tremont *Temple*, still at the same location in 2006, has had a much longer run than the Tremont *Theatre*.

Tom Ford, a supernumerary working in Boston theatres at the time, described the moment of conversion:

> Dr. Beecher *dedicated* the house, after its transformation from its original and legitimate purpose, to what? The eminent divine declared that the devil had been driven out of Boston, when the Tremont was closed.[3]

Beecher's tirade against the theatrical profession became a rallying point for actors, many of whom, throughout the country, wrote letters to

Introduction

their newspaper editors, objecting to Beecher's position and bitterly contrasting Beecher's and the public's view of clergymen with those of actors. One such letter by comedian Cornelius A. Logan is provided in Appendix One.

Throughout the nineteenth century, there were other clashes between church and stage. Prominent among them were two symbolic episodes occurring in 1854 and 1871. The first was the decision of Mrs. Mary Ann Duff, the first tragedienne of the American stage, to bury her identity as an actress so that her church would accept her. The second was the refusal of the Reverend W. T. Sabine to bury comedian George Holland from the church at which Sabine officiated. Each of the many episodes illuminates the theatre's inversion of traditions, customs, attitudes, and values which the most powerful institution in America had adamantly insisted upon from the time of the country's founding by Puritans right up to the church's partnership with the barons of industry in the nineteenth century.

The present approach, like those taken by many recent theatre histories, is a departure from the distinguished tradition of twentieth-century theatrical commentary. Up to the 1970s, the strength of the grand scholars, who shaped theatre history, was their preservation of stories of prominent actors and accounts of major theatrical events. But the tendency was to dismiss the ill repute in which the stage was held and to ignore the theatre's less savory aspects. Something was wanting, a reality that lay beyond and beneath the well-acted drama and the lives of popular performers. What was missing was a truth that could only be discerned by examining the theatre in greater detail, placing it in the context of the larger society of which it was a part. As Oscar G. Brockett writes, most theatre histories

Henry Ward Beecher, indisputably the most powerful minister in nineteenth-century America, with a gift, it was said, to reflect majority sentiment, was the pivotal figure in the Protestant Church's war on the stage.

Introduction

before the 1970s "did not connect their findings with what was going on elsewhere, with events before or after the time period being studied, or with the cultural forces within which the theatre existed."[4] The slowness with which the complete history began to emerge even suggested a degree of resistance to a picture that was often neither elegant nor beautiful, neither admirable nor felicitous.

The exception in this pre–1970s period was David Grimsted's 1968 *Melodrama Unveiled: American Theatre and Culture, 1800–1850*.[5] Grimsted adopted a broad approach, one in which drama was regarded (in the words of Joseph R. Roach) as "an autonomous category, transcending the sublunary sphere of power relations and ideologies."[6] Another of the earliest theatre historians to break from tradition was Benjamin McArthur in *Actors and American Culture, 1880–1920*, published in 1984. In his introduction, McArthur identifies three areas that had been slighted in histories: theatre structure, the occupational history of actors, and changes that shaped actor's social roles.[7] Other outstanding volumes of theatre history, theoretical and revolutionary in their placing of drama and the stage within a sociopolitical context, especially with regard to class and gender, include Bruce McConachie and Daniel Friedman, editors of *Theatre for Working-Class Audiences in the United Stages, 1830–1980*; McConachie and Thomas Postlewait, *Interpreting the Theatrical Past*; Bruce McConachie, *Melodramatic Formations*; Ron Engle and Tice L. Miller, editors of *The American Stage: Social and Economic Issues from the Colonial Period to the Present*; and Rosemary Bank, *Theatre Culture in America, 1825–1860*.

Histories in recent decades have acknowledged the darker side of the theatre, including the church's and the religious public's animosity toward the stage. But few have acknowledged the profound effect of the church's view of the stage. This volume focuses on the theatre's struggle within the complex contexts of theological, social, and economic ideas in the nineteenth century in an attempt to recognize the immense cultural significance of the church's war on the stage to those artists and members of the public who were impacted by it. A few important voices have been raised in the last twenty-five years to rectify this omission, beginning with Jonas Barish's in his 1981 *The Antitheatrical Prejudice*, in which he develops the philosophical basis for the bias against the theatre, notably as it is embedded in French literature and such classics as Jane Austen's *Mansfield Park*, William Thackerey's *Vanity Fair*, and Herman Melville's *Confidence Man* and "The Two Temples."

The church considered three terms in laying out their objections:

Introduction

drama meaning the literary work, the play; *the stage*, meaning the particulars and participants engaged in production; and *theatre*, which usually embraced all elements of drama, production, and audience. Still, stage and theatre were usually used interchangeably. While the following study touches on all three terms, its primary focus is on the actors, actresses, managers, and their audiences. It examines the dynamics that occur in the collision and interplay of two vastly different cultures, the ways in which the dominant religious world impacted the marginalized theatre world and the theatrical practices that fueled the church's attacks on the theatre.

The church promulgated the Victorian values of concealment, control, serenity, order, discipline and quiet acceptance, qualities that shaped personal life. These same values were demanded by the church, and the big business it supported, to keep workers acquiescently in their places. By its very nature, the stage was usually a repudiation of Victorian values. It was open, emotional, turbulent, uncontrolled, and unrefined. In its dismissal of social rank, it was recognized as a center of personal and political disruption.

In arguing that the collision of values engaged multiple aspects of American life, this study brings into the discussion such topics as the Protestant Ethic in the nineteenth century, the religious view of women and woman's place, the work of poor women, the work of children, the temperance movement, and the class struggle. Chapter 1 focuses on the history of the English theatre, especially the theology and class attitudes behind attacks on the stage in the late sixteenth and early seventeenth centuries in England, and the beginnings of drama in Puritan New England, in the light of Calvinist dogma, which shaped America's suspicion of the stage in the nineteenth century. Chapter 2 establishes the serious impact the church had on theatre by illustrating the clergy's power over nineteenth-century society—the standing of the clerics who were most critical of the stage—and the values that this powerful entity disseminated, values so incompatible with the stage. Chapter 3 lays down the particular religious arguments against plays, those who found employment in the theatre, and finally, the playgoing public. It concludes with the argument that these views of the Protestant Church in the nineteenth century had considerable impact on the theatre and the public, by showing the power of the church and the central roles held by the clergy who were most critical of the stage.

Chapter 4, using the words of managers and actors, illustrates just how deeply felt the religious public's attacks on the stage were and how detrimental they were to the survival of the theatre.

Introduction

Chapter 5 contrasts the Ideal Victorian Woman, that centerpiece of Victorian society, and the actress, beginning the discussion with the religious beliefs about women preached from the nation's pulpits, views which led to the church's characterization of women on stage as a threat to innocent playgoers and to society as a whole. The Protestant Church and the big business it supported were convinced that a Christian civilization was held together only if its individuals remained in their proper places. The middle-class woman's place was in the home, while her poor sisters, having no homes, were hidden away in factories and toiled at other demeaning jobs. But the actress was condemned, as Chapter 6 shows, because she made her own living by appearing in public. Chapter 7 continues with woman's violation of church dictates in assuming the roles of breadwinner and manager, roles she could assume in no other profession.

Chapter 8 covers how the religious public's hypocrisy was illustrated in the work of Elbridge Gerry, who lacked the determination to change the abominable working conditions of children in factories, yet went to great lengths to keep children from making their livings on stage.

Chapter 9 gives attention to those portions of the theatre world which provided the church with its most convincing proof of the theatre's sinfulness—the presence there of prostitutes and a bar—which led the church to the conclusion that the stage could never be reformed. Chapter 10 examines another strong argument against the stage—the violence and irreverence that was bred there. Great numbers of playgoers were dissatisfied working-class men and women who found a political rallying place in the theatre and posed a danger to social order, acquiescence and respect. The concluding chapter focuses on two events that hastened a change in the church's acceptance of the theatre in the last decades of the nineteenth century: the assassination of Abraham Lincoln in a theatre and the refusal of an Episcopalian minister to bury an actor from his church.

The underside of Victorian life in the dramatic arena is presented here primarily from the pens of those involved in the struggle, that is, stage people themselves, the clergy, playgoers, and those who observed the scene around them. Taken together, these primary sources reflect a subjective reality of how theatrical folk were perceived by members of American society, how theatrical folk saw themselves, and how they thought they were seen by others in that quite different world outside the theatre.

Clerical bias presented a constant hurdle to the stage throughout the century. Despite the impediments thrown in its path, the theatre

Introduction

was popular in nineteenth-century America. There is no denying that many businessmen and even churchgoers frequented stage performances, but definitely without the blessing or knowledge of their pastors. And the notorious image of all things theatrical, fashioned largely by the church, weighed on the profession like an ever-worsening bad review.

1

The English and Early American Beginnings

Ordained by the Devil
— Phillip Stubbes

The overwhelmingly Protestant nineteenth-century church in the United States had its cultural roots in a form of radical Calvinism which taught that the theatre — plays, actors, and audiences — was ordained by the devil. The cultural ancestors of nineteenth-century Congregationalists, Methodists, Baptists, Quakers, and Presbyterian's were members of a group of Puritans, introduced to the New World in the early seventeenth-century, who successfully banned theatre from New England, in the same way that their brothers in the English Puritan Parliament had closed the theatres on September 2, 1642, and kept them closed for eighteen years. The early English history of the Protestant Church's hostility toward the theatre, culminating in the official closing of theatres, is a richly documented story.[1] Although the church in Victorian America offered its own objections specific to the times, the foundation of an antitheatrical posture on social and political grounds was determined largely by dissenting Calvinists during the Renaissance.

The continuum of antitheatrical enthusiasm is apparent in selections from three works representative of the sixteenth, seventeenth, and nineteenth centuries. It was a bias that did not seem to have lessened significantly with the passage of time. As Jonas Barish observes: "Whatever the reason, it is evident that for most antitheatrical polemicists, playgoing tends to rank abnormally high in the hierarchy of sins."[2] The first passage is taken from

Church and Stage

Philip Stubbes' *The Anatomy of Abuses* (1583), written at the beginning of stage activity in England, in which he draws on the ancients to castigate plays, performances, and audiences:

> Playes were ordained by the Devil, and consecrated to Heathen Gods, to draw us from Christianity to Idolatry and Gentilisem.... It was decreed that no Christian man or woman shoulde resorte to Playes and Enterludes, where is nothing but Blasphemy, Scurrility and Whoredome maintained....
>
> [N]o player should be admitted to the Table of the Lord.... Playes were invented by the devil, practized by the **Heathen Gentiles**, and dedicated to their false Idols....[3]

The second excerpt is American, from *A Testimony Against Prophane Customes* (1687), by Increase Mather, (father of Cotton Mather, the well-known facilitator of the Salem witch trials), writing in New England in the seventeenth century:

> Stage-Plays had their Original from those Devil-Gods whom the Gentiles Worshiped. The Infernal Spirits did expressly command that men should use such Recreations, which we may be sure they would never have done, were not such Pastimes displeasing to God and dangerous to the Souls of Men....
>
> Hence, *Ancients* call such Theaters, the Devils Temples, and Stage Plays, the Devils Lectures, And *the Actors in them*, the Devils chief Factors.[4]

The third selections are from *Lectures to Young Men* (1850) by Henry Ward Beecher, a man just as renowned and respected in his day as was his sister, Harriet Beecher Stowe. His stress is on the theatre's alliance with vice, both on- and offstage:

> It is notorious that the Theatre is the door to all the sinks of iniquity. Half the victims of the gallows and the Penitentiary will tell you, that these schools for morals were to them the gate of debauchery, the porch of pollution, the vestibule of the very house of death.[5]

The great irony in the relationship between the church and the stage is, of course, the frequency with which performance had religious origins. In Greece, although the early drama was sexual in nature, it was held to be sacred in that it was essential to festivals devoted to the Gods, especially Dionysius. Dramas were comprised of recitations, musical concerts, and eventually dithyrambs or choral hymns, performed within a circle, with an

1. The English and Early American Beginnings

altar at its center for sacrifices to the gods. Even as Thespis inaugurated the theatre, in 534 BCE, by having speakers emerge from the chorus to dramatize stories of the gods, the theatre retained its position as a sacred place. In due course, not just the lives of gods, but the lives of mythic heroes were dramatized, even as it retained its religious purpose of effecting a purgation of its audience, as Aristotle wrote.[6]

The classic criticism of the stage in Greece would more aptly be described as philosophical rather than religious, coming as it did from the pen of Plato in the fourth century. In Book Ten of *The Republic*, his was a practical argument against the theatre because it presented gods as unheroic and the underworld as so terrifying that it impeded the learning of little children. Moreover, drama, like poetry, was founded in illusion rather than reality and it appealed to emotions that were better suppressed than nurtured. Aristotle agreed that the theatre did arouse unacceptable emotions, but only to purge them, an idea that antitheatrical clerics in England and America found to have no validity.

While the Medieval stage had its beginnings in the church, to resurgent Protestants of the sixteenth through the nineteenth centuries, like Stubbes, Mather, and Beecher, it was the wrong church. There was no entity regarded as so treacherous by both high and low Protestants as the Roman Catholic Church. And the theatrical interludes and plays, with their singing and dancing and ornamental costumes, smacked of the mass in which the English theatre had its beginnings. The mass had gradually grown to include small operas, in which the choir enacted scenes associated with Jesus' resurrection. To this was added the story of the shepherds, the Magi, the slaughter of the innocents and, eventually, stories of the prophets. The important issue is that the stage came to be synonymous with Catholicism in the minds of Protestant clergy.[7]

And the other progenitor of the stage — in addition to Catholicism — was of no better repute: this was an unruly, outrageous, out-of-control paganism: Druidic rites, tinged with witchcraft and held under cover of night at Stonehenge and the wild, erotic celebrations around the phallic May pole, from which it was said no maiden emerged a maiden. Stephen Gossen wrote in his *Plays Confuted* (1583): "May-games, stage plays and such like ... were sucked from the devil's teat to nurse up idolatry."[8]

The commotion over Sabbatarianism highlights the clerical view (that would continue well into the nineteenth century) of the theatre as a rival, a threat, and an inversion of everything the church stood for. The religious argument was not so much that theatre desecrated the Sabbath, but that it rivaled the church. Philip Stubbes called the church God's Edifice and the theatre Satan's Synagogue. Gossen referred to actors as the dancing *chaplains* of Bacchus. Stages operating on Sunday mornings were devilish events luring folk away from church services. On such occasions, the actor undermined the preacher. Many unlicensed theatres, having been persuaded to refrain from performing on Sunday morning when church services were being held, were still free to conduct business as usual on Sunday afternoons. But, as far as the church was concerned, the problem remained, because in the afternoon, the stage undermined everything ministers tried to accomplish in the morning. A ban on all Sunday theatricals, passed in 1581, was never effectively enforced.

Whether theatres refrained from playing on Sunday or not, the question continued to be asked: What good could come of an entity that had the devil of Popishness for a father and a pagan witch for a mother? It was only to be expected that the offspring of such devils would be plays that romanticized subjects such as murder, cruelty, sexual misconduct, and revenge. Thomas Kidd's *The Spanish Tragedy* (written between 1584 and 1589) was not at all an exception but rather the model of revenge tragedies that dominated Renaissance and Jacobean drama and enraged reformed religious leaders. In Kidd's play, a casebook of lurid psychological quirks, there are eight murders and suicides on stage, including one public hanging and one dramatization of the biting out of a gentleman's tongue. The Puritans could hardly have been taken with William Shakespeare's *Pericles* (c. 1607), which included a scene in a brothel and has incest as its initiating circumstance. There is also Marlowe's *Doctor Faustus* (1587), in which the protagonist, a religious sceptic, sells his soul to the devil.

Such a monstrous child as the theatre naturally drew its priests from the ranks of devils and only the refuse of society worshipped at its shrine. Up until the end of the sixteenth century, before the church turned its attention to the criticism of dramatic literature as well, it was these priests — the actors — and those whom they instructed and attracted — the audiences — who most categorically unsettled religious zealots.

It was charged by religious reformers that plays were put to life on stage by the lowest, most despicable human beings in society: uneducated bumpkins in guilds who dirtied their hands with their labor, and vagabonds and thieves — little more than beggars — who were driven from place to place. Few could deny Anthony Munday's inventiveness in calling actors the "caterpillars of the commonwealth."[9] To make matters worse, these audacious rogues had the presumption — even with laws on the books reg-

1. The English and Early American Beginnings

ulating the attire of the lower classes—to parade around on stage in flowery, expensive finery, suitable only for the aristocracy. Nothing could be more repugnant, not to mention sacrilegious, than these coarse laborers and vagrants, whom God had placed in their proper lowly positions, taking it upon themselves to assume the characters of kings and noblemen on stage. Philip Stubbes, one of the prominent enemies of the stage, complained that costumes made it hard to tell a gentleman from (horror of horrors!) a commoner.

But it was the audience and others who held forth in the vicinity of theatres outside London who really alarmed religious reformers. Here they found bear-baiters, courtesans, dice and betting games of all sorts, pickpockets, rabble-rousers, and a low class of peddlers (who could provide dissatisfied members of the audience with fruit to fling at the actors). So much else was going on in the theatrical "yard" that much of the time scant attention was paid to the play in progress, or so the actors complained.

As the Protestant clergy's criticism of actors in noble roles might suggest, at the bottom of the unhappiness with the stage was, in addition to its violation of Holy Scripture, its contravention of a basic tenet of Calvinism that insisted on a religiously sanctioned rigid social hierarchy. The ultimate hypocrisy on the part of dissenters was that, up until the seventeenth century, most of them found the theatre perfectly acceptable if the plays were performed by court-supported groups in the city of London that existed to entertain the king, his courtiers, and others of high degree. It is true that the Common Council in 1574 insisted that all plays produced in the city of London receive a thorough going-over and be censored when necessary, and officially licensed, before they could be produced, but much that the church deplored found its way on stage anyway. Still, up until the last decades of the century, it was primarily the productions of the lower-class rabble outside the city of London that required reprimand.

The genuine terror for religious reformers was not so much that the audience was dissolute, but that it constituted a rowdy, disorderly mob, likely being schooled in subversion, even revolution, by the stage and its surroundings. Colin Rice, in his study of the church's war on the stage, appropriately titled *Ungodly Delights*, concludes that "the general theme of obedience to authority [meaning magistrates and churchmen] had always been fundamental to anti-theatrical complaint."[10] There was little in the screaming, milling horde surrounding the theatres that suggested order or obedience. The 1642 antitheatrical ordinance was actually issued at the end of a declaration against "unlawful tumults and insurrections."[11]

Church and Stage

The theatre was damned if it did and damned if it didn't in sixteenth- and seventeenth-century England. The clergy castigated it for the practice of casting boys in female roles. At the same time, the thought of the appearance of a woman on stage was also beyond the pale. And while some clergymen scolded the stage for failing to continue its role as a moral teacher—condemning through personification such qualities as sloth and greed—as it had in its home in the church, others went on about the theatre's having no business trying to be a moral teacher and taking the role away from clergymen. "They are not called of God to any such publike function, as to be teachers of religion…. They are forbidden to meddle with religion."[12]

More than that, clergymen complained that theatres presented a great inconvenience to the business community and men of means because the working classes were seduced by the stage, resulting in shiftlessness, job absenteeism, and even pilfering.

In the last half of the Renaissance, with London drama continuing to be sponsored and embraced by the Crown, the theatre began to turn publicly on its critics. The form was satire, and the targets were those dissenting reformers sometimes inaccurately labeled Puritans. Puritanism in England was a broad term, ranging from John Milton, (who enjoyed the theatre, advocated freedom of speech, and tolerated divorce), to the poor, wild-eyed evangelical. Stage versions naturally reverted to the sour killjoy, the stereotypical hypocrite. These scurrilous portrayals of Puritans in their dramas, of course, fueled the church's outrage. One of the first was William Shakespeare's *Twelfth Night* (c. 1600), in which a major character, Malvolio (a Puritan) is an obnoxious, laughable busy-body. During the festive holiday of twelfth night, when most of the characters are singing, joking, dancing, drinking, and feasting, Malvolio takes it upon himself to lecture and moralize, even threatening to call the police as a strategy (unsuccessful) to dampen the high spirits of the party. The revelers analyze him as a hypocritical egotist and social climber who adjusts his behavior according to how the wind blows. After he leaves, they vow revenge. Malvolio falls for their trick, believing that the Countess Olivia is madly in love with him and wants him to appear in public in a ridiculous costume of yellow stockings and cross-garters.

The Puritan or The Widow of Watling Street, written by Thomas Middleton in 1607, is another prime example of a satire of Puritans on stage. The Widow Plus grieves for her husband, a Puritan who made a vast fortune for his thoroughly materialistic, snobbish family. The family's spiri-

1. The English and Early American Beginnings

tual leaders are Minister Fullbelly, who has been known to eat a whole pig in one sitting, and Parson Pigman, who rails against actors because on one occasion actors brought him up on stage drunk. Several scoundrels who plot to defraud the rich widow include two named for Puritan churches and two who are devout supporters of Parson Pigman. Pigman and Fullbelly have taught them that they may lie but not swear. Conveniently, you can lie with a woman but not swear that you did so. Captain Idle, a highwayman master-minding the hoax, declares in Act I, Scene IV:

> I'll sooner expect mercy from a usurer when my bond's forfeited, sooner kindness from a lawyer when my money's spent, nay, sooner charity from the devil than good from a Puritan. I'll look for relief from him when Lucifer is restor'd to his blood and in heaven again!

Ben Jonson's *Bartholomew Fair* (1614) has several Puritans in its cast, most prominently Zeal-of-the-Land Busy, a Puritan divine, who begins raving and preaching at the fair and finds himself thrown down a well for his behavior. He manages to emerge in time to interrupt the fair's puppet show, damning it as a cross-dressing stage abomination. Jonson's *The Alchemist* (1610) and John Marston's *The Dutch Courtesan* (1605) are also among the plays that parodied Puritans.

In the seventeenth-century reigns of James and Charles, church toleration of court theatre changed, as Puritanism came to take an upper hand and as the stage-loving monarchy and nobility found it hard to conceal their odious love of the Catholic Church. King Charles and his play-addicted wife even went so far as to appear in court plays themselves, and undisguised! For most of the sixteenth century, the vitriolic objections raised by various clergymen against the theatre were restricted to particular stage practices: the staging of plays on Sunday, the elaborate scenery and costumes, the rabble who gathered in and around it, and so on. But after 1603, objections began to be raised by a variety of clergymen to all theatre on principle, including all plays. A couple of decades later, the Puritans, realizing that their power was in the ascendancy and that certain political disruption would no longer work to their advantage, saw the necessity of doing away with these theatrical breeding grounds for revolutionaries, who were much more politically radical than they.

After forcing many unofficial closings of theatres, the Puritan Parliament, the Houses of both Lords and Commons, enacted the official — legislated — closing of theatres on the second of September, 1642, securing the ordinance with further statutes in 1647. The theatres were not allowed to reopen until the restoration of the monarchy in 1660.

The New World

The Calvinists who descended on the New World — Plymouth, Massachusetts, in 1620 and Boston in 1630 — put their English counterparts in the shade when it came to intolerance: intolerance of amusements, art, music, Christmas celebrations, May Day festivities, dancing, wearing apparel inappropriate to one's class, making love on the Sabbath, religious beliefs remotely different from the authorized Puritan doctrine of the moment, among others. English Puritans, of the kind that closed the theatres, actually expressed how appalled they were at the extremes to which their New England co-religionists carried their peculiar doctrines and behavior, especially their intolerance. Thomas Dudley, Massachusetts Bay's first lieutenant governor, provides a grim idea:

> Let men of God in courts and churches watch
> O'er such as do a toleration hatch
> Lest that ill egg bring forth a cockatrice
> To poison all with heresy and vice.[13]

Tolerance was sinful, weak, and made God angry. If you wanted to please God and have Him further the prosperity of New England, you needed to root out, banish, and punish any behavior that you believed might offend the Lord.

For well over forty years (until the appearance of the first English play, *Ye Bear and Ye Cubb* in Virginia), and for well over sixty years in New England, there was no need to legally prohibit theatre because it was such an impossibility in Puritan society, and passing an antitheatrical law would have been like legislating against trips to the moon. Stage plays were not only unthinkable in New England's Puritan world, where church and state were one, but even the church service, once known for its thunderous anthems, hypnotic chants, and ornate art, had to be expunged of all theatrical elements. Anything that might in any way allow the senses and emotions to run amok had to be monitored carefully. The church building itself had to be plain and unadorned, with no icons, no stained glass, no statues that might please the eye and distract from the sermon. The only music was to be unaccompanied, sing-song renditions of the Psalms, with

1. The English and Early American Beginnings

no pleasing melody so as not to allow the congregation to be carried away emotionally.

But, from the first, lurking (or prancing) in the misty forest, were intolerable activities that could eventually lead to dreaded stage plays. Well-known among these were the May Day celebrations that the Puritans had never been able to wipe out of Old England. To the New World Calvinists' disgust, other Utopian exiles besides themselves had also found their way to New England. There were Quakers; there were Baptists; there were Catholics; and, most loathsome, there were the Merry Mounters who had the brass to settle in the very backyard of the Plymouth Puritans in 1626. Led by Thomas Morton, an ex-lawyer in London turned libertine, Merry Mount, with a maypole as its icon, was a place for perpetual pleasure: festivals, wine, free love, dramatic interludes, moving songs, and, most of all, abandoned dancing in the lap of Mother Nature. Incidentally, it was also a place where the residents were told there would be no social distinctions. William Bradford, leader of Plymouth Plantation, reports that Morton told his community that "I, having a parte in the plantation, will receive you as my partner and consociats; so may you be free from service, and we will converse, trad[e], plante, and live together as equals, and supporte and protecte one another...."[14] They also began to arm the Indians to hunt for them. But the Salem and Plymouth settlers' real objection to them seemed to be their way of life, as Bradford reports:

> They also set up a Maypole, drinking and dancing about it many days together, inviting the Indean women, for their consorts, dancing and frisking to gather, (like so many fairies, or furies rather,) and worse practices. As if they had anew revived and celebrated the feast of the Roman Goddes Flora, or the beastly practises of the madd Bacchinalians.[15]

The Plymouth settlers began harassing Morton's settlement almost at once, but the serious crackdown did not come until two years after Morton's arrival. Then Plymouth sent Myles Standish (was he perhaps already soured by Priscilla Mullins' preference for John Alden?) to move on Merry Mount with a vengeance and a well-armed militia. Standish, who was dubbed "Captain Shrimp" by Morton, surged through the settlement with his men, who found it unnecessary to use much force because the well armed Merrymounters were reportedly too drunk to fire their weapons. Morton was roughed up, arrested and shipped back to England. The ever-persistent Morton returned two years later, but, again, the Puritans reacted by burning Merry Mount to the ground.

Church and Stage

The point here is that the Merry Mounters, in their theatricality, were counter in every particular to New England Puritans. Morton was their lascivious priest; the maypole dance was their religious ritual, their joy the inversion of Puritan gloom. Hawthorne, in his story of the historical clash, draws on this contrast with Merry Mount in summarizing Puritan culture:

> Their festivals were fast-days, and their chief pastime the singing of psalms. Woe to the youth or maiden, who did but dream of a dance! The selectman nodded at the constable; and there sat the light-heeled reprobate in the stocks; or if he danced it was round the whipping-post, which might be termed the Puritan May-Pole.[16]

The General Laws and Liberties of the Massachusetts Colony of 1672, in reaction to such groups as the dancing Merrymounters, includes a prohibition against "disorders arising in several places within this jurisdiction by reason of some still observing such Festivals, as were Superstitiously kept in other Countries, to the great dishonour of God and offence of others."[17]

But by 1684, the maypole outrage resurfaced, and the enemy was literally and metaphorically in the streets of Boston. The Charter of Massachusetts Bay was revoked, British soldiers began to be quartered in Massachusetts, an Anglican Church would be established in this Puritan stronghold, and the people of Massachusetts Bay would be inflicted with a resident governor appointed by the king. On May 1, 1685, with British troops now in Boston, celebrations were spotted on the islands off the coast of Boston where British troops were quartered. A May Pole was even erected in Charlestown, flaunting its colors in the face of Boston residents. The Bostonians' horrendous rioting in reaction was not a sufficient admonishment: a week later, there appeared a bigger, more decorative May Pole than before.

The law against dancing had also been recorded in the 1672 Colonial Laws:

> Nor shall there be any Dancing in Ordinaries upon any occasion, on the penalty of five shillings for every person that shall offend; and any Magistrate may hear and determine any offence against this Law.[18]

But in 1685, the year of the Charlestown Maypole, a dancing master named Francis Stepney was brazen enough to set up shop right near Boston Common. The danger to decency was so alarming that ten ministers in Boston met on November 12, 1685, to complain of Stepney's mixed dances—on lecture day no less. Samuel Sewall was outraged to learn that Stepney had

1. The English and Early American Beginnings

declared that one play could teach more divinity than the Old Testament or Samuel Willard, pastor of the Old South Church. Stepney was arrested, jailed, and fined on charges of blasphemy and reviling the government. His trial dragged on throughout January and February of 1686, and he fled town in July of that year.[19]

In February of 1686, while Stepney's case was being argued in the courts, Increase Mather was provoked to reissue his 1684 "The Arrow Against Dancing" in a new work entitled *Testimony Against Prophane Customs*. Mather says his specific objection was to *gynecandrical dancing*, an unhappy term which he defines as men and women dancing together.[20]

It is worth considering, in passing, what place dancing had in setting off the 1692 witchcraft terror: the catastrophe was set into motion when young girls in the Reverend Samuel Parris' household (who diverted attention from their own misbehavior by accusing other citizens of witchcraft) were caught playing in the forest. One has to wonder if it were not so much the games they were caught playing, not so much their revolting fortune-telling, but their *dancing*— some reports said naked dancing — that alarmed their pious father.

By 1716, with the English presence solidly in New England, the official prohibition against dancing had been lifted. Moreover, Edward Euston, the organist in Boston's despised Anglican Church, King's Chapel, actually began giving dancing lessons. On November 29, 1716, news got around that he had issued invitations to the governor, like-minded British officers, and influential Tories to attend a dance at his house, on the evening of lecture day, no less. Samuel Sewall and one other man of importance were selected by the Puritan leadership to call on the governor to urge him most solemnly not to attend. After considerable persuasion, he promised "at last" not to attend.[21] By 1720, Euston felt sufficiently confident to advertise his services in the *Boston Gazette* and move to larger quarters.

The importance of all this to the subject at hand is that the two activities— the May Pole celebrations and dancing were regarded as curses by New Englanders, not only in themselves, but precisely because they were looked upon as precursors of theatrical performance. Increase Mather makes this crystal clear in his preface to "An Arrow Against Profane and Promiscuous Dancing," a preface solely devoted to the evils of plays, to which the toleration of dancing leads. A few excerpts follow.

> Stage-Plays had their Original from those Devil Gods whom the Gentiles Worshiped.... *Hence Ancients call such* Theater, *the* Devils Temples, and

Stage Plays, *the* Devils Lectures, and *the Actors in them*, the Devils chief Factors.

For Men who call themselves Christians, to do that which is contrary to their Vow in Baptism, must needs by very Evil.... The *Devil* is in his *Pomps and Plays*. If then thou dost return to *Stage-Plays*, thou dost leave the Faith of Christ, and return again to serve Satan.

'Tis the usual practice of *Stage-Players* to make themselves and others merry with the Vices and Wickedness of men.

The Natural Effects of Stage-Plays have been very pernicious. *Not to speak of the loss of precious Time, and of Estate, which might be better Improved; Multitudes (especially of Young Persons) have thereby been Corrupted and everlastingly Ruined.*

The generality of good Men, both in former and in latter Ages, have looked upon *Stage-Plays* as abominable Vanities.[22]

Learned Puritan minister Increase Mather cautioned against the toleration of May Day celebrations and dances because, he believed, they would lead to an even more despicable practice — the production of plays.

Mather ends the preface with his fear that dancing will lead to stage plays.

In some colonies in the late seventeenth century, especially in cavalier Virginia and South Carolina, the occasional amateur theatrical performance was tolerated, but not in Quaker Philadelphia, Dutch Calvinist New York, and Puritan New England, that cradle of conventional nineteenth-century society. In 1699, both Massachusetts and Philadelphia found it necessary to outlaw the theatre. In 1726 Cotton Mather, a literary force in New England, published *Manuductio ad Ministerium*, a handbook, in which he, like his father, warned against the evils of even reading plays, much less performing them. Remember that this was directed to a class of people who were assumed to be far better fortified against

1. The English and Early American Beginnings

evil: divinity school students. The truth was that the Harvard lads needed these warnings more than most because their chief amusement was mounting private theatricals of their own:

> Most of the modern plays, as well as the romances, and novels and fiction, which are a sort of poems, do belong to the catalogue of this [the devil's] cursed library. The plays, I say, in which there are so many passages that have a tendency to overthrow all piety.... They are national sins, and therefore call for national plagues; and if God should enter into judgment, all the blood in the nation would not be able to atone for them.[23]

Perry Miller and Thomas H. Johnson, in volume two of *The Puritans*, sum up the three political and social reasons for the rejection of the drama:

Cotton Mather, the most prominent minister in support of the Salem witchcraft trials, warned his Harvard Divinity School students of the evils—"Egyptian Toads"—of the imagination as they emerged in poetry, novels, and dramas.

> Drama they banned, because they evidently gave great weight to the injunctions urged against it by the primitive church, and also because they knew it in their day as an art supported by a court which they disapproved, and as a theatre which, in the words of Chesterfield on decorum, combined the useful appearance of virtue with the solid satisfaction of vice. There was still bitter with them the caricatures of Puritans in Malvolio and Zeal-of-the-Land Busy.[24]

Theatre finally got a solid foothold in the English colonies when the first English theatrical troupe appeared in 1703 in Charleston, South Carolina. Not until 1732, did theatricals establish themselves in New York. And not until 1750, eighteen years later, did a stage performance (of Thomas Otway's *The Orphan*) slip by the magistrates in Boston, performed by two

Englishmen in the Boston Coffee House. This atrocity set off riots in the streets of Boston, and provoked the General Court of Massachusetts to enact further legislature forbidding playacting, even making playgoers subject to fines.

An Act to Prevent Stage-Plays, and Other Theatrical Entertainments

> For preventing and avoiding the many and great mischiefs which arise from public stage-plays, interludes, and other theatrical entertainments, which not only occasion great and unnecessary expenses, and discourage industry and frugality, but likewise tend to increase immorality, impiety, and a contempt of religion.[25]

Arthur Hornblow, theatre editor and historian, writes that, in 1754, although some Philadelphians were eager for theatre, "the majority of the inhabitants were bitterly opposed to play-acting of any kind."[26]

In the eighteenth century, with private theatricals having become a mainstay of entertainment of British officers and their Tory sympathizers, patriots joined the clergy in objecting to the stage. Just before and just after the Revolution, the theatre, where the players were British, became symbolic of the English crown and aristocracy, of dissipation, and of irresponsible spending. In 1766, for example, a theatre in New York City was torn down by protestors of the Stamp Act. Hatred of the British may have lain behind the passage in 1774 by the Continental Congress of a sentiment against all stage shows and especially the importation of British theatre. Historian Bruce McConachie writes that Colonial Republicans saw theatre as a corruptor that provided the new country with unsavory examples.

In the middle of the Revolutionary War, one of the first items of business of the newlyformed provincial government of the colonies was to confirm a resolution outlawing theatre and other entertainments. Nineteenth-century clergy were fond of quoting this resolution of the founding fathers to buttress their own denunciations of the stage:

> WHEREAS, True religion and good morals are the only solid foundation of public liberty and happiness,
>
> *Resolved*, That it be, and it is hereby, earnestly recommended to the several States to take the most effectual measures for the encouragement thereof, *and for the suppressing theatrical entertainments,* horse-racing,

1. The English and Early American Beginnings

gaming, and such other diversions as are *productive of idleness, dissipation, and a general depravity of principles and manners.*

WHEREAS, Frequenting play-houses and theatrical entertainments has a fatal tendency to divert the minds of the people from a due attention to the means necessary for the defense of the country and the preservation of their liberties,

Resolved, That any person holding an office under the United States who shall act, promote, encourage or attend such plays, shall be deemed unworthy to hold such office, and shall be accordingly dismissed.[27]

The state of Pennsylvania repealed its ban on entertainments in 1789. The old Massachusetts prohibition was reaffirmed in 1790 and, in 1792, Governor Hancock, who had a reputation as an enemy of the stage, seemed to be behind the arrest of several theatre folk in the middle of a play in Boston, exciting the fury of the audience. According to actor–manager William Clapp, although there were no further arrests, "the law was to remain in force till 1797."[28] But scholarly opinion seems to agree with historian William Dunlap that the law was repealed in 1793, only seven years before the nineteenth century, a time when American theatre blossomed into a lively, internationally recognized art form. Violence and politics were played out on the American stage in the eighteenth century. At Boston's Haymarket, the stage was dominated by British actors, who took pleasure in ridiculing the French, with whom the British were then at war. This excited tension between pro–British and pro–French factions in America and in 1796 caused a riot which "did considerable damage to the benches, doors, and windows."[29] In 1798, a fire in the Haymarket Theatre was seen as an act of God's displeasure and triggered renewed public sentiment against the theatre, several citizens agreeing to put up money to have the Haymarket razed to the ground.[30]

John Hodgkinson, an actor-manager and contemporary of William Dunlap, referred to opinions held by the general populace, not just the clergy, in writing of the actor's station at the turn of the nineteenth century:

> The situation of a Theatrical Performer seems here to be peculiarly unfortunate: Strong Prejudices are entertained against the Profession, and against the Drama itself by many ... and so wide is the Prepossession against the Calling, that *many* look upon an actor as something different from his fellow Men.[31]

Obviously, the prevailing, long-standing influence of Calvinists in the New World caused widespread animosity against the theatre to continue much longer than it did in England. England had at least reopened its theatres in 1660, after the restoration of the monarchy, despite continuing antitheatrical sentiment. And the arguments of Puritan divines had a far greater and more enduring impact on the American public than did the English Puritans on the English, partly because the culture in the New World, dominated by Calvinism, was unrelieved by a long-standing national poetic and courtly tradition. The *legal* fight against theatres, not only by Puritans, but Quakers, Lutherans, and other denominations, persisted in the colonies until the end of the eighteenth century.

To fully grasp the nineteenth-century American's prejudice against the theatre, one must, regretfully perhaps, tackle the tedious matter of the points of Calvinist doctrine from which it stemmed. Lying at the heart of religious intolerance were the Calvinists' views of the quality of mankind's faculties, the nature of pride and idleness, and the system of the callings, involving caste, class, station and place.

At the heart of religious intolerance, not only of the theatre, but of novels and poetry as well, was the Puritans' belief that the imagination was a dangerous faculty. With mankind's disobedience and expulsion from the Garden of Eden, every aspect of human nature became thoroughly depraved. The saving grace was that most faculties could be balanced or modified by others. So reason, flawed though it was, could be balanced by emotion, for example. But there was one faculty that was free to operate without the modifying influence of other characteristics of human beingness: this was the imagination, which was free to go wild without correction by the head or heart. English clergyman Thomas Wright wrote the following in his 1604 *The Passions of the Minde in General:*

> The body and soul suffer pain.... The understanding hath its errors, the will her irregular inclinations, the memory her weakness.... The senses are seduced by Objects, these help to abuse Imagination, which excites disorders in the inferior parts of the soul, and raiseth Passions, so as they are no longer in that obedience, wherein original Justice kept them; and though they be subject to the Empire of Reason, yet they so mutinie, as they are not to be brought within the compass of their duty, but by force or cunning.[32]

In the seminal work on the imagination in New England, the 1625 *The Soul's Conflict and Victory Over Itself*, Richard Sibbes wrote: "*[I]magination* of itself, if *ungoverned*, is a *wild* and *raging thing*"[33] Thomas Hooker, another of New England's prominent Puritan writers, underscores the danger of the imagination in typical highly colored language:

1. The English and Early American Beginnings

> A mans imaginations are the forge of villany, where it's al framed, the Warehouse of wickedness, the Magazine of al mischief and iniquity, whence the sinner is furnished to the commission of al evil, in his ordinary course; the Sea of abominations, which over-flows into al the sences, and they are polluted into all the parts of the body, and they are defiled and carried aside with many noysom corruptions.... The Imagination of our mind is the great Wheel that carries al with it.[34]

The ungovernability of the imagination was bad enough, but there was another reason to be wary of it: Satan operated more actively through the imagination than any other of mankind's faculties. So what was created by the imagination, in this case the playwright's drama and the actor's performance, were the results of Satan working through them to advance his own evil purpose—visiting his wickedness on the artist and using his influence over participants and viewers of the theatre.

William Perkins, an English cleric cherished by the New World Puritans, based his argument against the imagination on Genesis 8:21: "I will not again curse the ground any more for man's sake; for the Imagination of man's heart is evil from his youth." Imagination, he concluded, damaged the church, the Commonwealth, and the family, encouraging unwarranted ambition in readers and viewers of drama, tempting them to disorder and rebellion against authority, and fueling a hunger to be greater in the eyes of the world than God intended.[35]

If further proof of the seriousness with which seventeenth- and even eighteenth-century American divines regarded the imagination, one only has to glance at the alarm with which Cotton Mather wrote of its effects in his 1726 warning to Harvard's young divinity students:

> How much do I wish that such Pestilences, and indeed all those worse than EGYPTIAN TOADS ... Might Never Crawl Into Your Chamber! The UNCLEAN SPIRITS that COME LIKE FROGS OUT OF THE MOUTH OF THE DRAGON, AND OF THE BEAST; and GO FORTH unto the young People of THE EARTH, and in THE BATTLE OF THE GREAT DAY OF THE ALMIGHTY. As for those WRETCHED SCRIBBLERS OF MADMEN, my son, TOUCH THEM NOT, TAST THEM NOT, HANDLE THEM NOT: Thou wilt PERISH in the USING of them. They are THE DRAGONS WHOSE CONTAGIOUS BREATH PEOPLES THE DARK RETREATS OF DEATH. To much better Purpose will an Excellent but an Envied BLACKMORE feast you, than those Vile rhapsodies....[36]

The Puritan doctrine regarding pride and idleness also fed the antiliterary and antitheatrical argument. Pride was, essentially, the sin of aspiring to be like God. It was the sin of Satan, himself, who, in wanting to be like God, was banished from heaven. And it was the sin of Eve, who yielded to temptation by Satan, in the form of a snake, when he told her that she would take on the knowledge of God if she tasted the forbidden fruit. In the world of the Puritans, pride was nowhere more apparent than in the imaginative creation of a world by fiction writers and poets. It was blatantly apparent in the theatrical performance where a playwright, manager, and actors created a world of their own on stage, making a lie seem like the truth.

Practically speaking, the worst sin in the Calvinist work ethic was idleness. English writer Owen Feltham wrote in 1628 that "Idleness is the most corrupting fly that can blow in any human mind."[37]

Those involved in theatrical activities were neither glorifying God nor benefiting man: they were idlers. And they were tempting others to abandon their proper work and loaf. There was, the Puritan argued, nothing productive in the process of creating or attending a theatrical performance. In New England in 1730, Josiah Smith, in *Solomon's Caution,* preached that entertainments led to the neglect of business: people "not only lose their *time* but lose their *disposition* for Business."[38] Of course, let us not forget that an idle mind was the devil's workshop, wherein carnal desires were hatched.

New England Puritans even formally legislated against idleness in 1672 in *The Colonial Laws of Massachusetts*:

> It is Ordered, that no person, House-holder or other, shall spend his time Idely or unprofitably, under pain of such punishment, as the County Court shall think meet to inflict.
> And the Constables of every Town are required to use special care to take notice of Offenders in this kinde, especially of common Coasters, unprofitable Fowlers, and Tobacco takers, and present the same to the next Magistrate, who is hereby impowered to hear and determine the cause, or transfer it to the next Court.[39]

Finally, Protestantism was founded on the Doctrine of the Callings, which insisted that God intended a specific work and place or class for every individual and that God's essential charge was for all persons to remain in the stations in which they were born. There were several ways in which the doctrine of the callings shaped antitheatrical attitudes. In the first place, the doctrine lent a godly, theological sanction to social stratification. The effect of this, in the argument against the theatre, was felt by actors, who were despised merely because they were so lowly as to be outside any caste. Nor did lower-class audiences escape the consequences of this dictate. The doc-

1. The English and Early American Beginnings

trine also taught women and children their places, and their places, according to the clergy, were not on the American stage.

The Reverend Samuel Willard, revered Boston pastor, emphasized these key elements in rules that were and would later be employed in the war against the theatre, linking imagination, idleness, and the callings. One of his basic rules was to "lay a strict restraint upon our fancies or imaginations." Another was to "let us beware of idleness." And another was to "let us keep the station which God hath set us in."[40]

Hostility toward the theatre continued in nineteenth-century America from this theological foundation in reference to the radical Calvinists' views of human nature, sin, and the hierarchical structure of one's proper place.[41]

2

The Power and Values of the Church

> [T]hose who condemn the stage ... constitute a respectable and powerful body....
> — Southern Literary Messenger

The ignominious stage, so bereft in the colonial period and even outlawed by the newly formed country built on the separation of church and state, grew rapidly into a rich form of entertainment in the nineteenth century. It flourished in New York City, Boston, Baltimore, and Philadelphia, each eventually supporting numerous theatres. It easily moved to the less Calvinistic southern cities of Richmond, Charleston, and New Orleans, and out West, after the discovery of gold, to San Francisco. Traveling theatrical troupes traversed the frontier, playing in mining camps, barns, and, in a case reported by Joseph Jefferson, in a pig sty. It was an arena where an impressive, internationally respected cast of native stars of the stature of Edwin Booth, Charlotte Cushman, Lotta Crabtree, Joseph Jefferson, Edwin Forrest, Anna Cora Mowatt, and many others were as capable as their British counterparts of presenting classical roles of every age, playing them as readily as they did light comedies and melodramas. The colorful, spirited character of the stage has typically overshadowed the darker side of the story: its failure to find a comfortable place in the larger society of which it was a part. The historical irony argued here is that it flourished, but only as what was then understood to be a tainted underside of a society, incontrovertibly dominated by a powerful church hostile to the theatre. For the theatre was perceived as being anathema to all the religious values and virtues so

2. The Power and Values of the Church

fundamental to the prevailing Victorian society. Even in Charleston, South Carolina, considered to be a Mecca of theatrical art in the Southeast, and where the Dock Street Theatre had opened as early as 1736, antitheatrical sentiments were acknowledged. A writer for *The Southern Literary Messenger*, a journal which had a theatre-friendly home in Charleston, sees an "uncompromising hostility of the religious world to the theatre." The writer sums up what he sees as the religious public's view: "I am aware that those who condemn the stage in all aspects and influences constitute a respectable and powerful body, and that they conscientiously believe it repugnant to religion and injurious to the best interests of mankind."[1] The frontier, less tradition bound and less religious, might be expected to be less biased against the theatre, but actors met with disfavor even there.

To have a full appreciation of what the theatre was up against, it is essential to recognize the power of the Protestant Church in nineteenth-century America; to understand the personal religious values the church promulgated; and to grasp the socio-economic policies the church shared with big business, all of which affected the religious public's negative attitude toward the theatre.

After 1800, religious institutions in America had no official legal authority in the federal government to actually legislate wide-scale legal prohibitions of the theatre, but until the last decades of the nineteenth century, their opposition had as much forceful conviction behind it as it ever had. Not until 1833, did separation of church and individual states become official, when the Congregational Church was separated from the state of Massachusetts. But even though the United States was no longer a theocracy, it is almost impossible to over estimate the Protestant Church's far-reaching influence in nineteenth-century America. Sidney E. Ahlstrom writes in *The Religious History of the American People*, "Despite the legal separation of church and state, this American Protestant mainstream would enjoy the influence and self-confidence of a formal establishment."[2] Henry F. May draws attention to the church's refusal to relinquish the right to "supervise the morals of the nation."[3] And as early as 1835, Alexis de Tocqueville observed the same anomaly, an unofficial institution that could pervade and direct multiple diverse segments of American life:

> Religion in America takes no direct part in the government of society, but nevertheless it must be regarded as the foremost of the political institutions of that country.... I do not know whether all the Americans have a sincere faith in their religion, for who can search the human heart? But I am certain that they hold it to be indispensable to the maintenance of

republican institutions. This opinion is not peculiar to a class of citizens or to a party, but it belongs to the whole nation, and to every rank of society.[4]

There is no lack of first-hand testimony to the power of the church in the records of European observers of American society such as de Tocqueville, Mrs. Anthony Trollope, and Thomas Colley Grattan. The supremacy of the church is also borne out in histories of religion in America by Ahlstrom, May, Winthrop S. Hudson, and Charles Cole.

Traveler to America, Thomas Colley Grattan, who observed American society in 1859, was impressed with the sheer numbers of people and the intensity of activity in American churches:

> In no country of the world is there more religious fervour, than in America, and nowhere a more strict observance of forms. The true religious sentiment, that has its source and life in the hearts of men, is out of the pale of calculation; but the numerical force of observers of church discipline, in all its varieties, is, I have no doubt, greater in the United States than anywhere else.[5]

Grattan's impressions have the ring of truth, because Protestantism had grown by leaps and bounds in the first half of the century. Between 1800 and 1850, membership in Protestant churches increased tenfold. According to one estimate, the 40 percent of the population who were church members in 1800 had risen to 75 percent by 1835.[6] Even this high percentage of church members probably fails to reflect the real impact of the church on the population because almost three times as many people attended church as joined it.

Much of the church's hold over the public can be laid to its extravagant veneration of the clergy, many of whom were the superstars of their day. The always critical English visitor, Mrs. Frances Trollope, contended that the clergy, in assuming inordinate power, had woven an unwholesome spell over the public. Once you had joined a sect in America, she wrote, "your next submission must be that of unqualified obedience to the will and pleasure of your elected pastor."[7] The opinions of the clergy were made known, not only from the pulpit on Sunday, but through the many revivals, religious education classes, prayer meetings, and charity and missionary societies of all kinds which occupied much of the churchgoers' time. Mrs. Trollope quipped: "Every evening that is not spent in the churches and meeting houses, is devoted to what would be called parties by others, but

2. The Power and Values of the Church

which they designate as prayer meetings."[8] Church opinion was also transmitted through a rapidly growing religious press, which outstripped the secular press from 1840 to 1860 and was "widely and avidly read."[9] The Reverend G. Lewis, a Scottish observer of American churches, noticed this marvel in 1848: "Everything connected with a congregation," he wrote, "is reported through the religious press.[10] Through increased organization and religious activity, as Winthrop S. Hudson concluded, the church became the major force in nineteenth-century society:

> [It] had established undisputed sway over almost all aspects of the national life. It was a Protestant America that had been fashioned by the churches; and the influence of the churches ... extended far beyond their somewhat narrowly defined membership. The vast majority of Americans, even when not actual communicants, regarded themselves as "adherents" of one church or another; and among the populace at large the patterns of belief and conduct — private and public, individual and corporate — were set by the churches.[11]

The values that this prevailing institution and its mainstream religious public, especially its middle class, promoted are at the root of antitheatrical fervor in the United States. The church's unqualified insistence on concealment, order, tradition, self-control, self-denial, industry, and rigid class stratification frequently resulted in physical repression, prudery, and repressive attitudes toward women, children and the poor.

The churchgoing mainstream had its foundation in the ideal family living quietly and orderly in its Victorian home. Here deportment and order took on the force of moral value. For those who could afford to dine, meals were taken at precise times. To sleep late was to be a laggard, to bed late was profligate. Good habits, genteel manners, and a predictable routine were signs of moral stability in the sacrosanct home. The whole of Western civilization seemed to hang in the balance as one chose the right fork or the right hat. How different was the life of the actor. Theatre people rarely had the luxury of stable homes, moving as they did from place to place in search of work. A painful line from a letter by America's first lady of the stage, Mary Ann Duff, illustrates: "I wish to return home when it please my children to let me know where that home is."[12]

The Victorian insistence on concealment was epitomized by the multiple layers of clothing that concealed the human body. There was the long-sleeved shirtwaist, worn often in the heat of summer, the long skirts, the fear of exposing an ankle in alighting from a carriage, and, for men, cravats, suit coats, and sometimes overcoats for gentlemen, even in summer.

Parallel to concealment of the body in long clothes was the concealment of what was deemed unpleasant or coarse in language, particularly matters regarding the body or remotely suggesting sensuality. This was the age of euphemism, the use of words to mute realities. Thus, *leg* became *limb*; *chicken breast* became *white meat*; *weathercock* became *weather vane*; *cock* became *rooster*; *prostitute* became *fallen woman*; *cow manure* became *good rich earth*; *hell* became *Hades* or *Guinea*.

For men and boys, especially, emotions had to be concealed, especially those that would naturally tend to evoke tears, for tears were a sign of weakness reserved for women. Loss of emotional control was undignified and betrayed a "common" up-bringing.

The clergy also preached the necessity of holding excitement and emotion at bay. So, for example, leisure activities were carefully supervised and kept to a minimum. Typical activities of ideal wives consisted of making afternoon calls, doing needle work and attending Bible and missionary meetings. The reading of fiction, poetry, and philosophy were not encouraged as pastimes for women because it stimulated the emotions and intellect and was known to cause, not only dissatisfaction, but both mental and physical ailments. Some educated women allowed themselves the self-indulgence of keeping diaries.

Like their mothers, little girls were allowed only the quiet diversions of sewing, playing with dolls, sometimes painting, restrained piano playing, and readings of a moral or religious nature. Physical activities were forbidden as unladylike. Little boys were allowed the latitude of highjinks on the playing fields and in swimming holes, but all children, when in adult society, were to be seen and not heard.[13]

Victorian economic values, as well as personal ones, affected the reception of the theatre by the church and its supporters. The howling dogs of disorder and misrule were as apparent and as threatening to society at large as they were to individual character. Power in America was held by well-born men, successful businessmen, and prominent men of the cloth who were the darlings of big business. By the nineteenth century, as sociologist Max Weber so convincingly argues, the Industrial Revolution, begun in eighteenth-century England, had progressed to America, and the Protestant church joined forces with the new industrialism and capitalism.

Now it was not enough to work hard in one's calling. One had to succeed and succeed remarkably. The old Puritan attitude evolved into the

2. The Power and Values of the Church

conviction that the accumulation of wealth was both patriotic and virtuous. Making money became a religious duty, and economic success became a prominent subject of sermons.

The church encouraged certain behaviors and condemned others with the purpose of assisting capitalism in working smoothly and productively as God intended. For businessmen certain conditions had to prevail: individuals, particularly women, children and members of the working classes, had to remain quietly in their proper places, had to avoid idle pleasure seeking, turbulence, and disruption; tradition and order had to be maintained; and the moral requirements of the clergy and religious public had to be respected. The mere existence of such an inverse subculture as the theatre posed a constant threat to the civilization built by the values of the Protestant Ethic.

Proof of the alliance between church and big money can be seen in the numbers of highly visible leaders, in both conservative and liberal church denominations, who were well-published and widely read political theorists, the large majority of whom were dedicated to a system designed to encourage moneymaking on the part of already wealthy capitalists and to underpin the prevailing structure, not alter it.[14] Institutions of higher learning in the United States were largely run by the most conservative of religious sects (Harvard being something of an exception), and political economics courses, which communicated religion and conservative social views, were at the core of their curricula. The students of these divinity school professors presumably spread these economic views when they went out to preach.

The alliance of church and big business was in keeping with the new Protestant Ethic that taught that God smiled upon business success, that the rich man was the greatest glory to God, and that the poor deserved their poverty. An address by clergyman Elijah Parish is typical in praising "the rich men of this country that took time out for nothing in their work.... These are the great men, — these are the rich men, to whom the idle go for a piece of bread."[15] Clergyman Thomas Hunt betrays his political theology in the title of his tract, *The Book of Wealth; in Which it is Proved from the Bible, That it is the Duty of Every Man, to Become Rich*. And, if you did not become rich, it was your own fault. The Reverend Lyman Beecher, father of Henry Ward, called the poor (who wanted to band together for better conditions) "vicious" and called the Workingmen's Party an "infidel trumpet-call."[16] Social tranquility, obedience, acceptance, and industry, especially with regard to the lower classes, kept disorder and violence in check. Values that promoted social order rendered the country into a well-oiled productive machine of which God approved.

The theatre posed a danger in that it was frequently a magnet for political violence offstage. In the theatre — this inverse world — significant power was in the hands of women, children, and economically and socially dispossessed men. The mere existence of such an inverse subculture posed a constant threat to the society built by the values of the Protestant Ethic.

At a time of unspeakable poverty and owners' abuse of workers, churches fervently undertook reforms, not primarily to alleviate the suffering of the poor, but to convert them. The great reform issues addressed by the clergy were temperance, sexual behavior, and the proper role of women, children and the lower classes. But behind the religious public's mask of morality and order lurked an ugly reality, an undeniable hypocrisy. One is led to ask, "Who wore the mask? Was it the players or was it the clergy?"

The Protestant Church, in all its own magnificence and buttressed by its alliance with big business, used its influence to thwart the theatre, an institution that negated those moral standards that glued Victorian society together. Evidence is overwhelming that the Protestant Church in America pooled its vast resources to speak with one loud voice against what all agreed was tantamount to the anti–Christ — the villainous, ubiquitous theatre. We know that the denominations that most consistently objected to the theatre were the direct and indirect descendents of the New World Puritans — Methodists, Baptists, Quakers, Congregationalists, and Presbyterians — and that they far outnumbered Anglicans, Unitarians, and Roman Catholics, who *theoretically* tolerated theatre. Furthermore, it was the impression of clergymen that their views were shared by the substantial majority of their brethren and the religious public. As Benjamin McArthur's research tells us, as late as 1877 the Methodists Episcopal Church asserted that the church would scold or even possibly excommunicate church members found going to the theatre. The Methodist College, Ohio Wesleyan, disciplined some underclassmen and expelled some seniors who attended the theatre against the rules in the 1880s, and, in 1890, a major Baptist Association ordered their members to avoid the theatre.[17] The Reverend William Wallace Everts, a professor of theology at the Baptist-run University of Chicago, informed his readers that all the great American religious leaders were antagonistic toward the theatre. He mentions the Unitarian William Ellery Channing (who was a close friend of Ralph Waldo Emerson), Timothy Dwight, both a theological and literary figure, and Francis Wayland,

2. The Power and Values of the Church

president of Brown University.[18] The Reverend Thomas Ebenezer Thomas was sure that "few Christians of any eminence have failed to pronounce sentence against the stage."[19] Writing long after the Civil War, Josiah Leeds, a Quaker, claimed that his diatribe against the stage had been endorsed by *The Episcopal Recorder*, *The Lutheran Observer*, and the *Presbyterian Observer*.[20] James Monroe Buckley, a Congregationalist, agreed with Thomas and Leeds that Baptist, Quakers, and Methodists, as a matter of church policy, were opposed to the stage. "In general terms, it may be said, that all evangelical churches in this country, except the Protestant Episcopal, are opposed to the theatre." There is, he writes, complete unanimity on this position.[21]

In 1882, Herrick Johnson, who also mentions that "the Church, with remarkable unanimity ... has pronounced against the stage," broadens the sphere of the stage's enemies to include — not just the clergy — but the vast religious public as well, "the great mass of those who believe in the morals of the New Testament." Johnson says his stand against the stage has been endorsed not only by fellow Presbyterians in Chicago but by Baptists and Methodists.[22]

In 1871, John F. Ware, who argues that the theatre can be reformed, admits that he is rare among clergymen in support of the stage. In speaking of the reputation of actors, not just among churchmen, but in the general public, he finds an "ill-disguised, all but unanimous public opinion against performers."[23] Even Anglican, Unitarian, and Catholic churches, while officially tolerant of the stage, actually condemned actors and argued vociferously for sweeping reforms. Stories persist of Episcopal and Catholic clergy refusing to officiate at the funerals of actors or to allow them burial in church cemeteries. The Rev. William Wilberforce Newton, an Episcopalian minister in Boston and Pittsfield, Massachusetts, was, along with others of his denomination, a member of the Society for the Elevation and Purification of the Stage.[24]

The marginalization of the theatre by the church is made abundantly clear by the statue of those ministers who led the assaults on the theatre. The ferociousness of their rhetoric might lead one logically to assume that the antitheatrical campaign was waged by a fringe group of illiterate religious extremists. But this was far from the truth. The real eye-opener is that among the most vociferous adversaries of the stage were the most highly educated, highly regarded, influential ministers of the day.[25] For example, chief among the critics were the Reverend Timothy Dwight and the Reverend Henry Ward Beecher. Dwight, who published *An Essay on the Stage* in 1824, was the grandson of Jonathan Edwards (whose sermons reportedly made his congregation suicidal), and he, himself, was a Calvinist scholar, a preacher, a widely read publisher of numerous sermons, and the president of Yale College from 1795 to 1817. The century's most respected religious scholar, a leader of the Second Great Awakening, and a member of the literary school known as the Connecticut Wits, Dwight had published a popular five-volume work on Christian theology. He was scarcely an uneducated crackpot.

Beecher, who castigated the stage in *Twelve Lectures to Young Men* (1879), was an internationally known lecturer and from 1847 to 1887 the pastor of one of the largest churches in America — the Plymouth Congregational Church in Brooklyn. His sermons were published weekly in newspapers throughout the country. The *Dictionary of American Religious Biography* proclaims that he had "an ability to reflect majority sentiment" and enjoyed "unequaled popularity and influence,"[26] an influence scarcely dented when a husband dragged him into court on the grounds that Beecher had committed adultery with his wife.

Beecher and Dwight, prominent for their antitheatrical opinions, can scarcely be dismissed as insignificant. And they weren't the only ones. A brief look at a few of the other prominent sermonizers and tract writers confirms the contention that antitheatrical sentiment came from the pens of men who carried weight in mainstream society.

The Rev. Justin D. Fulton, author of *Theatres and Their Pernicious Influence*, was the Baptist pastor of Boston's renowned Tremont Temple, and subsequently the founder of the foremost church in Brooklyn, a place known at the time as the City of Churches.

The Rev. John Berry M'Ferrin, author of *The Pulpit and the Stage or the Two Itinerancies by One Who Knows*, was editor of *The South-Western Christian*

Timothy Dwight, Connecticut Wit and president of Yale College, was one of the many learned divines who believed that everything about the theatre was evil.

2. The Power and Values of the Church

Advocate, head of the Methodist national publishing house, and an extremely popular national lecturer, with a reputation as the best platform speaker in America.

The Rev. William Wallace Everts, author of *The Theatre* and *Temptations of City Life* (in 1868), was a Baptist minister and one of the founders of the University of Chicago.

The Rev. DeWitt Talmage, author of two books castigating the theatre, *The Average Theatre* and *Sports That Kill*, was pastor of the Presbyterian Tabernacle in Brooklyn, New York, the largest Protestant church in the world.

Maurice Francis Egan, author of *The Theatre and Christian Parents* (1885), was a professor at Notre Dame and Catholic University, and was later a diplomat to Denmark.

The Reverend C. C. Everett, who warned young people against the theatre in his *Ethics for Young People*, was a Unitarian minister and Bussey Professor of Theology at Harvard University.

In conclusion, the Protestant Church was not just one of many forces in nineteenth-century society; it was the most powerful force. Nor were the clergymen who preached against the stage a small number of ministers on the fanatical fringe; they were the most educated and illustrious figures of their time, who brought to the excoriation of the theatre an explosive rhetoric that they lent to little else.

3

Plays, Playgoers, and Actors

> *The gate of debauchery, the porch of pollution, the vestibule of the very House of Death.*
> — Henry Ward Beecher

As learned and influential as we have seen antitheatrical clergy to be, as a general rule they did not base their arguments on actual observation or first-hand experience, a failing that they were compelled to justify. At the same time that they generalized about what went on onstage or in greenrooms offstage or in theatre audiences, they boasted that they had never set foot in a theatre. The Reverends Justin Fulton and Thomas Ebenezer Thomas, for example, bragged that they didn't have to enter a theatre to deliver their maledictions on it. Thomas's admission is a familiar one among the clergy:

> I bless God, that through the early instruction and pious example 'of parents passed into the skies,' I never saw a play, never even entered a theatre. You might have asked me, then, — what can you know of the stage? I might, indeed, have answered, — one need not eat a joint of tainted meat to ascertain its putridity. One need not have a loathsome disease to understand its character and consequence.[1]

Along these same lines, the Rev. John Angell James warns young people not to enter the theatre, even once, in order to see for themselves what it is like:

> Taste not the poison to ascertain how you like it, and to form an opinion of its deleterious power. Touch not the fang of a serpent, to ascertain by examination the sharpness of its tooth. These are matters which it is safer and easier to decide by testimony; and a cloud of witnesses can, and do

3. Plays, Playgoers, and Actors

depose, that of all the avenues to destruction, not one is more seductive, or more direct, than the theatre.[2]

With or without first-hand knowledge behind it, the antitheatrical text—sermons, tracts, and books of advice to the young—became something of an art form in itself, raising the same alarms and often repeating the same horror stories to warn that the stage was a den of iniquity to be avoided at all costs. The model antitheatrical sermon reaches a pitch of hysteria as the writer, having outlined the theatre's psychological and social perils, flings down his horrific statistics and dramatizes his case studies of souls addicted and lost to the world through association with the theatre.

It was all right for religious writers themselves to take flights of fancy and play on the emotions of the gullible, resorting, as they did, to excitement rather than reason, and then to denounce the theatre for doing the same things. One of the most theatrical techniques was throwing out alarming statistics about the result of playgoing. Henry Ward Beecher alleged in 1850 that half of those in jails and half of those executed for crimes were first led astray by the theatre.[3]

The Rev. DeWitt Talmage, writing in 1875, had reached the same conclusions, taking some of his evidence from an English divine:

> How often has a condemned man on the scaffold in his dying speech, said: "*The Theatre ruined me!*" The Bishop of Carlisle examined the records of a penitentiary, and found that the majority of the inmates were first seduced from rectitude by theatres and races. Almshouses, insane asylums, and state prisons have gathered the corrupt fruit of this corrupt tree.[4]

The *pièce de résistance* of the antitheatrical tract or sermon was the case study: the repetition of unspeakable fire-and-brimstone stories—not so much of eternal damnation, but of hell on earth. Apocryphal stories were usually about young men who live tormented lives and die early deaths as a result of their first attendance at a theatre. In 1866, the Rev. William Everts relates several stories that crop up in other sermons:

> A few months since a young man came to this city with the purpose and means of pursuing a professional education. For a time he succeeded well. But, persuaded by a companion, he attended the theatre, neglected his studies, incurred the reproach of his teachers, parted with all his funds in a gambling house, and attempted suicide.[5]
>
> While the Tremont theatre, in Boston, was in course of transformation

into a place of worship, an aged man entered, and was observed to bow his head and weep. Being asked the cause of his tears, he said with deep emotion, "Oh! I was thinking of my two sons that were both ruined here."[6]

A dying young man says, "In an evil hour I was asked by a friend to go with him to the theatre, and accepted his invitation. From that hour I trace my wandering and my ruin."[7]

In 1841, in a sermon in the Tremont Temple, the Rev. Justin D. Fulton had also told the story of the old man crying in church over his two ruined sons. He blames the suicide of another young man, once a member of Tremont Temple, on playgoing, and quotes a bereaved mother who claims her son was killed by the theatre: "His thoughts were polluted, his speech evidenced it, no more than his life."[8]

When a frightening example was not sufficient, ministers offered their own imaginative stories of what *could* happen to a young man or woman who attended the theatre. Talmage imagines a young man who visits the theatre for the first time when his defenses are down. "At first he sits far back, with his hat on and his coat-collar up, fearful that somebody there may know him."[9] But soon, after attending several performances, he has "started on the long road which ends in consummate destruction.... You will be tossed, and dashed, and shipwrecked, and swallowed in the whirlpool that has already crashed in his wrath ten thousand hulks."[10]

The Reverend DeWitt Talmage, renowned speaker, writer, and leader of what was regarded as the most powerful Protestant church in the world, saw theatrical people as "the outscourings of society."

Despite the horror stories about young men who had dared to enter the theatre, many

3. Plays, Playgoers, and Actors

clergy were convinced that women were more likely to be led astray by viewing dramas than were men and that the consequences were even worse. An unsigned article in *The Christian Spectator* reflects this view:

> A mother might fear the polluting comedy for her son but the more absorbing tragedy for her daughter. Pride, ambition, and revenge, lust, seduction, and murder are, I need not tell you, the materials of which the tragedy is composed; and it is not to be imagined that the delicate mind of a female, young and imaginative as she may be, can be agitated by scenes like these ... and yet suffer no depravation.[11]

One reason why play-going was so bad for women, according to Francis Wayland in *The Elements of Moral Science,* is because it took up time that a woman should more properly have been devoting to her household duties,[12] but the danger in the theatre for women was more serious than neglect of domestic chores. The wife, that moral rock of the American home on whom the nation's economic system rested, might become dissatisfied with her life as she witnessed a play, realizing that her own quiet home was dull compared to the adventures enjoyed by the female characters she saw on stage. Even if she were not provoked to desert her home, even if a young daughter did not resort to prostitution to support her habit of theatre-going, woman's awakening to her own dull lot, as a result of seeing plays, was not deemed likely to strengthen the ideal home. The Rev. Robert Turnbull wrote that the theatre could cause women to develop a "distaste for simple and home born enjoyments, as well as for sober everyday duties!"[13] In short, "the sweet charities of home will lose their attraction. Ordinary scenes of social joy and fireside satisfactions will be exchanged for resorts of more tumultuous excitement."[14] A gentleman, writing advice to his sister in 850, admonished her to "keep a constant watch over the imagination ... since this is the medium through which temptation comes, never suffer your fancy to rove without control."[15]

Poor men pilfered and stole for the price of a theatre ticket, but women, who had poor-paying jobs, or no jobs, turned to prostitution to support their addiction to the theatre. This is the warning of a Professor Griscom, who was frequently quoted in tracts and newspaper columns:

> In the case of the feebler sex, the result is still worse; a relish for the amusements of the theatre, without the means of indulgence, becomes too often a motive for listening to the first seducer; and this prepares the unfortunate captive of sensuality for the haunts of infamy and a total destruction of all that is valuable in the mind and character of woman.[16]

Church and Stage

The Rev. Winchester goes on to express the same sentiment in his own words: "The excitement produced by the theatre's attractive introduction to the female mind of licentiousness and her eagerness—addiction to it—for which money is necessary, starts many a young woman toward the fall."[17]

While the weak young woman was easily seduced by plays, the upstanding young woman had sound judgment and was on her guard around what she knew to be the evils of the theatre. Fulton relates the extraordinary reaction to the theatre of one such young lady:

> A young girl had for the first time gone to a theatre. The play had been full of suggestive vileness. Men and women talked of what they saw and thought. The girl endured it as long as she could, and then putting her fingers in her ears—shrieked out these words, saying, "Take me anywhere; to the smoking car or baggage car; anywhere to be way from this vile talk."[18]

What aspects of the theatre produced these horrific consequences? The typical adversary of the theatre damned its every component, starting with the plays themselves. Both classic and modern plays were supposedly sacrilegious, immoral, and false. Shakespeare's comedies were lewd, therefore unacceptable. His tragedies had no moral messages. The Rev. Turnbull leveled particular complaints against *Hamlet*'s failure as a moral drama: Polonius's wise advice, he charged, is ridiculed; the only really good character, Ophelia, is shown as impossibly weak and demented; and King Claudius, as wicked as he is, is allowed to keel right over without any real physical suffering.[19] A Baptist minister, the Rev. Jeremiah Jeter, afforded Shakespeare the benefit of a strange doubt in attacking his plays: "For the honor of his genius, I am willing to believe that Shakespeare was not the author of the profane and obscene language in his plays."[20] Far too many plays, both old and new, were thought to portray vice of all kinds, present loose women and licentious men in a sympathetic or comical light, and mock ministers or religion in general. The Rev. James Monroe Buckley analyzed popular plays in typical fashion. He disparaged Oliver Goldsmith's *She Stoops to Conquer* as an example of "profaneness" and "vulgarity," a play which "sneers at temperance and religion."[21] His amazing comment on *School for Scandal*, a frequently produced play, was that "no woman could read it to any but her husband, or some other near relative, without giving grounds for a presumption against her purity."[22] *The Ticket of Leave Man*, another popular play, was to be avoided because it presented "scenes of vice" and "coarseness."[23] The play *Saratoga*, was "unchaste" and filled with *double entendres*. Finally, he attacks *East Lynne* as a typical example of the theatre's

3. Plays, Playgoers, and Actors

sympathetic treatment of such evils as adultery, infidelity, and murder.[24] Few plays escaped without criticism of some kind. Buckley also announced his disapproval of the use of "slang" and portrayals of remarriage. Others objected to plays that showed dueling.[25]

Even if a play had a moral message and represented the triumph of virtue over vice, the mere fact that it was presented in dramatic form obviated any Christian value it might have:

> It is true, villainy is commonly punished in these plays, but the villainy is often given such dash and daring and bravado, and is so set round with attractions and is pursued with such utter abandon and intoxication of delight that many a youth is led to prefer the way to destruction and the devil; because the journey can be made in such a blaze of glory.[26]

John Angell James sums up what many thought to be the perils of staged dramatic literature.

> As to the staple matter of which the ordinary run of dramatic representations are composed, it is altogether adapted to corrupt the youthful mind, by appealing to the most inflammable, the most powerful, and the most dangerous of its passions[27]

The moving of dramatic literature into live production colossally magnified the deleterious effects of the drama's subjects. Joseph W. Leeds, a Quaker, pointed out that it was impossible to *dramatize* Christian virtues. As a Quaker, he interprets those virtues as silence, moderation, poverty, patience, and humility. In contrast, the production of a play is noisy, extravagant, lavish in display, and proud.[28] Timothy Dwight makes the same argument by stressing the production's anti-Christian displays of self-conceit, pride, arrogance, haughtiness, and disdain.[29] The Rev. James writes that it is not only the subject matter of the play itself that is corrupting, but the representation of it upon the stage.[30]

Curiously, the church made little distinction in severity between what went on onstage and what went on before and around the stage, even though there was more obvious need of meaningful reform touching the audience and the environs of the theatre. Yet, again, the clergy attacked the problem with overheated rhetoric and exaggeration, leveling its ammunition against the whole audience without question and assuming that it was the theatres themselves that shaped the neighborhoods of squalor and dens of vice they inhabited — the theatre — rather than the greed of the church's most ardent parishioners who lived well from their workers' poverty.

Church and Stage

A sense of the usual floor plan of the theatre is essential to an understanding of the clergy's case against the audience. The typical inside of a theatre was constructed for a highly stratified audience. Except in aristocratic theatres, the pit was frequented by theatre critics, other literary sorts, and working-class ruffians. The dress circle, which was an elevated arc around the edge of the theatre, was frequented by the middle classes, occasionally even families. (However, J. B. M'Ferrin called it the "undress circle,"[31]) Just above and on either side of the stage were boxes for small private parties, the occupants of which were understood to be better heeled than others in the theatre. A bar was maintained on the second tier. The third tier was identified with prostitutes. Sometimes theatres had a "sky parlour" for African American patrons. Otherwise these patrons were relegated to a special section of the third tier. It was the theatre's accommodation of the bar and prostitutes, both to be discussed in subsequent chapters, which provided the church with its most inflammatory objections.

But clerical critics preached that the whole audience, not just the prostitutes in it, was "profligate," like a deserted castle "left to the habitation of bats and owls, unclean beasts, and poisonous reptiles."[32] The Rev. Fulton claimed that "vile boys and girls" crowded around the doors of theatres, waiting to get in.[33] M'Ferrin enlivens his antitheatrical argument with a little verse about the audience:

> Like ants on Mole-hills, thither they repair
> Like bees to hives, so numerously they throng,
> It may be said they to that play belong.[34]

The Rev. Thomas's assumptions were couched in especially colorful language:

> [T]he mass, from Athens to New York, are the ignorant, the dissipated, the debauched, the scum and refuse of society.... From pit, box, and gallery of theatres innumerable here — they are congregated in countless throngs of lost souls, under an everlasting doom, as lovers of pleasures more than of God![35]

Talmage summed up his view of the audience, including some especially damning evidence — that horse jockeys could be found there!

> Husbands who have lost all love for home go there. Horse jockeys go there. Thieves go there. The lecherous go there. Spendthrifts go there. Drunkards go there. Lost women go there.... An institution that nightly draws together from the lowest haunts of vice so many of the leprous, and unwashed, and abandoned, must have in it a moral taint.[36]

3. Plays, Playgoers, and Actors

Some insisted that audiences were comprised solely of the lowest social and moral orders. And it was true that members of the working class found a home in their own theatres and, in their political struggles, frequently erupted in violence.

Others wrote that upper-class men cheated on their wives by bringing their "paramours" to the theatre and proceeding afterward to the bars of "Five Points," one of the roughest New York City neighborhoods where working-class theatres were located.

The church also used the argument that theatres attracted vice to the neighborhoods around them, gambling dens (as they were then called), saloons, grog shops, and houses of prostitution. Talmage writes: "Aye, the theatre would have died long ago but for the surrounding evils that keep adding fuel to these wasting fires of hell."[37]

People who attended theatres not only exposed themselves to moral pollution, but to criminals, chiefly the thieves, pimps, prostitutes, and pickpockets who, clergymen insisted, inevitably wandered through the audience and waited outside in the general neighborhood for prey.

One of the strangest clerical reasons given for the need to avoid the theatre was that it was bad for one's health. Consider what the Rev. Everts has to say that could as easily be applied to prayer meetings:

> Protracted exposure to the impure atmosphere of a crowded auditory, and subsequently to the cold or damp night air, often sows the seeds of disease, including premature death, or protracted and hopeless decline.[38]

The Rev. Talmage also describes graphically how the theatre can blast the physical health of an individual and a nation:

> I charge upon the average American theatre *much of the unhealthy of this country*. The man who sits night after night, until ten or eleven o'clock, in the theatre, and then takes his oysters and ale, and crawls into his bed at twelve or one o'clock, will be a sick man. No physical constitution can endure it. The nerves shattered, the imagination excited, the strength exhausted, he will be eaten up by disease, and sink into an early grave. The American theatre has filled the land with an army of invalids. We see them dying with dyspepsia, with neuralgia, and liver complaints, and consumptions, and there is congratulation in hell that the theatre killed them. It is death to a man to be busy all day in a store, the air poisoned and corrupt, and then, as a usual thing, to spend three hours at night in a theatre, the atmosphere of which is made up of ten parts of cologne, fifty parts of tobacco, one part of oxygen, and three hundred and seventy parts of poor whiskey.[39]

Church and Stage

The church's condemnation of plays, productions of plays, and audiences, was without exception, but it was particularly the indiscriminant labeling of all actors as scoundrels and scourges that reduced an entire profession of artists to one of the lowest ranks in nineteenth-century America. Ministers, who assumed the roles of guardians of America's youth, damned actors as unsavory characters bent on corrupting those who attended the theatre. For instance, DeWitt Talmage's primary objection to the stage is what he calls the unsavory employees of the theatre. He asks a rhetorical question: "How many of you would like to have your sons and daughters grow up and launch out in the association of play-actors?"[40] In his mind, the bad character of most actors is proven by the existence of the greenroom offstage: "The associations of the greenroom are blasting. It is a terrific ordeal, through which but few can pass unsigned. The whole land ever and anon rings with some outcry of shame or cruelty."[41] And what has poisoned the characters of actors? Talmage was convinced that, with few exceptions, actors were unable to be good people because of the parts they played. "The man who so often assumes a bad character, after awhile becomes that which he represents."[42] The Rev. Fulton had the same idea: actors become the villains they impersonate.

Timothy Dwight raised a familiar charge when he wrote that theatre people were "a nuisance in the earth, the very offal of society."[43] He was convinced that the public unanimously viewed acting as a "tarnished profession," the fact that actors "are notorious for wickedness is undeniable."[44] And William Everts was confident that the reputation of actors was lower that that of "any other profession of equal talent and advantages."[45]

But it is Henry Ward Beecher's tirade against actors that is the masterful example of the loaded and incendiary language adopted by the stage's clerical enemies:

> Those who defend Theatres would scorn to admit actors into their society.... Where there is one [great actor], how many thousand licentious wretches are there, whose acting is but a means of sensual indulgence? In the support to gamblers, circus-riders, actors, and racing-jockeys, a Christian and industrious people are guilty of supporting mere mischief-makers—men whose very heart is diseased, and whose sores exhale contagion to all around them. We pay moral assassins to stab the purity of our children.[46]

3. Plays, Playgoers, and Actors

The actor, among other entertainers, is doomed to hellfire, according to Beecher, just by virtue of his blighted vocation:

> Oh! Thou CORRUPTER OF YOUTH! ... Thou shalt draw near to the shadow of death.... Images of terror in the Future shall dimly rise and beckon; — the ghastly deeds of the Past shall stretch out their skinny hands to push thee forward! Thou shall not die unattended. Despair shall mock thee. Agony shall tender to thy parched lips her fiery cup. Remorse shall feel for thy heart, and rend it open. Good men shall breathe freer at thy death, and utter thanksgiving when thou art gone. Men shall place thy grave-stone as a monument and testimony that a plague is stayed; no tear shall wet it, no mourner linger there! And, as borne on the blast thy guilty spirit whistles toward the gate of hell, the hideous shrieks of those whom thy hand hath destroyed, shall pierce thee — hell's first welcome. In the bosom of that everlasting storm which rains perpetual misery in hell, shalt thou, CORRUPTER OF YOUTH! Be forever hidden from our view: and may God wipe out the very thoughts of thee from our memory.[47]

Despite the overblown rhetoric and stereotyping, some of the clergy's opposition to the theatre was justified, but only up to a point. Major urban theatres did recruit prostitutes, but others struggled successfully to discourage them, and there is no evidence that prostitutes were involved with the many traveling shows outside urban areas. It is also true that outbreaks of violence, rowdiness, and petty crime were common in and around urban working-class theatres and, on occasion, spread from there to upper-class theatres. But this was not the general character of upper- and middle-class theatres or road companies.

Some of the church's complaints about actors had legitimacy. Managers and actors acknowledged that alcohol was a problem in theatre companies. But it was no less a problem among all the working poor, many of whom drank themselves into insensibility after long, grueling hours on the job. The drinking among actors was much more apt to be on display. The question could also be asked if syphilis, known to plague some actors, was more prevalent among members of the profession than it was in other areas. It was true, as Benjamin McArthur's statistics bear out, that there were more divorces among actors than in other professions.[48] Still, as managers and actors argue in the following chapter, it was inaccurate and unjust to assume that all, or even most, actors had loose morals. In short, the clergy zeroed in on the lowest urban theatre imaginable and presented it to the religious public as a portrait of all theatres throughout the city and country. All actors, they argued, were identical in character to the worst reprobate on stage.

Church and Stage

In trying to assess the success with which the church determined that larger climate of opinion with which actors had to contend, one has, of course, to acknowledge that the church constituted only one of many voices in a large nation. Nevertheless, the voice of the church was the loudest and most strident one in the nation, a voice to which the majority of the people listened as if their souls depended on it.

4

The Impact of Clerical Attacks on Actors and the Profession

You are a preacher of the Gospel; I am nothing but an actor....
— Solomon Smith

The conflict between church and stage was violently rhetorical but clearly went beyond rhetoric: It created open hostility, as primary testimony of nineteenth-century actors and managers substantiates. The clergy, as God's chosen leaders of the religious public, not only created the theatre's lowly reputation, it did its best to broadcast and keep alive in nineteenth-century culture the view of the theatre as the devil's temple wherein Victorian values were repudiated. But did the antitheatrical clergy exaggerate the schism between church and stage? Was the theatre's bad reputation among the respectable citizenry really as bad as the clergy declared it to be? And did the scorn for the theatre of religious society actually have significance in the lives of actors?

The argument put forward in this chapter is that clergy scarcely exaggerated the reputation of the theatre and that the words and actions of the clergy and their followers *did* take on profound significance in the professional and personal lives of theatrical workers for most of the nineteenth century. At least two recent distinguished theatre historians have used the memoirs of Noah Ludlow, Solomon Smith, and specific pages of the introduction to William Wood's memoir to argue that nineteenth-century actors had no difficulty fitting into polite society.[1] Yet Wood, Smith and Ludlow give evidence not only of social ostracism but also a full range of problems endured by theatre people as a result of the enduring conflict between church and theatre: social humiliations, aggressive animosity toward their profession, their lowly reputation, and their bitterness toward the church, which, with its powerful influence, had turned religious America against the stage. William Wood has this to say about the actor's standing:

> Indeed, none but an actor can conceive how much he may be made to suffer and often most undeservedly. He commences his career in doubt and terror; pursues it in constant anxiety; trembling at every step for the preservation of the little reputation which his toil and privations may have gained him, and which he feels may be destroyed by even the slightest and most unintentional offence.[2]

An incident from William Wood's memoir epitomizes and illuminates the effect that the church's antitheatrical bias had on actors, an episode that, in itself, contradicts the idea that the church's view was of little consequence. As a manager working throughout the northeast, Wood's company, appeared in Baltimore in 1816, in a production of *Bertram*, a play that normally would not have been expected to anger religious leaders because it had been written by a minister and edited and approved by English censors. Despite clerical attacks on the play as immoral, Wood decided to produce it and cast his wife, the company's leading lady, in the starring role. The play was produced, and, on Sunday, his actress wife went to her regular church, little suspecting that her pastor would attack actresses the next Sunday while she was in the congregation. This is how he describes it:

> The tragedy of "Bertram" had proved highly attractive throughout the last season, in spite of a merciless attack upon its immoral character. It may appear strange that a play written by a clergyman, authorized for performance by the Lord Chamberlain, and again revised by the licenser, a gentleman remarkable for his rigid treatment of pieces defective in moral tendency, should have become the object of so much remark and reproach, as it will be remembered by any that this piece was. There severe strictures were not confined to occasional essays or notices, but in our case, at least, proceeded from the pulpit, no doubt from the error of referring only to the original printed edition, unaware of the fact that every doubtful line or allusion had been carefully struck out by the licenser, whose authorized copy alone we followed. On one occasion the speaker became so much carried away by a mistaken impression, as boldly to appeal to his audience, and asked what estimate could anyone make of the feelings or the principles of that woman — of her perceptions of right

4. The Impact of Clerical Attacks on Actors and the Profession

and wrong — who could be found capable of representing the heroine of this shameful production. I know not whether the gentleman was aware that the unfortunate person who the week before, in discharge of her professional engagements, had been representing this character, was at the very time a regular member of his own congregation, and was seated on that Sunday, as she usually was, in her accustomed place at church.[3]

Other first-hand accounts of actors and managers are bitter testimonies to the impediments the church threw up to the successful exercise of the theatrical profession. To a much greater extent, actors faced the same frustrating dilemma that other artists, to a much lesser degree, had to contend with in much of the century. That is, many actors felt *called* to pursue a life on the stage, but saw that men of God damned their calling as satanic. The establishment of theatres in many parts of the country and the greater acceptance the stage began to enjoy in the last decades came with continual, painful struggle against the church and the religious public. Actors, in their own words, provide clear evidence that the religious attitude toward theatre not only hampered the profession as a whole but also humiliated them as individuals.

In exploring the actor's response to antitheatrical religious attitudes, this chapter relies heavily (but not exclusively) on the memoirs of comanagers Solomon Smith and Noah Ludlow because their accounts cover a wide geographical area and include significant details. Both were prominent managers (sometimes comanagers in conflict with each other) whose engagements took them to the frontiers of New York State, Ohio, Missouri, South Carolina, Alabama, Louisiana, and Mississippi during a period ranging from the 1820s into the 1840s; and they also often established theatres in some of those areas. Religious attacks on the stage were apparent from the early days of the century, recorded by the English-born Francis Wemyss, to the later headier days of Albert M. Palmer and Daniel Frohman. As Benjamin McArthur points out, the problems concerning the social position of actors and clerical objections to the stage were still hot topics in magazines and newspapers up to the twentieth century.[4]

Workers in the theatre contended that, unlike other professionals, they were all damned on the basis of the bad behavior of even one of their number. Even as a young man, Noah Ludlow had quickly found that the public in general had a low opinion of actors. "I discovered that when an actor or actress gave offence, the 'outside world' were always ready to involve the whole fraternity, or at least all associated immediately with the offender, however clear of censure their conduct might be."[5] Wemyss also highlights the same problem:

> And here let me ask. Why an actor should not receive from society the honors due to talent? The physician, the barrister, the clergyman, the soldier are all received with the honor due to their occupation. The player, whose toil is equal, and whose task to gain eminence is more severe, is only received as a clever buffoon, tolerated, but not accepted in the bosom of society. It is true, the Kemble family form an exception to this general rule of exclusion; but even they hold their position upon sufferance, not upon right.[6]

James H. McVicker, a theatre professional in Chicago, also acknowledged the impediments thrown up in the 1830s to actors. In his younger days in Chicago, he had seen "a child refused admittance to a school, for the reason that the parents were connected with a theatre."[13] Prejudice against the theatre was glaringly apparent to McVicker as late as the 1860s.

In many places even on the frontier, scorn of the stage and actors persisted as relentlessly as it did in cities like Boston and Philadelphia. Noah Ludlow found in 1854 that Pittsburgh's view of the theatre was just as backward as he had found it many years earlier in 1817:

> In a limited population, such as Pittsburg contained in 1834, a large portion of which were church-people opposed to the theatres, the absence of 20 or 30 well-known and influential supporters of the drama, their families and friends, made a very important deficit in the receipts of the theatre.[7]

Anna Cora Mowatt, an actress born into wealth and prestige, who acted throughout the 1840s, recognized "the prejudices of the world against the profession as a body."[8] The actor, she wrote, dwells "on the outer side of a certain conventional pale of society, which he is allowed to enter only by courtesy, unless it is broken through by the majesty of transcendent talents."[9] Clara Morris, born and reared at the opposite, lowest end of the social spectrum from Mowatt, reached the same conclusion — that members of her profession had labored under a cloud of disapproval throughout most of her career, which had begun in the 1860s: "Even the people who did not think all actors drunkards and all actresses immoral did think they were a lot of flighty, silly buffoons, not to be taken seriously for a moment."[10] Although the cloud of public suspicion was slowly lifting during the last decades of the century, Morris left no doubt about having felt its presence in the 1860s: "The actor had no social standing; he was no longer looked down upon, but he was an unknown quantity."[11] By the 1880s and 1890s, she believed that *some* members of the profession had "won *some* social recognition"[12] (my emphasis).

4. The Impact of Clerical Attacks on Actors and the Profession

Albert M. Palmer, one of the most successful theatre owners and managers in the last half of the century, estimated that at least until mid-century, seven-tenths of the population looked on stage attendance and acting as "almost a sin." He observed some improvement in the public's attitude toward the profession by the 1880s and 1890s.[14] Daniel Frohman, another outstanding producer of the period, known as the "star maker," corroborated Palmer's conclusion that, as late as the 1860s, antitheatrical bias was far-reaching: "Within my memory, play-going had been considered unethical not only by the clergy, but by church-goers."[15]

In the last decades of the century (which will be discussed in more detail in the final chapter), one finds several developments and continuations. The general public's condemnation of actors was not as widespread, and more people, including ladies, attended the theatre. But paradoxically, sermons condemning the theatre increased, perhaps for the very reason that the public was no longer as hostile to the stage. Still, *social* acceptance of actors was still extremely rare. The names of the same few actors are repeated again and again as proof of the general acceptance of actors in America, prominently the Kembles, Charlotte Cushman, and Anna Cora Mowatt.

For most of the century, experienced actors and managers made plain that they attributed the public's hostility toward the theatre specifically to the church. Noah Ludlow speaks bitterly of how the church had brainwashed the public and "stigmatized" his fellow actors to produce the situation he found in Ohio in 1828:

Noah Ludlow, co-theatrical manager with Smith, leaves a bitter account of his personal and professional struggle against the church's antitheatrical attitudes. From George C. D. Odell's 1927 *Annals of the New York Stage* (courtesy of the University of California–Berkeley).

Church and Stage

> No attraction could bring together a succession of full houses in a city where many persons were afraid to go to a theatre, lest they should be "talked about" by those who were members of churches where the clergy were continually consigning *actors* and those who supported them to the *Infernal* regions.[16]

Without going into great detail, Ludlow claims that churches interfered in the private lives of two actors. One, Cornelius A. Logan, Ludlow writes, had been branded as an ungodly undesirable by his own Roman Catholic church in which he had been reared.[17] And a former actor, Charles B. Parsons, was forced to withdraw from his post as minister in a Methodist Church because of "an objection from some narrow-minded members on account of his having been an actor."[18]

Harry Watkins, a minor touring actor who worked for Ludlow and Smith on occasion but met with little luck or money throughout his career, left fragmentary notebooks which were edited and augmented by actors Maud and Otis Skinner, and in which were recorded the obstacles that the actor encountered put up by the church. In New York state in the 1850s, he "[h]ad a long article published in the *Williamsburg Times* written in answer to several articles by a Methodist clergyman ignorantly abusing the stage."[19]

Another theatre professional, William Davidge, author of "The Drama Defended and *Footlight Flashes* challenges the church's view of the stage. Other professional people, he notes— especially those in the clergy and the law — are never branded by the behavior of one or two individuals, while in the theatre, on the other hand, the entire profession is sullied by the behavior of occasional individuals, "their *entire race* tabooed and stigmatized as ... unworthy."[20] He claims that more improprieties are "glaringly evident to any observer who will take the trouble to watch the retiring crowds from the several churches."[21]

Speaking of the public's opinion of the stage as the embodiment of the Devil and hell, Smith relates a strange (and no doubt hilarious to the company) story concerning an 1829 appearance in Tuscaloosa, Alabama, in a production of *Don Juan*, supported by devils and flames. In the process of the performance, a piece of wood on the set caught fire and began spurting real flames. Panic ensued as everyone dashed for the door and alarm ran through the community that God was punishing those who attended the theatre:

4. The Impact of Clerical Attacks on Actors and the Profession

> The bigoted portion of the Tuscaloosans seized upon the circumstance, and held it up as a warning to all play-goers, and shaking their heads ominously, said they knew all along that no good could possibly come from encouraging profane stage plays in a Christian community.[22]

Immediately after the fire, Smith had gone into action himself and had had a carpenter replace the burned piece of wood, then quickly invited the public in so they could see that there was no evidence of fire. Many came and were duly impressed, not knowing that Smith had pulled a devilish trick of his own.

This religious enmity, recorded by actors, had a negative impact on both their professional and personal lives. The low repute in which stage folk were held by the religious public impinged on the growth of theatre in many areas where townspeople were scared away from theatrical performances. The difficulty in attracting audiences naturally resulted in inadequate proceeds and the inability to pay actors living wages, forcing some to abandon what they saw as their rightful calling, and reducing many of those who persisted to live from hand to mouth.

Traveling companies were invariably crippled by the competition forced on them by religious groups. The church's presence on the frontier made itself known in small churches and in camp meetings, which figure prominently in Solomon Smith's account of the trials of management. Frequently, a short distance away from the camp meeting, a touring theatre group would be trying to make a living by enlivening the air with a performance — one that might be noble or ignoble, but was always, by its very nature, flamboyant and enticing. In *Huckleberry Finn*, Mark Twain's satiric portrait of the frontier, he includes both a camp meeting and a stage frolic as typical cultural entities. Traveling theatre companies, especially those trying to make a living by producing much nobler and more highly regarded fare than that represented by Mark Twain's pair of egregious frauds, often found that camp meetings had sprung up as if by magic, at the same time that announcements appeared advertising that a play was being produced. Their purpose was to remind one and all that duty, as well as their own sense of well-being, demanded their presence at the camp meeting or the revival, not the play, which was the enemy of Goodness. Solomon Smith describes one such incident as it occurred in his travels through Kentucky in the 1820s: "[T]he Methodists had raised their banner before us, and had got possession of all the money and all the hearts of the young folk. They fairly conquered us and drove us from the field!"[23]

Church and Stage

Smith's theatrical company collided with churches in Alabama, Tennessee, and Georgia as well. For instance, citizens were warned by their pastors to stay away from the theatrical company in Huntsville and Florence, Alabama, in 1829:

> We performed only four nights in the week; but I find by a memorandum made at the time that there was "preaching every night." The preachers carried the day — and the night too, and we were very glad to escape from Huntsville without a serious pecuniary loss. Yet our performances were not without their moral effect, though the preachers endeavored to make their hearers believe that all who visited the theatre would certainly be eternally roasted in the hottest sort of fires, the heat of which was to be intensified by liberal supplies of brimstone![24]

Solomon Smith, a widely known theatrical manager, is one of the primary sources of information on the extent and painful effect on actors of religious America's loathing for the stage. From George C. D. Odell's 1927 *Annals of the New York Stage* (courtesy of the University of California–Berkeley).

Returning to Huntsville in the same season, Smith declared that he and his company would never return: "The drama *may* flourish here at some distant day, but it will be when religious meetings ... shall have lost their attractions."[25]

In Tuscumbia, Alabama, Smith's company encountered similar religious competition: "We tried a week over at Tuscumbia; but a religious excitement prevailing there at the time (one lady, a Mrs. Goodlow, hanged herself in her ecstasy), we played but six nights to an average of $42 per night and quit."[26]

He also found his company in a clash with reli-

4. The Impact of Clerical Attacks on Actors and the Profession

gious meetings in Greenville, Tennessee, where their production on the first night drew a total of six people:

> My landlord, the carpenter, attributed the slim attendance to a *camp-meeting* that was in successful operation about two miles from town, and "reckoned" that if I would "hold on" until that broke up, we should have full *shops* every night.[27]

Harry Watkins is blunt about his fellow players' lowly station and the difficulties in the life of the itinerant actor. Watkins found that the displeasure with actors and the theatre was as strong in mid-century in Boston as it was on the frontier. He also found the peculiarity existing in New York and other cities that stands as one of the memorable oddities of the nineteenth century — entrepreneurs, faced with the stigma of public distrust, defused the problem of "theatre" and allayed public fears by merely calling their establishments "museums" rather than theatres, announcing that their functions were educational rather than entertaining, thereby pulling in the religious public. Watkins, who had utter scorn for the practice, points out that in every way the Boston Museum, for example, was actually a theatre. "But it is *called* a Museum, and under that title, is visited by members of the church, who would not enter its walls if it was called its right name — Theatre. Such conduct they call religion. I call it hypocrisy."[28] Maud and Otis Skinner, Watkins' editors, go on to explain that these so-called museums actually did have a chamber of horrors in their upper halls which were intended as

Harry Watkins, a poverty-stricken traveling actor, kept a journal of his experiences, including candid stories about the church's humiliation of theatrical folk. Maud and Otis Skinner's 1938 *One Man in His Time: The Adventures of H. Watkins, Strolling Player, 1845–1863* (courtesy of the University of California–Berkeley).

hellfire warnings to sinners and so, by refiguring and renaming the establishment, "rendered this sacrosanct establishment the more tolerable to Mrs. Grundy, [Mrs. Grundy being the stereotypical killjoy] and permitted the clergy to enter its doors without sin."[29]

The theatre faced many impediments on tour because of religious objection. One way in which religious attitudes of the day frustrated the work of traveling companies lay in the reluctance of locals, whose help was essential for the production of plays, to involve themselves with theatre groups. Before the advent of trains, of course, companies traveled by means of horse-drawn carriages or by boats on navigable rivers, and their "companies" most often consisted of the manager(s) and a core of actors. Then, once they reached a town, they had to secure the cooperation of locals to find a place for the company to sleep and secure a suitable place in which to perform, sometimes barns, sometimes attics, at least once in a meat locker. They had to round up carpenters to do necessary and basic work, and, concomitantly, find at least some small troupe of musicians to perform as needed, along with miscellaneous others to serve as choruses or supernumeraries. These were, in short, primitive times for the traveling players and they could scarcely operate without local help, who often regarded actors as smelling of sulphur.

Smith writes of one such instance that occurred in western New York, where the man who rented the company a ballroom for their theatre always hid backstage so the word would not get around to his church that he was doing business with actors.[30] Ludlow records the same problem in Pittsburg in 1817, when he was a young man. The bias against theatre was especially strong in the community, making it almost impossible for the company to find the necessary extras and supernumeraries among the young people in town. "Seamstresses and shoe binders would have as soon thought of walking deliberately into Pandemonium as to have appeared on the stage as 'supers,' or 'corps de ballet.'"[31] The boys they were finally able to attract to be supers were, Ludlow remembers, glad that their hats were too big because "they were ashamed of being seen in such company."[32] Watkins and Smith both describe an appearance in Columbus, Ohio, where the local musicians hired for the performance insisted that they would only play if they were not seen.

Because of religious attitudes, another obstacle acting companies had to confront in some areas was a stiff charge for licenses to perform, levied by the local authorities. James Herbert McVicker, a theatrical manager, critic and historian of the Chicago stage, notes that in Illinois

4. The Impact of Clerical Attacks on Actors and the Profession

local licenses had to be purchased from the city at prices designed to keep actors from working there.[33] Joseph Jefferson, son of a theatrical family and the most famous comic actor of his age, also wrote of citizens using high fees as a discouragement of theatre, using as an illustration an incident in Springfield, Illinois, where a religious revival was in progress when the theatrical company arrived to play to the citizens. Largely to keep the company from drawing souls away from the revival, they were hit with a tax which they were unable to pay. "[T]he fathers of the church not only launched forth against us in their sermons, but by some political maneuver got the city to pass a new law enjoining a heavy license against our 'unholy' calling."[34] Jefferson reveals that the young Springfield attorney who volunteered to represent them in court, and managed to get the tax dropped, was none other than Abraham Lincoln.

There were, then, significant barriers, chiefly arising from religious disapproval, which hindered theatrical companies and caused their work in their calling to be arduous and unprofitable. Moreover, the actors' choice of a theatrical profession damned them to disruption and scorn in their personal lives.

Except for those born into theatrical families (like Joseph Jefferson), family and community bias made it difficult for would-be actors to even enter the profession. Many young people who were determined to pursue a theatrical calling did so only at the expense of family connections and support, often running away from home and losing contact with their parents for many years.

Solomon Smith's first introduction to the theatre came when he was a young boy, having to sneak out at night and hide himself backstage because his brothers had forbidden him to attend the theatre. He follows a stage company out of town, having determined to become an actor, but when he returns home for his clothes, he is forced to stay with an uncle rather than his mother, father, and brothers. Later, ironically, one and then another brother joined him in his theatrical endeavors.[35] Noah Ludlow, Smith's co-manager, attested to an even worse family conflict, created by his choice of a career. His mother and father so deplored the theatre, out of religious convictions, that the young Noah, who was intensely attracted to the stage, had to flee home to follow his calling and did not return for ten years. Even after he married, Ludlow continued to have family problems because of his career. His wife's family put the young couple under immense pressure to abandon their careers on stage:

> But my own and my wife's connections were pleased to look down upon this latter course of life with something like feelings of contempt; they

seemed to think that the "blood of all the Stuarts" had been disgraced. Alas! For poor, weak, narrow, human understandings.[36]

McVicker was another of those young people who attended the theatre and took up acting against the wishes of his parents: "My mother sympathized with all the prejudices that existed at that time against theatres and actors, and was lavish in her advice that I should avoid them."[37]

Having decided to devote themselves to a scorned profession, theatrical folk learned that the general public shared their families' disapproval of the stage. They personally felt these indignities and recorded them in their memoirs.

Early in his career, for instance, young Ludlow faced an enlightenment when he and his fellow actors stopped in Franklin, Kentucky, in what appeared *initially* to be a rare instance of welcome for the company: "The theatre was attended by the best educated and most respectable people of the town and country around about, and the performers, many of them, received into some of the first families. I mention this latter fact, because it is somewhat singular in the history of the stage...."[38] The young actors were thrilled to be invited to the community's Christmas Ball, and excitedly planned what they would wear. They soon learned that certain "gentlemen" of the town, men who had at first pretended friendship, put out the word, with an implicit threat of violence, that the young actors would not be welcome at the ball because, they claimed, the young ladies of the community would refuse to attend if actors were present. Ludlow confronted the men who finally confessed to starting the rumor. This may have given him some emotional satisfaction, but the humiliation embittered Ludlow for the rest of his life: "Having had my temper soured by what I had recently passed there in Frankfort, and my personal respect brought into question because I was an *actor*, I resolved on a life of seclusion from society...."[39]

Similarly, wherever Sol Smith went in those early days, on the east coast as well as the frontier, he was constantly reminded of the lowliness of his position as an actor. In 1824, after some sporadic experiences in the frontier theatre, Sol went east where he was asked by the members of a New Brunswick Episcopal Church to teach the singing of anthems and set religious pieces. He eagerly agreed but kept his meager theatrical experience a secret: "It must be remembered that no one had any idea that I was connected with *the stage*. If they had known I was an actor, my reception and treatment in New Brunswick would most likely have been widely different."[40]

4. The Impact of Clerical Attacks on Actors and the Profession

Even years later, in Natchez, Mississippi, after he had made his mark as a successful manager, he again felt wounded by malicious injustice and bias when he went to court to testify against a boy charged with stealing his watch. When the judge learned that Smith was in town working as an actor, he screamed, "At the THEATRE! ... [S]erved you right, then — served you right! Boy you may go; I dismiss the case." He then informed Sol that he was in a *"criminal profession."*[41]

Nothing made life so difficult on the road and was such a cruel reminder of the public's opinion of actors as being turned away from boardinghouses. Some owners of boardinghouses barred actors from their premises on personal religious grounds. Others, who had no particular animosity toward actors, refused to house them because they feared the ill will of their community or were anxious that other "respectable" boarders would not give them business if they knew that actors had been admitted to the boardinghouse.

In 1815 Noah Ludlow sought to escape opprobrium by renting a room in a boardinghouse not frequented by the rest of the company. Later, his landlady told him that if she had known from the first that he was a member of a theatrical company, he would never have been allowed to rent a room in her house.[42] Twenty-six years later, when Ludlow was a theatrical manager of good national repute, he ran into the same bias from a landlady in Vicksburg, Mississippi, who sent him packing when she learned that he was a member of a theatrical company.[43]

J. H. McVicker also records having trouble finding a boardinghouse to stay in. In one instance a woman who ran a boarding house hesitated to allow actors to stay there because she was afraid her other boarders would leave.[44]

Even at the end of their lives, actors were often not treated with decency and respect by the clergy. The most egregious expression of antitheatrical bias—one that had long been observed in England and France, and that had never ceased to be an outrage to actors and managers—was the refusal of clergymen to provide their fellow actors with religious burials, or, if they did officiate, managed to malign the actor and his or her profession in their funeral sermons. Harry Watkins records this behavior on the frontier in Ohio in the 1840s:

> Attended the funeral of Reeves. He was an Irishman. They went to a priest to pray for him, but he would neither pray nor allow him to be buried in Catholic ground, so they got a Universalist preacher, who in his *sermon* took upon himself to slander members of the profession.[45]

Church and Stage

Shortly after this episode, Collins, another actor in Watkins' company, died of alcoholism, and Watkins reports the incident, (which neither Ludlow nor Smith includes in their memoirs) that, being again unable to secure a minister for an actor's funeral in New Orleans, the company's manager, Sol Smith had to officiate:

> Having no minister, Sol Smith officiated. He spoke very feelingly, and with more sincerity than a minister would, for the latter would undoubtedly have slandered the profession.[46]

In their various defenses of the stage, actors and managers make clear that the church had broadcast views of them that were completely unwarranted. These defenses outline the clerical arguments and answer them point for point, proclaiming that the church and its members—without foundation—were responsible for much of the suffering of actors. One example is Noah Ludlow's defense of his profession on the occasion of a major stop in Nashville, where their success was impeded by a wealthy town matron who insisted that all Nashville's churchgoing population must stay away from the theatre:

> A profession requiring the highest degree of intellectual power, the most elevated and refined taste, the combined excellencies of the poet, the painter, and the sculptor, added to those of the rhetorician! A profession, too, in which there is less deceit, less roguery, less cheating, less dishonesty, than any other of which I have knowledge.
>
> And now, while on this subject, I wish to record my most solemn affirmation that, take them as a class of men and women,—I mean *actors* and *actresses*,—I believe them to be as good, as moral, and as truly religious in thought and act as any other of the same number of beings on the face of the earth. I have lived among them and associated with them in all the relations of life for more than half a century, and I emphatically make this declaration unbiased by fear, favor, or reward. I do not wish to be understood as saying that they are free from faults,—for they are human, and subject to the frailties of human nature,—but I mean to say that they have not *more* or *greater* faults than many other classes I could mention.[47]

Some actors, including Cornelius A. Logan, Harry Watkins, as well as Sol Smith, felt so keenly the injustice of the clerical attacks on the stage that they answered specific sermons and had them printed in newspapers. Sol Smith chose to include in his memoirs several lengthy defenses of the stage. The first, published in St. Louis in 1841 as his letter to the editor, replies to a sermon preached by the Rev. Artemus Bullard upon the death of President William Henry Harrison. Bullard had used the occasion to attack many

4. The Impact of Clerical Attacks on Actors and the Profession

national policies and institutions, including the theatre. But although he makes some exceptions regarding groups of other professions, his damnation of all members of the theatrical profession is unmitigated. "*'Our theatres have become too degraded for any purpose but the exhibition of brute animals and the most abandoned of the human family, male and female.'*"[48] Sol counters:

> If there be *one* of the ONE HUNDRED employed in the St Louis Theatre who can be justly charged with any offense against the welfare of society — with any crime which would render him or her deserving of being termed the "most degraded of the human family," or with conduct calculated to bring disrepute upon the dramatic profession, *let the proofs be given*, and that individual shall be "cast out" from the community of players just as surely as you would "read out" an offending brother from your church.[49]

Sol (who was often mistaken for a minister) alludes to Holy Scripture in castigating the Rev. Bullard, and closes with a sharp rebuke: "Recommending to you the cultivation of more charitable feeling toward your poor, sinful brethren of the human family, I remain, reverend sir, your well wisher."[50]

In 1841, the *New Orleans Picayune* published an editorial written in full support of one of Smith's letters to that paper in defense of the theatre. The interplay of church and theatre is seen in the editor's ironic assertion that "one would be apt to mistake the preacher for the player, and the player for the preacher."[51] The editorial confirms the acrimony and irrational rhetoric of the clergy which so affected the public and the actors:

> A letter from Manager Sol Smith appears in the *St. Louis Bulletin*, in which the worthy humorist defends manfully his profession from the violent abuse of some ill-advised preacher.... Old Sol addresses the reverend gentleman in a strain of caustic but polished reproval, and the style, thoughts, and Christian-like spirit of his letter all present so forcible a contrast to the fire and brimstone character of the sermon, that, without close attention, one would be apt to mistake the preacher for the player, and the player for the preacher. It is a sad error theologians fall into in launching these loose and ill-considered thunder-bolts at the drama; they betray by it their superficial knowledge of the subject....[52]

In a similar manner, numerous actors responded in 1843 to Henry Ward Beecher, the country's most eloquent cleric, who delivered his notorious and publicized antitheatrical speech at the dedication of the Tremont Temple. Among those responding was Smith, who had business in Boston shortly after; he wrote a brilliant 2,000-word rejoinder to Beecher which was published in several newspapers. This time Smith took a no-holds-barred approach, attacking Beecher personally and the antitheatrical clergy generally in his analysis of Beecher's speech. He also compared actors favorably with clergymen, playing on the antipathy between two cultural polarities: the highly esteemed religious establishment and Smith's own profession, whose members were social outcasts:

> *You* are a preacher of the Gospel; *I* am nothing but an actor, and a *poor* one at that, in every sense of the word. *You* are in possession of a princely income, as payment for advocating the cause of the meek and lowly Jesus; *I* am struggling for a precarious subsistence in my capacity of a stage-player, occasionally adding a little to my income by appearing "in the character" of a *lawyer* in the courts of justice. I may add that *you* stand at the head of a powerful sect of professing Christians in the United States, while *I* am content to claim membership in the lowest rank of artists called histrions.[53]

Smith "bluntly" goes on to declare that he has absolutely no desire, under any circumstances, to meet Beecher who, in his dedication, had called the Tremont Theatre the seat of Satan and his works, and claimed that all actors were evil, and the sources of all vice, who stole the souls of good people and delivered them to Satan. Smith turns the tables in a withering attack on the clergy: "[W]e might retort upon the pulpit, and point out instances (and not a few either) where all the wholesome restraints of society have been broken through and trampled under foot by preachers of eminence."[54] Smith then points out that one of the consistent vices of prominent clergymen is adultery; ironically, almost thirty years later, Beecher himself would be charged with adultery in one of the longest, most notorious trials of the nineteenth century.

In the 1845–1846 theatrical season, Smith again wrote a letter in defense of the theatre in response to the diatribe of a clergyman, this time the Rev. W. G. Elliot of St. Louis. Smith answers each of Elliot's objections to the stage: that it is too exciting; that it is too expensive; that other evils are associated with it; and that it leads young men astray. Smith counters that the play's moral message rather than excitement should be the real issue. On the second point, he writes that, with larger audiences, the price of a ticket to see a play has been cut in half. On the third point, he writes that the bar and third tier for prostitutes have not been a part of the St. Louis theatres since the 1830s. And, on the final point, he claims that "'Dissipation' has

4. The Impact of Clerical Attacks on Actors and the Profession

no more connection with the theatre than with the church."[55] The effect of the antitheatrical religious bias on actors is suggested in his last line where he charges the clergy with attempting to "consign" theatrical people to "want and starvation."[56]

In his epilogue, written fifteen years after his retirement from the stage, Smith suggests reforms that need to be made in the theatre, but still renews his condemnation of the antitheatrical clergy:

> The persecution the stage and its professors have been subjected to from certain ministers of the Gospel, so called — those "I am better than thou" teachers of God's law, who delight in crushing and belittling all professions but that to which they belong — must be stopped.... Let every actor — yea, and every actress— who can wield a pen — ... turn upon their assailants ... and the bigots will soon cease their railing against the STAGE, which ought to be, and *is* (with all faults of both considered), of equal standing with the PULPIT as a teacher of morality.[57]

In conclusion, it must have been hard for theatrical people, like Ludlow and Smith, to write about the lowly state of their profession and the mortification to which they had personally been subjected. Still they left undeniable proof in their records of the effect the church and the religious public had on the profession as a whole and on the lives of those who saw the stage as their rightful calling.

5

The Church and the Actress

> *[A]s a temptress, she has not abandoned her vocation*
> — Justin D. Fulton

Nothing dramatizes the collision of the church and the stage so strikingly as the situation of the nineteenth-century American actress, branded a harlot by religious society. One haunting story sets the stage for the discussion for the necessity of the actress to choose between her profession and her religion. On the sixth of September in 1857, two women, one middle-aged, the other about sixty-three, lay in the receiving tomb of Greenwood Cemetery in New York City. When the two women died, seemingly within a few days of one another, the certificate of burial identified the younger woman as Mrs. Matilda I. Reillieux. The older woman was listed on the certificate only as "& co." Both women were eventually buried in the same grave, the older woman still unidentified. The tombstone that was finally erected over the common grave bore only these words: "My Mother and Grandmother." The older woman's death in 1857 was not discovered by her friends and the general public until 1874. At the time, stage historian Joseph N. Ireland could find no clear answer as to why the elder woman's granddaughter would so thoroughly wipe out her grandmother's and her mother's identity. Both had been actresses and the older woman had, seemingly, lived a respectable life as a faithful and self-sacrificing wife and a loving mother of ten children. The "dishonor" of this woman, finally identified as Mary Ann Duff, lay elsewhere: For twenty-eight years, until she was forty-four years old, she had been an actress on the American stage. Moreover, she had been the first great tragedienne of the American theatre, praised by none other than Edwin Booth as the greatest tragic actress in the

5. The Church and the Actress

world. In middle age she had left her profession and converted to a straight-and-narrow life as a devout Methodist, successfully burying her theatrical past.[1] Noah Ludlow writes, "It was said at the time that she had become a member of some church that forbade their communicants attending theatres."[2] The only reason Ireland could finally give to explain her burial without a name was that her devout family was taking every precaution to conceal their kinship with an actress.[3] Mary Ann Duff's and her family's decision to give up her identity as an actress to win the acceptance of her church painfully illustrates the church and stage divide.

The close dependency of most American women on their church at this time illustrates just how alienated actresses were, for they were denied the religious comfort and supportive connection that most other women enjoyed with their clergymen. The church provided most middle- and upper-class Victorian women with their only social life outside their homes, somewhat independent of their husbands.[4] To English and European travelers, the zeal and single-mindedness with which other American women were expected to, and did, turn to religion and clergymen was an extraordinary matter deserving of special attention. Mrs. Trollope found that women crowded the churches from east to west. "Surely," she wrote, "there is no country in the world where religion makes so large a part of the amusement and occupation of the ladies. Spain, in its most Catholic days, could not exceed it."[5] Not only did hundreds of women crowd into individual Sunday morning church services and revivals, but they spent a great deal of the rest of their time at religious meetings. According to Mrs. Trollope, in Washington, D.C., Presbyterian women went to church three times on Sunday, and on the edge of the frontier "no evenings in the week but brings throngs of the young and beautiful to the chapels and meetinghouses."[6] J. S. Buckingham also referred to "the frequency of religious meetings, almost every evening of the week, engaging all the leisure of the women."[7] Mrs. Trollope was convinced that the relationship between women and the clergy had reached the point of being downright unhealthy:

> The influence which the ministers of all the innumerable religious sects throughout America, have on the females of the respective congregations, approaches very nearly to what we read of in Spain, or in other strictly Roman Catholic countries. There are many causes for this peculiar influence. Where equality of rank is affectedly acknowledged by the rich, and clamorously claimed by the poor, distinction and preeminence are allowed to the clergy only. This gives them high importance in the eyes of the ladies. I think, also, that it is from the clergy only that the women of

America receive the sort of attention which is so dearly valued by every female heart throughout the world. With the priests of America, the women hold that degree of influential importance which, in the countries of Europe, is allowed them throughout all orders and ranks of society, except, perhaps, the very lowest; and in return for this they seem to give their hearts and souls into their keeping.[8]

But there was one class of women who were automatically refused the comfort of the church and its clergymen — those who worked as actresses. Will Rossiter defends and advises the actress that she has to prevail without the comforts of the church, and must resist temptation without the support and teachings of the church:

The influence of the home; the teachings of the church, and the association with good and noble people are a power for good which cannot be over-estimated. The absence of these incentives to an honorable life are a negative reason for some of the ruined lives whose mistakes are so graphically pictured in the daily papers. All honor is due to the actress, who without these moral supports, and in the face of temptation, is able to come out unscathed, with no blemish upon her character.[9]

The center of the ideal woman's life was not only her home but her church; however, Clara Morris asserts that the "exclusive spirit" of churches ostracized actresses. They were not welcome there. The public falsely assumed that actresses were not capable of being religious at all and, as a class, were regarded as the enemies rather than the champions of religion.[10] Because of this, the actress seemed to bear a heavier burden than did other working women in her deviation from the ideal: she was regarded not simply as failing to live up to the ideal, but as being symbolic of all that the ideal was not. In the minds of many clergymen and churchgoers, no woman could remain on the stage and remain pure, as the Rev. Robert Turnbull contends:

The effect of the kind of life led by players is peculiarly pernicious to female character. It strips it of all its loftier attributes, its softer and more delicate charms. Sensibility, modesty and refinement are gradually extinguished by the unfeminine and indelicate business of the stage, and nothing is left but the hackneyed and haggard form of injured humanity, covered and bedecked perhaps, by false and tawdry ornaments. A few female actors may have preserved their virtue, but, alas! How many have lost it forever by their connection with the stage. And if others have not been entirely ruined by this means, how greatly must their characters have

5. The Church and the Actress

suffered in purity and elevations, by the dark forms of evil with which they come into such close and continual contact![11]

To understand the magnitude of the condemnation of actresses by the church, one first has to know what the church's general view of women was. The predominant stance maintained by the church was that women were depraved by nature and needed heavy restrictions to keep them from tearing down Christian society because, it was argued, by virtue of their profession, actresses escaped necessary limitations and controls; they insured their own damnation; and worse, were allowed to corrupt individuals and the whole of society.

The basis of the church's view of women began from the beginning — the story of Adam and Eve in the Garden of Eden in the book of Genesis. God, according to scripture, created Adam, placed him in the Garden of Eden, and only later created Eve as his companion. Even though the pair was warned not to eat the fruit of the Tree of Knowledge, Satan, in the form of a serpent, was able to persuade Eve to take a bite of the forbidden fruit and she, in turn, convinced Adam to partake of it, provoking God to throw them both out of the Garden into the cruel world, at the same time rendering humankind eternally depraved according to prevailing church doctrine. In 1860 John Angell James, a clerical railer against the theatre, expressed his view of the nature of woman, derived from scripture, in the ironically titled *Female Piety. A Young Woman's Friend and Guide*. On the first page of his guide, this pastor and "woman's friend" began with the widely accepted church view: "Woman was the cause of sin and death in our world."[12] Later, in enlarging on the idea, he writes that "Events have justified the sagacity of his [Satan's] malice; for to her influence how much may be traced of the crimes and calamities which desolate our earth."[13] Some ministers claimed that the necessity for woman's subjugation to man was proven by God's failure to have woman in his original plan. She was a second thought, required by Adam's need. The Rev. R. W. Patterson even went so far as to claim that there was a fundamental flaw in woman's nature from the first (not present in Adam), even before she met the serpent. "That is, there is a certain element in the female constitution, which induced the tempter to first assail her as more likely to be beguiled...."[14] It is startling to remember that, before it was printed, the Rev. Patterson delivered this address as a sermon to a congregation likely made up chiefly of women.

Frances Power Cobb, an author who defends women against the defamation of the church, notes that ministers insist to women that their very nature leads them to love the devil more than their families, "that we are desperately wicked above all things and destined to everlasting misery.... [T]hat we and all that are born of us, are under the curse of an avenging God."[15]

From the pulpits of America, women learned that they were, by nature, not only depraved, but weak-minded, frivolous, intemperate, and fickle. And, as the biblical story makes clear, when Eve compelled Adam to eat of the forbidden fruit, woman was exposed as a temptress. The combination of her depravity and her role as temptress made her doubly dangerous to men and society. "[A]s a temptress, she has not abandoned her vocation," wrote Justin D. Fulton, a pastor at Tremont Temple in Boston. Woman is still involved in "leading astray the unwary."[16] It is she, primarily, who is responsible for the moral failings of men, tempting them into evil and intemperance, and eventually destroying them on this earth and damning them to hell in the hereafter. So what could be done to protect humankind from the devil's accomplices? Clearly society had to place severe controls on women. The most elemental of these was confinement to her domestic sphere when her economic status permitted it. Next was to forbid her from appearing and speaking in public. Then she must be required to conceal her body, modesty being a vital quality of the Ideal Woman. As nearly as possible she must be shielded from excitements like novel-reading and play-going. And, to keep her pure, her social contacts with men must be minimized, her physical activity limited, and her sexual nature repressed.

The first imperative was to insist that her sole, true calling was, and must be limited to, the domestic sphere as wife and mother. Many published ministers and religious men and women throughout the century turned to the Apostle Paul to buttress the conviction that women should not assume a public role, that, in so doing, she invariably took on the role of Eve, working hand-in-claw with Satan.

After 1800, the idea of "woman's place," as it was defined by means of the Protestant Ethic, grew increasingly strong, increasingly rigid, and idealized.[17] Religious female writers of very different persuasions acknowledged the idea of woman's place and woman's duty as their age dictated it. Eliza Farrar, a nineteenth-century woman, wrote in her book of advice, *The Young Lady's Friend*, that whether a woman were rich or poor, housework was "her express vocation, her peculiar calling."[18]

Women should not even give consideration to becoming missionaries of the Gospel, or engaging publicly in charity work or reforms. Andrew P. Peabody, a theology professor at Harvard College, scolds those who have

5. The Church and the Actress

"forsaken the home-sphere for those most conspicuous ministries in which so many highly gifted and conscientious but, as I think, misguided women are now courting the public eye."[19] For woman to leave her rightful place would be catastrophic for all humankind, according to John Y. Gholson, rector of St. Bartholomews Church in Baltimore: If woman seeks work outside the house, "the domestic circle [will] be broken, society disorganized, chaos reign, and hell rule on earth."[20] Many women, working closely with the clergy, seconded the need for placing controls on themselves. One example is Mrs. A. J. Graves, obviously a devoutly religious soul, who in 1841 contended that there is scriptural support for the necessary confinement of women to the home, though the author provides nothing but generalities for that claim.

> Oh! That the mind of woman were enlightened fully to ... appreciate her true position in society; for then she would be in no danger of wandering from her proper sphere, or of mistaking the design of her being. That woman should regard home as her appropriate domain is not only the dictate of religion, but of enlightened human reason.[21]

If women were kept in their own true calling, they would naturally be less able to damage others by appearing or speaking in public. Although Puritan women had more vocational freedom than their daughters in the nineteenth century, the prohibition against women being heard in public was an even greater atrocity than it was later. It is at the heart of two notorious cases of heresy against the church: Anne Hutchinson and Mary Dyer, one of whom was banished and one executed because they dared "preach" in public, although Hutchinson's public platform was her own house. When women in the nineteenth century sought church platforms in their work for abolition and temperance, causes that many of the clergy supported, they were invariably turned away because of the ban against women "exposing" themselves in public by speaking before mixed audiences of men and women. The extremity to which this could be carried was recorded by Matilda Gage, a nineteenth-century suffragette: "In 1843, the Hopkinson Association of Congregational Divines of New Hampshire unanimously enacted a statute in opposition to women opening their lips in church, even to 'sigh' or 'groan' in contrition."[22]

Mary Lyon, founder of Mount Holyoke College for women, is one of many examples of a woman who was strongly admonished by the clergy to cease her speaking appearances before "mixed meetings."[23] To further their causes, Mary Lyon and others, pressing for education for women, and those who met at Saratoga to work for women's rights, had to recruit men to do their public speaking for them.

Another restriction that curbed woman's potentially evil nature was the requirement for her to be modest by curtailing her encounters with men. Polite society had even adopted the custom of having ladies retire to drawing rooms, separated from gentlemen, a practice that was more strictly adhered to in America than it was in England and Europe.[24]

With the church's position on the nature of woman in mind, it is easy to see why religious people equated actresses with harlots. Fundamentally, the actress had overthrown all the fetters that kept the depraved nature of women in check and prevented her from endangering humankind. The actress had taken herself out of the sheltering concealment of domesticity, not only working outside the home, but, for most of her life, not even having a home. She lived on the road, traveling from town to town in the provinces, or performing in different cities. Instead of working in silence behind the walls of her house, the actress had chosen a calling where appearing and speaking in public were the very essence of her work. It was her job to be on display. Rather than carefully avoiding excitements, as the clergy warned all women to do, the actress was surrounded by, and part of, the excitement—the music, and costumes, and lights, and romantic tales connected with theatrical entertainment. Instead of having minimal contact with men, she traveled with them when shows went on tour, rehearsed with men, changed costumes frequently in the same general backstage area with men; and onstage she would play love scenes with men. Ministers described her as dispensing "lascivious smiles, wanton glances, and dubious compliments."[25] She assumed "indelicate attitudes," kissed men on stage, and engaged in a "variety of vain and sinful practices," undoubtedly betrayed by "heaving bosoms, languishing glances, voluptuous attitudes, falling into the arms of men,"[26] and, as the Rev. David Agnew writes, allowing herself to be scantily attired and "twirled and handled on stage."[27] She danced instead of heeding the warning that she avoid physical activity, and her dress displayed more of her arms, neck, and upper chest than would have been remotely approved by Victorian churchmen.

Stories about the church's displeasure with actresses abound, the story previously told about the wife of William Wood being one of them. Another example was star and playwright Anna Cora Mowatt who was harshly criticized by the religious press in 1842 for appearing publicly before men and women. Her biographer, Eric Barnes, notes a general public attitude that "it was bad enough that Mrs. Mowatt should read poetry in public, but that

5. The Church and the Actress

she should do so before mixed audiences seemed nothing less than depravity."[28] With appropriate sarcasm, Noah Ludlow tells another story about an actress who loses her past to please her in-laws and their church. When an actress of his company married a steamboat captain, "the parents of Capt. H____ were much displeased with the marriage, on account of the lady having been an actress, such was the stupid prejudice of those days.... She ... became an exemplary member of a church, and *of course* the *sin* of her having been an *actress* was atoned for."[29]

The actress's most egregious deviation from female decency in the eyes of the religious public was what it regarded as her personal "impurity" or immorality, labels attached to her because of her profession. Not all ac-

Anna Cora Mowatt was an upper-class woman forced on stage to support her family after her husband suffered financial reverses. Mowatt wrote plays and books about the stage as she knew it.

tresses were morally upright. Certain carefree stars like Adah Isaacs Menken, who had multiple affairs, one of them with Alexander Dumas, père, buttressed the religious argument against actresses. The divorce rate was higher among actresses than among women in most other segments of Victorian life. And not all actresses resisted the advances of stage-door Johnnies and mashers who were ready to pounce on them outside the stage door. But the memoirs of theatrical folk defend actresses as a class and deplore the tendency of the church to damn them, one and all, and to automatically assume that the bad conduct of one or two actresses was always worse than women in other segments of society. Olive Logan deplored the fact that "the name of the poor stock actress is a synonym for what is lax in the sex."[31]

This misconception that equated most actresses with prostitutes, or "what is lax in the sex," originally arose because of the conditions on the

Restoration stage to which critics alluded rather frequently. John Harold Wilson, in *All the King's Ladies*, recounted the genesis of a reputation, developed during the Restoration, that plagued actresses for two hundred years thereafter. From the time when actresses were introduced to the English stage, around 1660, until the eighteenth century, the theatre was a means by which poor women could marry into wealth, but more often, become kept mistresses of wealthy men. Of the eighty women who are known to have been actresses in London between 1660 and 1689, at least twelve, according to Wilson's research, left the stage to become mistresses or prostitutes. Twelve others who continued to work as actresses had reputations as harlots. Of the eighty, probably no more than twenty-four led respectable lives. As a result, Wilson wrote, "'actress' and 'whore' were effectively synonymous."[31] It was the reputation established at this time that stuck to members of the profession in nineteenth-century America, long after it had ceased to be accurate and had instead become a slander. It did not help matters that prostitutes were encouraged by managers to frequent the theatre and that many of them, when they were arrested, identified themselves as actresses. In what is largely a defense of the actress, Will Rossiter, in 1903, enlarges on an unhappy practice that one assumes went back to the nineteenth century:

> Few people realize how continually the theatrical person stands in the white glare of publicity. Details of life which would pass unnoticed in ordinary circles are picked up and commented upon in a manner little less than disgusting when the subject is an actor or actress. Read the daily papers—half the disreputable women who are carried to the police courts claim to be actresses.... [T]hese poor drabs try to cloak themselves in the mantle of theatrical respectability to mislead the officers of the law.... [S]mall wonder these poor professionals [actresses] bear a bad name, when every street walker can assume a professional standing and does not hesitate to do so.[32]

The men of the American theatre defended actresses, not only as more humanitarian than other women, but even in terms of a very narrowly defined morality, as being as respectable as other women. W. W. Clapp, a historian of the Boston stage, claimed that there was "no class in the community more remarkable for constancy and devotion in their domestic relations" than were actresses.[33] Another actor, William Davidge, supported actresses in a book entitled *The Drama Defended* by writing that "there are now in the city of New York, who have returned from the duties of their profession, those whose chastity, truthfulness, and domestic accomplish-

5. The Church and the Actress

ments, as daughters, wives and mothers, are second to none, not even the most opulent in this vast metropolis."[34] When actresses and ballet girls did become immoral, he continued, it was not the fault of the theatre. "A young woman seldom falls or loses her self-respect because entrusted to her own guidance behind the scenes of a Theatre; it is from without that the spoiler comes. It is very rarely from the profession, but from the followers of inexperience."[35] Nor, wrote Davidge, was there any truth in the argument that actresses were just naturally sinful because they worked in close association with men: men and women worked together in factories and churches without being corrupted or compromised. Furthermore, he insisted, what seemed to be true on-stage was not necessarily true offstage, as many ignorant critics of actresses thought: An actress who was affectionate toward an actor onstage might dislike him intensely in real life and scarcely be on speaking terms with him after the curtain fell.[36]

Theatrical women were particularly quick to rise in defense of their sister actresses, including the lowly ballet girls who were so often the prey of stage-door Johnnies or "mashers." Anna Cora Mowatt, a latecomer to the stage, who had been suspicious of actors in her youth and felt insulted when a manager first offered her a stage position, defended actresses after she had acquired some firsthand knowledge of the profession. She indicated just how very wrong she had been in her self-righteous disdain. To her surprise, she had found "refined and accomplished ladies, exemplary wives" in the theatre, and said, "My views concerning the stage and my estimate of the members of dramatic companies had undergone a total revolution. Many circumstances had proved to me how unfounded were the prejudices of the world against the profession as a body." Women in the theatre, she found, led lives of "unimpeachable purity, industry, devotion to their kind, and fulfilled the hardest duties of life with a species of stoical heroism."[37]

Clara Morris saw the bias against the actress, which had been promulgated by the church, in the attitude of her mother, who had struggled all her adult life in the most menial and demeaning of domestic positions, as housekeeper and seamstress, but was "stricken with horror" when her daughter turned to the theatre as the only likely means of sharing the family's financial burden.[38] Her observations as an adult actress belied everything her mother had assumed about the theatre. Morris probably went a bit too far in claiming that, in all her years in the theatre, she had seen only one instance of even a breath of scandal in the theatres where she had been employed.[39] The outstanding stars of the American stage rarely, if ever, complained of the acute personal distress they must have suffered from the injustice of social snubs or false accusations or their inability to move comfortably in polite society, outside the protective circle of their profession. But, here and there, we find hints of just what these actresses endured. We read of Fanny Kemble's shock at being told after her marriage to a rake from an aristocratic Quaker family that she would be forbidden from entertaining old friends because her husband would not allow actors in his house.[40] We find Anna Cora Mowatt being accused of betraying her class when she decided to become an actress, and finally, after her remarriage, suffering the snubs of Richmond society, not only because she was a Swedenborgian, but because she had been an actress.[41]

It has often been observed that in Victorian society women were either angels or harlots. There was no middle ground. No matter what her character, this forced the American actress, who could never fill the role of the ideal woman, into the unfortunate ranks of the fallen women. To deviate from the qualities of modesty, purity, and piety, even once, was to put her reputation, her marriage, her very life in jeopardy. For the actress's choice of the stage, she paid dearly. By relinquishing those qualities that her society valued in woman, those limitations that protected her from damnation, she could not turn for spiritual sustenance to her church or depend on the high regard of polite society as her Victorian sisters did.

No matter her personal behavior, the actress was tainted solely by her association with a profession seen as a temple of the harlot. The careers of Mary Ann Duff and Clara Morris illustrate the ambiguity of the actress's position: She was able to anticipate professional rewards which few other women in the age enjoyed, but only at considerable sacrifice of intangibles precious to nineteenth-century woman — personal esteem and social acceptability.

The actress' reputation in nineteenth-century America, distorted and exaggerated as it was, was a reality she had to confront.[42] It is hard to escape a sense of the loneliness that she must have suffered in her exile, imposed by the church, from the mainstream of nineteenth-century womanhood, hard to underestimate the courage it took her to stick to her calling, which was the worst and the best of worlds.

6

Trading Religious Approval for Work

Everything in the theatre's make-believe — except salary day....
— Clara Morris

As one broaches the subject of why American women would want to ostracize themselves from mainstream society and bring on themselves the opprobrium of the church, with its alliance with capitalism gone mad, one returns to the Protestant Ethic and the church's insistence that every person — the poor man or woman included — remain in his or her proper place. In light of this, one of the many dangers of the stage, in the eyes of the church, came in the theatre's empowerment of the dispossessed, like working-class women, whom it invited or enticed. These women of the theatre posed a double threat: The theatre handed woman authority of a real *economic* character, which allowed her to take on real life roles inappropriate to her sex, the most significant of which was the role of breadwinner.

While the church was insisting that Eve's story proved that woman should be subservient to man, this disparaged profession gave her, if she were ambitious and talented, the possibility of economic independence and professional equality with men which she could find nowhere else.

Benjamin McArthur, in *Actors and American Culture, 1880–1920*, finds in the census of 1900 "that the stage offered women more opportunities than did other professions. In 1900 the traditional professions contained a comparative handful of women, and discrimination against them was nearly universal. The theatre, by contrast, had no long-standing barriers against females, and successful actresses stood on equal footing with men."[1]

Church and Stage

The nation as a whole was experiencing vast commercial awakenings and enlargements, but the vocational growth of its women in other professions was stunted by greater church-inspired psychological, social, and economic limitations, which somehow placed them outside of life's mainstream and forbade them to compete with men for wages and for positions of professional prominence. Only within that larger context of women and work in the nineteenth century can one appreciate a woman's good fortune in the theatre in being able to circumvent many of the barriers placed before most others.

Whether a girl grew up in the first or the last of the century, one constant paradoxical trap remained, an impossibly complex situation that placed her between Scylla and Charbydis: While economic changes lured her, even forced her, out of the home to work, more often than not, middle- and upper-class attitudes placed a moral stigma on her for venturing out of the sphere of her own home. It is curious to look back over the religious admonishments offered to women to remain in their stations.

Clara Morris, daughter of a domestic worker, went on stage to make a living. She become a star, a fiction writer, and a recorder of life on stage.

Vary rarely does a clergyman take into account that a large segment of the female population had no home in which they could remain and had no choice but to work outside the house. Most actresses, even the highborn Anna Cora Mowatt and Charlotte Cushman, were among those who could not financially afford the luxury of remaining in the domestic sphere. Inventions and the growth of machinery were robbing woman of the traditional homebound work, while Holy Writ, capitalistic dictates, and her very nature, as the century viewed it, dictated that she was created to stay at home and grace it with the performance of special, limited duties.

The church's support of capitalism, (see Russell Con-

6. Trading Religious Approval for Work

well's *Acres of Diamonds* and Horace Bushnell's *Prosperity Our Duty*) added to special readings of the Bible. And singular beliefs about woman's nature also served to limit her options as a worker. The new capitalist proved his success by his accumulation of material goods, which included a wife who could be maintained in "ornamental idleness."[2] In short, the ideal woman was an object meant to grace the home of the successful businessman. As Mari Jo Buhle, Ann D. Gordon, and Nancy E. Schrom wrote in their history of working women in America, "The older traditions of feminine usefulness, strength and duty were cast aside for moral and decorative functions."[3]

To look at the mere numbers of jobs available for uneducated women, however, without recognizing the conditions under which they worked, is to have an incomplete picture. From the vantage point of the worker, that picture was almost universally harsh. Even the famous textile mills of Lowell, Massachusetts, built to meliorate the gross abuses of the industrial revolution and shown to European visitors as model establishments, were themselves heavily paternalistic and restrictive, and whose working conditions deteriorated as the century wore on.[4] Conditions in most factories, moreover, were distinctly less than model and, in many instances, hardly humane.

In 1817, a day in the cotton mills of Fall River, Massachusetts, began around five in the morning and lasted until seven-thirty at night. One-half hour was allowed the girls at midday to rush home, eat, and return to work; and when they finished in the evening, they were usually too weary to eat at all. Everywhere the cotton mills were generally unventilated and filled with cotton dust and the fumes from oil lamps. If a young woman were lucky, she could perhaps go into domestic service, generally considered a step above factory work. But here, too, the situation was hard and demeaning. Servants were on call twenty-four hours a day, seven days a week.[5]

The more highly regarded jobs as white-collar workers or salesgirls were scarcely better and not so readily available. Saleswomen had to stand behind their counters throughout the long day, 5:00 A.M. until 10:00 P.M. for six days a week, and half day on Sunday, when inventory was taken. Like factory workers, they were fined for tardiness or for overstaying their allotted three to five minutes in the company bathrooms.[6] Even at the close of the century, when industrial barons enjoyed unparalleled luxury, the conditions of their workers were still abominable.

A report by Helen Campbell of the 1893 findings of the Massachusetts Bureau of Labor attests (as do other accounts of women's work) that, while

For factory workers who hadn't the option to live within the designated domestic sphere, life was dangerous and arduous, a marked contrast to work in the theatre.

the century needed women's labor, employers were scarcely willing to share the benefits of industrialism with them.[7]

As unlike as the educated and uneducated women might be in background and capabilities, when misfortune forced them onto the job market, they faced a common future of discouragement, limitation, and injustice. Whether the conditions of a woman's job were pleasant or hard, whether she were skilled or not, she could depend on one fundamental reality, so widespread and long-standing as scarcely to be noted: She would inevitably receive far less money than would men for the same kind and quality of work. She also faced another constant and discouraging reality, whether she worked outside the home or not and whether she were educated or not; that reality was servitude. The woman teacher, like the domestic worker, was inevitably under someone else's strict supervision. It was the rare situation, almost freakish, to find a woman in a position of school principal, or having positions of financial or political leadership, or working with any degree of independence.

In such a world, where the shopgirl was broken, the factory worker

6. Trading Religious Approval for Work

tied with the iron chains of poverty to machines that could kill her, where even the cultivated woman, cast out on her own, often felt the cold threat of nonexistence close in around her, in such a world designed to atrophy the courage and imagination of the hardiest women, one field stood apart as a viable aspiration for both educated and uneducated women of talent and ambition. That possibility was the stage. For the women who entered its portals, opportunities for financial reward, professional status, and even a surprising measure of equality with men were within reach, as they were almost nowhere else.

The history of the theatre's development in the nineteenth century suggests that a young woman who chose a career in the theatre allied herself with a rapidly growing, vital profession. The developing industrialization, the growth of cities, the expansion across the plains, the sudden opening up of the West, especially California — all worked to facilitate the spread of theatre, despite religious America's objection.

The sheer numbers of theatres and companies in the century, as well as the breadth and vitality of theatrical activity, is evidence that the theatre could be a feasible profession for many women in a time when the vocational choices as a whole were few and dismal. In the beginning of this burgeoning business, opportunities for women were relatively good. As theatres multiplied, so did the jobs for actresses. The stock company in William Dunlap's time, at the turn of the century, hired about eleven regular actresses as well as a number of supernumeraries, or "supers": the spearholders, the extras— members of crowds hired for a particular show, to be at a certain spot at a certain time and to shout, stand, or cheer.[8] A good example of the acting jobs available as theatre began to be established is the 1806 Philadelphia company that hired nine men and eleven women plus an undetermined number of supers, and the New York company, in 1798, that hired ten men and ten women.[9] John Bernard, an actor who recorded the American scene, in *Retrospections on America, 1797–1811,* looked back with pleasure on the profession in the first quarter of the century: An actor in those early years was easily employable and, when not called upon to appear in a production, could augment his or her salary by doing readings in small towns.[10] By 1843, a typical stock company, like Wallacks or the Boston Museum, hired as many as twenty men and twenty women.[11] Sol Smith apparently went on tour in 1833 with nine men and four women, and he and Noah Ludlow toured with seven in 1836, only four in 1845, and thirteen in 1850. On occasion they had 20 women and hired locals to supplement the cast.[12]

By the 1830s, when such professions as law, medicine, and business had been closed to women for some time, jobs in the theatre were more accessible than they had ever been. Statistics collected by Joseph A. Hill in *Women in Gainful Occupations, 1870-1920,* show that in 1870 there were more women in the theatre than in medicine, including nursing; twenty times more actresses than newspaperwomen; four times more women in the theatre than in literary and scientific vocations combined; about one hundred forty times more actresses than women lawyers. The only profession that had more women than did the theatre was teaching. By the 1880s, only teachers and nurses outnumbered actresses.[13] Positions for women as well as men were defined by rather rigid lines of business. The basic female positions were a leading lady, a second lady, a juvenile lead, an old woman, a heavy, one or two singing chambermaids, a character actress, and several women known, in descending order of importance, as "walking ladies," "responsible utility actresses," and "utility ladies."[14] Most actresses began at the bottom as supernumeraries or utility actresses. In the 1840s those with talent and initiative could move up in the cast after a three- or four-month apprenticeship, although later in the century, it took longer and longer, sometimes as much as a year, for a super to become a utility actress. One avenue an actress could take to gain notice was to appear in afterpieces, playlets given after the main attraction. Benefits also allowed the eager young actress to demonstrate her abilities. On those nights when established actors were given the opportunity to put together a performance from which they garnered most of the profit, apprentice actors were often requested to take longer roles than they normally were assigned. In any case, a novice who got beyond the supernumerary line had an excellent opportunity in a stock company to learn her craft by playing many different kinds of small roles, and if her performances were promising, earning promotion.[15]

A development in the 1830s opened up many more jobs for women in the theatre: the trend of introducing pageantry, musicals, and operas.[16] Eventually these productions led to the development of one of the largest groups of employees in the theatre — the ballet corps, frequently mentioned by actresses Anna Cora Mowatt, Olive Logan, and Clara Morris. Morris had actually begun her own career as a member of the ballet corps. In 1882, J. J. Jennings, a professional stage watcher, who sensationalized his account of the theatre, drew attention to a theatre's call for fifty ballet girls for just one St. Louis production — a number that he said was not unusual. They were drawn from the unemployed working force, the lower classes: "The

6. Trading Religious Approval for Work

majority of girls who answer for 'ladies for the ballet,'" Jennings wrote, "are shop girls, girls who take work to their homes, girls thrown out of employment, poor girls who had no other way of honestly earning a dollar."[17] Like supers, some ballet girls could expect eventual promotion to acting jobs, even stardom. Clara Morris is a shining example. She was, while a member of the ballet corps, given a small secondary speaking role, then assigned boys' parts, later given a chance to understudy more important roles, and finally, after proving her abilities, given a regular acting position in one of the "lines" of business.[18] Naturally the stage did not guarantee instant stardom to every woman who presented herself at the door. Nor could every woman even expect an immediate place in a theatre company as an actress. But many women did find instant employment in the theatre in various other capacities, primarily as costumers. As early as 1792, the stage was recommended as an answer for unemployed women by those who did not share the usual prejudices against the stage. It could be a means of preserving "the indigent helpless female from the necessity of earning bread by improper means."[19] Nineteenth-century actresses who wrote memoirs of the stage (Anna Cora Mowatt, writing in the 1830s and 1840s; Olive Logan, writing about the 1850s and 1860s; and Clara Morris, about the 1870s and 1880s) all agreed that the stage offered women one of the few self-respecting occupational alternatives. Morris stressed it as a realistic choice in a limited world that demanded servitude of its women:

> Some impetuous young reader who speaks first and thinks afterward may cry out that I am not doing justice to this profession of acting, even that I discredit it, in thus comparing it with humble and somewhat mechanical vocations; so before I go farther, little enthusiasts, let me remind you of the wording of this present query. It does not ask what advantage has acting over other professions, over other arts, but "What advantage has it over other occupations for women?"[20]

Although Olive Logan was more candid about the adversities of acting, a way of life in which she had been reared and to which she returned solely from necessity, she was as convinced as Morris that the living offered women by the theatre was not to be taken lightly. In light of all the difficulties of the stage, wrote Logan, a man's desire to become an actor was not as understandable as a woman's desire to be an actress. In one of her stories, an experienced woman challenges an aspirant actor: "But, why do you desire to go upon the stage, Mr. Pennyweight? You cannot wish thus to earn a livelihood. If you were a woman — or even a poor man, I might understand it. The channels in which woman can work are few, and obstructed by numberless toilers."[21]

One reason why women were unable to enter so many other vocations was that they were often thrown into the workforce so suddenly that they had neither the time nor the funds to acquire the training demanded by those open occupations that might be suitable otherwise. A woman could not even do the humble work of sewing or teaching painting and music without some training period. Meanwhile, no income could be realized until the skill was mastered. If she had the funds to wait, she might be able to train herself. But many could not wait. Logan dramatized the situation in her story of "Carrie Lee, an American Debutante":

Olive Logan, from an acting family, defended her profession, but, at the same time confessed that she hated working as an actress, but was compelled to do so from economic exigency.

Being suddenly left fatherless, motherless and penniless, Carrie Lee was made painfully conscious of the fact that landladies, whatever their sympathies, do not keep boarders for nothing; and that the only irresistible music in this world is the jingle of a well-filled purse. Knowing then that she must do something for a livelihood, Carrie Lee investigated the subject of women's employment. But what could she do? Alas! here was the trouble. Carrie Lee had received a good boarding-school education, such as young ladies of the present day commonly receive — a smattering of French, a smattering of algebra, a smattering of drawing, a smattering of music and a smattering of various other genteel accomplishments — all of which were of very small use to her now. They would not, or so it seemed, bring her in five cents a day. In fact Carrie had never been taught anything useful in the world — there is

6. Trading Religious Approval for Work

not one girl in a thousand who ever *is* taught anything useful, or anything which she could turn to practical account if she were obliged to earn a livelihood. What *should* she do? Coloring photographs, dress-making, plain sewing, all these things require time and instruction before a livelihood can be made from them; and in the case of Carrie Lee the material wants were immediate, and must be immediately supplied.[22]

Of course, Logan, herself an actress, suggested the stage at mid-century as the solution to the problem of a girl such as Carrie. Not only could she be employed immediately, but she could also be paid as she learned. Clara Morris, writing of a later period, agreed: "The theatre is, I think, the only place where a salary is paid to students during all the time they are learning their profession; surely a great, a wonderful advantage over other professions to be self-sustaining from the first."[23]

The stage not only provided many women with jobs; it also gave them fair wages — sometimes even extremely good wages — compared with other occupations. As Clara Morris was told by a young ballet girl when she first entered the theatre, "everything in the theatre's make-believe — except salary day."[24] A comparison of the standard wages paid to stock company actors, including ballet girls, with wages paid to female workers in other occupations in America gives the contemporary reader some idea of the economic life of theatrical women. It takes little imagination to see a very bleak life for working women in the salary figures throughout the century. For example, Matthew Carey, a philanthropist interested in the plight of seamstresses, found that in 1831 the earnings of these women rarely exceeded $1.12 a week. At times they cleared only $.04 a day for food, fuel and clothing.[25] Barbara Wertheimer, in her study of working women, indicated that the wages for Lowell mill girls, "about the highest that women could command in the early part of the century," were $.35 to $.50 a day plus room and board. She discovered, further, that in 1845 half the women workers in New York City earned less than $2.00 a week.[26] Dr. William Sanger, who made a study of prostitution in the city in 1858, found that female domestic servants, often on call twenty-four hours a day, made $5.00 a month or less. Seamstresses, tobacco packers, and book folders, many of whom eventually turned to prostitution out of sheer weariness and desperation, averaged only a dollar a week.[27]

In the 1860s, thirty thousand female factory workers in New York City received an average salary of $.33 a day. At the same time, sewing machine operators earned from $5.00 to $8.00 a week, out of which they had to pay $3.00 or $4.00 for "a bed in a wretched room, often with several other occupants, and without a window...."[28] By 1868, another large group of women employees, milliners, were averaging from $4.00 to $7.00 a week, saleswomen from $6.00 to $7.00.[29] As late as 1893, the average salary for working women in New York City was still only $.60 a day, ranging from $2.00 a day for cashiers to $.30 a day for East Side factory workers, who, incidentally, worked from twelve to fifteen hours a day.[30]

Nor were educated women who worked as teachers earning living wages. A Horace Mann report of 1847 indicates that the average pay per month for female teachers in the United States ranged from $4.75 in Vermont to $10.09 in Pennsylvania. It stands to reason that they also received board in addition to this wage.[31] A writer for the *Nation* in 1867 claimed that few women teachers ever earned more than $600 yearly.[32]

Compared with these salaries, the wages of women in the theatre appear to be very good, indeed, especially when one considers the less grueling, less demeaning work.[33] While factory girls were making $.33 a day in the 1840s, supernumeraries, at the very bottom of the theatrical salary scale, were paid from $.25 to $.50 a night for relatively light work and few hours and, as has already been indicated, the promise of moving up to better roles and better salaries after several months, if they were talented and interested.[34] The beginning salary at mid-century for a ballet girl was, it is true, only $3.00 or $4.00 a week and she had to provide her own costume, but even that was four times what skilled female labor was being paid by many employers. In short, the work of a ballet girl was not nearly so unpleasant or so hopeless and demeaning and physically arduous as domestic and factory work.

For those on the next step up the theatrical ladder, the ordinary actresses, available figures reveal an even more extraordinary situation in light of women's wages throughout the century. In the 1798–1799 season, William Dunlap paid his various actresses weekly wages of $25, $37, $20, $14, $13, $12, and $16. In the next season, furthermore, the salaries of continuing actresses were raised.[36] Female stars could even then, at the turn of the century, command from $50 to $100 a week.[37] And in addition to their regular salaries, most actors and actresses were allowed to hold about two benefit performances annually. The actress who held a benefit reaped most of its profits; she might net $500 to $1,000 annually from benefits alone.[38] As the century wore on, moreover, the salary of the actress improved, despite fluctuations in the national economy. Olive Logan reported that an ordinary actress in 1850 could expect from $40 to $60 a week, and a popular actress in good demand could command from $5,000 to $20,000 a

6. Trading Religious Approval for Work

year.[39] At mid-century, Lester Wallack's Theatre in New York City was paying its male and female employees from $6.00 to $55.00 weekly, with guarantees of benefits written into the contracts.[40] Nor did this situation prevail only in the East. According to George MacMinn, a theatre historian of the Far West, women took home immense salaries in the inflation-ridden frontier; the lead actress in a California mining theatre could earn $200 a week in 1849, and amateur secondary actresses could earn $60 a week.[41] There is even an account of a Swiss organ girl who accumulated $4,000 in the course of five or six months on the California stage.[42]

In fact, the salaries of actresses in any part of the country were so good that the women were often preyed upon by unscrupulous men looking for small fortunes or steady incomes. For this reason, both actors and actresses repeatedly warned the young girls in the profession to be wary of prospective suitors:

> It is astonishing with what blindness and reckless disregard of results young ladies on the stage, after having by their industry acquired handsome sums of money that with their talents would make them independent, pecuniarily, for life, will throw away those blessings and destroy their comfort, perhaps their happiness, by bestowing their hands and fortunes on heartless adventurers who have nothing to recommend them, but, perhaps, goodly persons, and subtle tongues to plead their suits.[43]

The high-salaried Lucille Western, much in demand on both coasts, is a good example. Her husband certainly knew that he had a good enterprise in having married an actress, and he knew her income from night to night. It was his custom to gauge the house before one of his wife's performances, estimate the receipts within $5.00, and gamble it all away before her performance was over. During one session he managed to gamble away three nights of his wife's work.[44]

Even the lowly ballet girl was game for unscrupulous men. One actor, William Davidge, observed that "she at times ties herself to one whose means are not of that positive and satisfactory nature represented (in domestic dramas) and awakes to the fact when too late, to know that the evening of her life will be consumed in laboring for the support of him and his offspring."[45]

Even more unusual than the better salaries was the theatre's custom of paying women salaries equal to those of men, for this policy of equality of payment in the theatre prevailed at a time when gross inequality was rampant in other professions. In the 1840s, for instance, male teachers had average salaries almost three times those of female teachers.[46] In the 1860s female teachers were still paid only half of men's salaries.[47] In 1860 saleswomen in department stores were paid less than half the wages paid to men for the same work.[48] In the 1870s and 1880s, women doing mill work were paid only half the wages paid to men, and in heavier, outdoor work the disparity was even greater.[49] Matilda Joslyn Gage wrote in 1893 that in the 1880s and 1890s, a male factory worker received $14 a week for performing the same work for which women were paid $4.[50]

By contrast, actresses and actors were paid on the same scale according to their talent in the company. Women came closest to economic equality in the arts and especially in the theatre, according to historians Vera Brittain and Elizabeth Dexter.[51] "Actress and actor," wrote Elizabeth Dexter, "advanced side by side."[52] Olive Logan, writing in the nineteenth century, was firmly convinced of this from firsthand experience: "An actress is a woman who, from the moment she steps her foot on the stage to the moment she leaves it, is in receipt of a salary as good as that of an actor of the same degree." In the theatre, she noted, men and women "stand on an absolutely equal plane in the matter of cash reward."[53] When a difference in salary did occur, it appeared to be based on differences in talent and public demand, not gender. If one performer were more valuable than another, he or she received more money, regardless of gender. Thus, a successful actress very often took home much more salary than her male counterpart. In the records of William Dunlap's 1801 season in New York, one finds that Mrs. Merry, Dunlap's female lead, drew $100 a week, while the company's male lead, Thomas Cooper, drew $38.[54] Many times the wife of an acting team, if she were more talented and popular, received more money than her husband. Two actresses, identified as Mrs. Seymore and Mrs. Johnson, for example, were paid more by the Park in 1800 than were their actor-husbands, also employed by the Park.[55] George C. D. Odell recorded a number of similar cases in New York throughout the century.

This unusual economic position of women in the nineteenth-century theatre resulted in an extraordinary domestic situation for a number of them: They were the principal or only breadwinners in their families. Since the church-created taboo against women working outside their homes limited most middle-class married women to domesticity, a large number of housewives lived in total ignorance of even the most elementary financial matters and were cared for by their husbands. If a woman did work outside the home, the inadequate salary paid her was scarcely enough for self-support. This situation and, of course, the power of traditional role

6. Trading Religious Approval for Work

assignment, meant that one rarely found a female who was financial head of a household that included a male adult. Nevertheless, here, as in many other matters, the theatre was the reverse of ordinary society, for in the theatre many women were the principal or sole support of themselves and their families. Although the salaries of ballet girls were low compared to those of other women in the company, even many of these young people supported mothers, brothers, and sisters.[56]

Actresses, of course, could and did provide for themselves and their families much more easily than could ballet girls. Sometimes an actress supported her husband after he had suffered financial reverses, as in the cases of Anna Cora Mowatt, Emma Wheatley, Mrs. Hackett, and Mary Ann McClure. It was the financial collapse of Mowatt's husband that drove her to the stage in the first place. Similar reverses necessitated the return to the stage of Emma Wheatley, an actress who had retired the year after she married the son of a bank president. In the eighth year of their marriage, his business failed, and she once again turned to the theatre.[57] Mrs. McClure retired twice and returned twice in order to see her husband through financial crises.[58] Clara Morris tells a similar story of an actress named Sallie St. Clair, who, despite poor health, supported her invalid husband and two invalid female relatives. Mr. St. Clair, in a moment of poignant confession, revealed both her success and his despair: "I always see my wife, Sallie, with a helpless woman over each shoulder, and myself on her back like the 'old man of the sea,' a pretty burden that for a sick woman to carry."[59] In some cases, when husband and wife were both performers, the actress-wife, seeing her husband's fortune fail as he lost favor with the public for some reason, emerged bearing the entire financial burden of the family. Such was the case of Mary Ann Duff. She and her husband, John Duff, had come to the American stage together from Ireland — he as a leading actor, she as a novice; but as his alcoholism increased and his health and popularity waned, her career began to blossom, until ultimately they changed places. She was compelled to support herself, her husband, and their ten children.

Although the theatre's work, while not as demeaning nor as physically arduous as other labor, was not necessarily a romantic lark or even an artistic mission: It was an economic necessity. The motivations of actresses in particular, as they are revealed in memoirs and biographies, were accurately reflected in 1857 by Moncure Conway: "A few persons go on the stage from genius and strong inclinations; many more because they can get employment there; by far the majority are there simply to get a living, and if they should have fortunes left them, would not remain."[60] Quite a few actresses had no great passion for the stage. Anna Cora Mowatt began reading, then acting, in public only after her husband's financial ruin. After a long career, she left the stage when it appeared that she would no longer need to support herself, feeling "some decided attachment for the profession," but certainly no "passion" for it.[61] Olive Logan, born of a theatrical family, was much more outspoken in her assertion that economic necessity alone kept her on the stage:

> For myself, I am free to confess that I never liked the life of an actress. My mature judgment rebels against it, *for me,* as much now as it did when I was led on, against my infantile wishes, to personate Cora's child in the play of *Pizarro.* I know that this is equal to an acknowledgment to actors that I had not the sacred fire for dramatic art; and I candidly believe I never had. It was necessity which drove me to it in the first place, necessity which at different intervals in my life sent me back to it; and I trust such necessity will never come upon me again.[62]

Fanny Kemble, too, actually hated acting from the first — hated it while she was a star and hated it when she had to return to it. Her letters and journals suggest that one of her chief reasons for marrying was to be able to leave the stage behind:

> And so my life was determined, and I devoted myself to an avocation which I never liked or honored, and about the very nature of which I have never been able to come to any decided opinion.... I never presented myself before an audience without a shrinking feeling of reluctance, or withdrew from their presence without thinking the excitement I had undergone unhealthy, and the personal exhibition odious.[63]

Though some actresses had little artistic passion for the stage, they found in their profession artistic and financial status available directly to women, but less tangible benefits were also theirs — independence, freedom, and a profound dignity that could only come from self-esteem and self-accomplishment. Wives at home and women in other jobs were largely the servants of other people. From this servitude the actress was spared. As Clara Morris maintained, the actress might even say that she, of all other women, worked for herself:

> The actress's independence is comparative; but measured by the bondage of other working women, it is great. We both have duties to perform for which we receive a given wage, yet there is a difference. The working girl is expected to be subservient, she is too often regarded as a menial, she is

6. Trading Religious Approval for Work

ordered. An actress, even of small characters, is considered a necessary part of the whole. She assists, she attends, she obliges. Truly a difference.[64]

In spite of Olive Logan's distaste for acting, she also felt and cherished that independence and dignity that Morris saw in the profession. The idea of being able to depend on herself was to Logan as important as having a salary. The actress, she wrote, did not have to marry merely to have her "board and lodging paid"; she could support herself, "feel when she lies down at night that she is really thanking her Maker and not her husband, for having given her this day her daily bread."[65]

The actresses' vocation made them citizens of this extraordinary subculture in their century — one that expected of women the independence so untenable in the church and religious society at large.

In the opportunities the theatre gave women for work and equal pay, it reversed the gender roles and social and economic practices insisted upon by the church-led Protestant America. The theatre allowed itself to become a haven for individuals who were on the margins of life in America. This custom, as it included women, was possible because the theatre, while it subscribed to capitalism, did not share in its view of art and leisure and rank included in the Protestant Ethic. And this alone would have relegated the stage to the edges of religious middle-class society.

Because of the religious objection to the theatre in the nineteenth century, an aspiring actress was pulled in antipodal directions, for at the same time that she was excoriated as an actress and socially ostracized, she was afforded in the theatre one of the very few opportunities to earn independence and a living wage but also, ironically, to gain a measure of self-respect in a limited arena.

7

Wearing the Pants, Making the Choices, Writing the Plays

[P]erform[ing] functions which transcend her proper sphere.
—Justin D. Fulton

Women are not meant for public roles, wrote the Reverend Justin D. Fulton: "Nature itself shirks back from such offices; and God and man have uttered their veto on the subject."[1] And the Reverend R. W. Patterson wrote: "We injure the cause of truth, and practical religion as such ... if we encourage her to perform functions which transcend her proper sphere."[2] Another typical, biblical argument for man's supremacy over woman and the need for her to stay in her place was written by a nineteenth-century physician, Dr. L. P. Brockett:

> We can infer that it was not the intention of the Almighty to create as a help-meet for Adam one who should be in all his respects his peer or equal.... This very language of both Adam and the Creator implies, in some degree, a subordination to the man, whose helper she is to be. With the Divine approval, Adam assumes the right to assign to her a name, as he had previously done to the animal creation.... We have already noticed how this authority of the man, with subordination of the woman, is still more distinctly stated in the sentence pronounced upon the woman, after her temptation and fall, and in part, we must believe, because she had undertaken to act independently of her associate and head.[3]

7. Wearing the Pants, Making the Choices, Writing the Plays

But the theatre not only opened up work for decent pay to women, it paid little attention to the laws of female subordination to men preached by the church in collaboration with the growing numbers of industrialists and financiers. In the theatrical arena alone, women were not only independent but in charge — stepping out of their submissive positions to make decisions as actresses, to assume, as managers, the power of decision making and authority over men; to assume the grand male roles on stage, and to write plays for the stage, all of which buttressed the clerical argument against the stage in general.

The accounts of managers reveal that actresses as well as actors wielded significant influence in such matters as the selection of plays and the assignment of roles. And if one were a star of any magnitude, he or she enjoyed immense artistic and financial clout. Charlotte Cushman reigned supreme over the companies in which she played, choosing her supporting players and the dramas to be offered. Other actresses, like Adah Menken, Clara Morris, and Lotta Crabtree also had the authority to direct the ways in which scenes would be played and the persons to whom parts would be assigned.

The most dramatic evidence of the opportunities offered women in the theatre and of their assumption of men's business— the power to create policy and to enter business—lies in the impressive number of women who actually managed theatres (though perhaps not legally, in that such positions and property ownership was forbidden women by law). In the nineteenth century a number of women in the theatre were in full charge of whole companies of employees, and responsible for all personnel decisions regarding both men and women. They were also responsible for other financial as well as artistic arrangements which made or broke their businesses. They determined salaries, saw that salaries were paid, arranged loans, bargained with landlords, paid for the physical necessities required to stage a production, and, in some cases, designed and oversaw the construction of theatre buildings. The nineteenth century was indisputably the age of the female theatrical manager. In 1844 the trend was sufficiently widespread to impel Joe Cowell, a comedian of the day, to label it disparagingly "petticoat government."[4] The initial inspiration seems to have come from the career of the tyrannical Madame Vestris, in whose London-based company Laura Keene first received notice. Many American actresses followed Vestris's example, notably Sarah Kirby-Stark, Catherine Sinclair, Laura Keene, and Mrs. Drew.

The earliest successful managerial careers enjoyed by women in America began, appropriately enough, in the less structured, less crystallized society of the Far West, where the church had much less clout. Three women in particular emerged from this background as pioneers: Sarah Kirby-Stark, Catherine Sinclair, and Laura Keene. Keene, it is true, achieved her lasting fame at a later time in the East, but all three women initially made their marks in the turmoil of the early gold-rush days.

The first of these, Sara Kirby-Stark, arrived in California from the east coast in 1850. A consistent champion of melodrama, she had already become widely known as "Wake-me-up-when-Kirby dies."[5] During the following summer, 1851, Kirby-Stark toured California, opening theatres in mining towns and returning periodically to appear in San Francisco. With her determination to give that city the kind of drama it craved, and her own background in melodrama, tempered by a devotion to quality production, she promptly won the wholehearted support of San Francisco. What the public wanted more than anything else was spectacle, and Kirby-Stark was a master at staging it. One of her extravaganzas in the spring of 1852 was graced by a group of naiads who frolicked in several fountains before donning armor to march around the stage. In addition to such spectacles, the public wanted variety, to which she responded with high tragedy, low comedy, musicals, melodrama, and farce. She ran the gamut, often presenting a different play every night.[6]

A new personality, Catherine Sinclair, also arrived on the California scene in the early 1850s, first as an actress at Maguire's Theatre and then, only two months after her San Francisco debut, as manager of the Metropolitan.[7] Although her marriage to Edwin Forrest had brought her into contact with the American theatre, she had had no career of her own in her ten years of marriage to him. But she was compelled, after her acrimonious divorce from Forrest, to support herself. By borrowing funds, seeking training as an actress and declining to accept every offer, she eventually was able to lease the San Francisco Theatre (later known as the Metropolitan), took the lead in her own first production, and hired a talented young man named Edwin Booth. In 1855 she left the California frontier, which she had conquered, for another frontier in Australia.

In the wake of Kirby-Stark and Sinclair came Laura Keene, the manager supreme in an age of female managers.[8] Those who have studied her contributions to the American stage seem to agree with DeWitt Bodeen that she "probably did more for the growth of American drama than any other single person in the nineteenth century."[9]

Her first bit of luck, after returning to New York from the West, was finding the Metropolitan Theatre up for lease. Once she had secured it, she

7. Wearing the Pants, Making the Choices, Writing the Plays

decorated and named it for herself. She lost her theatre, likely due to the chicanery of her male rivals but, undaunted, she went ahead with plans to build her own theatre, a grand, comfortable structure, decorated in fine style with white and gold damask and satin. The newspapers called it the best in the city.

Her contributions to all areas of stage management are important. She staged productions, making every effort to produce the grand effect with as little money as possible. She valiantly fought against the star system that was forcing the closing of many companies, but she paid her regular actors well, often wooing the finest performers away from their companies by offering them better parts and more pay than they were receiving elsewhere. Edward H. Sothern and Joseph Jefferson were among those who graced her company.[10]

That Laura Keene's Theatre stayed open in the most difficult of national times — it was the only legitimate theatre open in New York during the summer of 1861 — is a testament to her extraordinary managerial skill. Odell gives her a special place of importance in his history of the New York theatre. Her years as a manager, he says, form "one of the bright chapters in the best of our drama."[11] The demise of her theatre came during the Civil War. Odell, a man of wide experience as a playgoer and chronicler of the stage, wrote, "A poem of epic proportions should have marked the exit."[12] Her career, like those of many other theatrical women, stands as a brilliant example of high accomplishment and achieved potential in a man's world.

The theatre establishment in cities other than New York seems to have been exceptionally hospitable to female managers. In 1860 the stockholders of Philadelphia's Arch Street Theatre asked, not *Mr.* Drew, but *Mrs.* Drew to assume the management of their theatre, the beginning of a career of great success and longevity. In her autobiography, Mrs. Drew made a special point of mentioning that her husband was out of the country, in Australia, at the time she received the stockholders' business proposition. When Mr. Drew returned from touring, he became a member of his wife's company. She retained control of the Arch Street from 1860 to 1892, retiring finally at the age of seventy-two. When she first became manager of the theatre, she was prepared to borrow funds to attract the most talented actors available, and borrow she did — for every week of her first season. As a result, business improved; she began to pay back the company debts; and the stockholders, in the second season, agreed to build a new theatre for her. By the fourth season, she was able to employ figures of the magnitude of Lester Wallack and Edwin Booth.

Mrs. John Drew was one of many who stepped out of woman's exclusive role to manage the business of a theatre.

She struggled with the star system and with larger theatres in the city. Nevertheless, with Joseph Jefferson, her sole attraction toward the end, she, as manager, held the Arch Street together through the years. In 1880, at the age of sixty, she took a company on a nineteen-thousand-mile tour.

7. Wearing the Pants, Making the Choices, Writing the Plays

Amazingly enough, she managed the Arch Street back in Philadelphia long-distance, even while touring, and kept it going until 1892 when she retired from management.[13]

The role reversal offstage continued on stage. The power of the lead actress and the rise of female managers helped sustain an unusual practice that was especially obnoxious to the religious public and stoked the fires of theatrical argument throughout the century: the assignment of leading male roles, or breeches parts, to women, noteworthy female leads being at a premium. This custom, while dating back to the introduction of actresses to the stage during the English Restoration, was widespread and endemic to nineteenth-century America theatre. If one dips into any part of the century, one commonly finds a woman playing Hamlet or Romeo or Puck or any number of other male roles from Oliver Twist to Cardinal Wolsey.[14] The practice enabled a good actress, who could ordinarily only look forward to the parts of vaporous heroines (who fainted and shrieked with regularity) to attempt the great tragic roles of world drama, thereby partially compensating for the universal scarcity of truly good female roles. It also allowed her to expand her own artistic perceptions. Breeches parts, furthermore, were found in all parts of the country and in all kinds of theatres. It was fairly rare to find an actress who did not at some time take a male role. The frequency of the practice provoked a few objections among some theatre people, and was damned by traditional moralists, on the grounds that breeches parts were unnatural, immodest, and unwomanly. The charge of immodesty stemmed somewhat predictably from the often requisite display of legs: All Elizabethan and certain other historical roles called for the use of tights—at a time when even the very word *leg* was avoided in many "moral" circles. Among the more vehement theatrical critics was the manager Noah Ludlow, who denounced breeches parts as "a series of Monstrosities" and "objects of disgust."[15] Many actors were far from happy with women in breeches, largely because as George Vandenhoff wrote in *Leaves from an Actor's Note-Book*, "they usurp men's parts and 'push us from our stools.'"[16] He especially resented Charlotte Cushman's portrayal of Romeo, despite his admiration for her as an actress:

> Romeo requires a *man*, to feel his passion, and to express his despair. A woman, in attempting it, "unsexes" herself to no purpose, except to destroy all interest in the play, and all sympathy for the ill-fated pair: she *denaturalizes* the situations.... There should be a law against such perversions.[17]

There can be little doubt, however, that any such law would have failed, for the public seemed to enjoy the spectacle. In fact, one of the odd hypocrisies of the day, as related by William Wood, was that, while the general public violently objected with some frequency to the costumes of female dancers, no matter how many absurd loose layers covered them from head to toe, audiences continued to support actresses costumed in tights while playing male roles.[18]

How breeches parts grew to have such importance at this particular time and place is a matter of speculation. Obviously one pertinent factor was the playgoers' insatiable demand for novelty on stage. The same impulse that caused the public to flock to see five-year-old Kate Bateman play Richard the Third, or to see a stage full of trained horses and dogs, or *Julius Caesar* in blackface, most certainly drew it to appearances of women in men's clothing. No doubt such roles had their prurient appeal — nowhere more apparent than in Adah Menken's popular portrayal of the supposedly nude *Mazeppa* in what appears to be a skintight body suit.[19] Actually, explanations of why playgoers encouraged the trend are no more than educated guesses, but some of the reasons why actresses and theatrical companies promulgated it are fairly clear. The policy operated to the advantage of both player and company. The company benefited especially from the assignment of juvenile's roles to actresses. The maturity and skill required to play a young boy like Oliver Twist, for example, were beyond the scope of most young boys. The mature actress with a slight build would be more likely to make a success of such a part: She could easily be made to look like a boy, and her years of experience would enable her to bring needed skill and insight to the part. Thus, the roles of Albert in *William Tell*, the Dauphin in *Louis XI*, Patrick in *The Poor Soldier*, and Puck in *A Midsummer Night's Dream* were frequently filled by actresses.[20]

The actress, in turn, benefited from the greater number of parts available. Classic plays in which a woman was the central character could almost be counted on the fingers, but the enviable male roles were inexhaustible. Most of the assignments of male *leads* to women, as opposed to male secondary roles, occurred in particular circumstances. One was an actress's benefit performance, when she could choose her own play and her own part. For a time at mid-century it appeared as though every actress in New York had chosen to play a male role for her benefit performance. For instance, Annie Hathaway played Richard III; Fanny Herring portrayed Richmond; Mrs. Battersby acted both Hamlet and Macbeth, and Mrs. Baldwin was cast as Marc Antony. Between 1821 and 1858 in New York City alone,

7. Wearing the Pants, Making the Choices, Writing the Plays

at least twenty-six women played some thirty to forty male roles, including Cardinal Wolsey, Richard III, Romeo, Richmond, Macbeth, Marc Anthony, and Shylock.[21] Another circumstance, besides the occasion of her benefit, gave a leading actress an extraordinary opportunity to play male leads: that was her undisputed position of power and influence in a company. When her talent and drawing power made her indispensable, she could play the coveted roles whenever she wanted, without benefit of benefit. In her long career, for example, Mrs. John Drew played the Duke of York, Dr. Pangloss, Richard III, and many other male roles.[22] Adah Menken played the male leads in *Mazeppa* and *Black-Eyed Susan*.[23] Helen Weston, who was the star of her company, played almost as many male as female roles.[24] The same was true of Clara Fisher, who even cast herself as Shylock, and in boys' parts was said to be "unsurpassed."[25] Charlotte Cushman took the prize as the queen of breeches parts, taking on every male lead imaginable, from Romeo to Cardinal Wolsey.[26] Always with one eye on the success of the entire production, Laura Keene would take whatever role needed filling, whether it was male or female, major or minor. She played Oliver Twist, David Copperfield, Romeo, Faustus, and the double male lead in *The Corsican Brothers*. When Joseph Jefferson, a member of her company, refused to play Puck, Laura, with her usual adaptability, took the role herself.[27]

The stage offered women another unusual path, much deplored by religious society: that was the opportunity to write plays for production in the theatre. Many such women, like female novelists, could ply their trade without disobeying the dictate to remain within the home. But, in most quarters, they were considered just as unsavory as the actress herself, in part because they performed a man's work, which work in itself (whether produced by man or woman) posed a threat to the acquiescence and emotional stability of the female exposed to it — the woman who had to struggle constantly to keep down her natural passions and frivolity.

Despite society's disapproval of her, the female playwright was another class of women who was offered the opportunity to win her bread in a way that did not break her body in a factory or a field or break her spirit by depending on relatives for her survival. Because theatres were clearly receptive to women in all sorts of work, women playwrights were numerous and highly successful in the nineteenth century. But in a matter largely irrelevant to the church's war on the theatre, we find that while producers and managers welcomed women playwrights, male playwrights and many historians in the first half of the twentieth century did not. It is

Many women made the decision to play male roles in the nineteenth century. Charlotte Cushman, a descendant of one of America's first families and shown here playing Romeo, was master of the art.

7. Wearing the Pants, Making the Choices, Writing the Plays

enough to mention that until 1907 *the* professional association of dramatists, the American Dramatists' Club, refused membership to women playwrights. Early drama histories rarely discuss women playwrights before the twentieth century, with the exceptions of Mercy Warren and Anna Cora Mowatt.

A typescript, dated 1944, written by Robert L. Sherman and entitled *Drama Cyclopedia: A Bibliography of Plays and Players*, is a list of plays produced between 1750 and 1940 in the major metropolises of the United States. Compiled from contemporary accounts and newspapers, Sherman records over 250 plays written by English and American women and produced during this time. Furthermore, among the dramatists on the list are some fairly prolific writers: Susanna Rowson, also the author of *Charlotte Temple*, whose seven plays were professionally produced between 1793 and 1810, and Louisa Medina, whose twenty-one plays were produced between 1829 and 1849.

Throughout the nineteenth century prominent actresses and managers also wrote plays for themselves or their companies. Their numbers include Charlotte Cushman, Laura Keene, Catherine Sinclair, Adah Menken, Mrs. John Drew, and Lotta Crabtree. Mrs. Sidney Bateman wrote five plays in the 1850s; Laura Keene, six in the 1850s and 1860s; Fanny Herring, eight in the 1860s and 1870s; Olive Logan, nine in the 1870s. Several women were prolific and popular playwrights at the end of the century: Marguerite Merington; Madeline Lucette-Ryley; Charlotte Blair Parker, whose *Way Down East* (1891) ran for two decades (one indication of its success: a single actress played the lead in Parker's play 4,000 times); and Frances Hodgson Burnett, an Englishwoman, whose eight plays produced in America between 1881 and 1897 included one of the century's favorites, *Little Lord Fauntleroy* (1888), a dramatization of her own novel.[28] Martha Morgan was the "dean" of women dramatists, in part because she was one of the first women to be commercially successful in the field and to articulate the difficulty that women had in writing for the stage. Her canon consists of thirty-five plays for which she received up to $350 plus a percentage of receipts.[29] The women mentioned here are not the sole playwrights writing for the nineteenth-century American stage, but only the most prolific ones. Few of their plays or reputations as playwrights have survived. The nineteenth-century theatre provided them with rare opportunities, but until the 1970s, with the rise of the Women Studies movement, they were largely lost to history.[30]

In the opportunities the theatre gave women for work and equal pay, it reversed the gender roles and social and economic practices of Protestant America insisted upon by the church. In this way, the theatre, itself being relegated to the edges of religious middle-class society, allowed itself to become a haven for individuals who were also on the margins of life in America and had little chance for economic positions in the larger culture dictated by the Protestant Ethic.

8

Children in Industry: Children on Stage

> *Childhood on Stage is Gerry's Bogey*
> — New York Dramatic News

The theatre's inability to subscribe to the superficial idealism of the church-dominated culture in which it thrived is more revealing of the dark underside of mainstream society than it is of the theatre itself. Much of society's hypocrisy, which the history of the theatre uncovers, is found to be a creature of economics, whereby, as we have seen, women were used as fodder for a system created by the Protestant Ethic, and then labeled whores for participating in one of the few professions which empowered them. The same can be said of child actors.

Capitalism, a cornerstone of the Protestant Ethic, thrived on the backs of the working-class poor, above all on the menial labor of children whose physical labor supported the system. Against this background the theatre alone, as it did with women, provided limited opportunities for some children to work, in most cases, for reasonable wages under good conditions, performing activities that were neither arduous nor demeaning nor corrupting. Benjamin McArthur quotes from the *New York Mirror Annual* of 1888 which published a list of the twenty-four different stage specialties for male actors (character actors, light comedians, etc.) and thirty-one for females. Of the number of individuals in the group of male actors, juveniles constituted 14.6%, the third largest group after character actors and comedians. Of female performers, juveniles and children made up 12.0%, second in number only to leading ladies.[1]

Church and Stage

In offering children work, however, the theatre again went against the grain of mainstream religious society, inverting customs and upending social roles that were seen as essential to the economic health of a Christian nation. In a word, children were to remain completely subservient to adults, were seldom to be seen, never heard, and were to stay in their God-given social stations. But the theatre reversed this dictate by inviting children to be seen and heard and enabling some of them to become the breadwinners of their families.

The conflict between the two sets of values, one promoted by the church and reformers and one which emerged from theatrical practices, surfaced in the press in the last three decades of the nineteenth century and continued into the early twentieth. A pattern of hypocrisy, with psychological as well as economic undertones, came to light when reformer Elbridge T. Gerry's obsession with banning children from the stage became, for four decades, an emotional topic of public discussion.

Few men have ever made such a dramatic appearance in the spotlight of history as Gerry. One day in 1874, some eight years after Henry Bergh established the Society for the Prevention of Cruelty to Animals, Gerry came into a New York City courtroom carrying a small, frightened child. Her body was a mass of old scars from daily beatings with rawhide and her face showed a fresh wound where she had been stabbed with scissors. She was eight years old. If she had been a dog, the perpetrators of

Elbridge Gerry, a founder of the Society for the Prevention of Cruelty to Children, spent more time and energy in keeping children off the stage than in addressing the abuses of child laborers.

8. Children in Industry

this horror would have been punished; but since she was a human being, the law was silent. It was only by classifying this girl, Mary Ellen, as an animal that Gerry could argue that a crime had been committed. After Gerry's courageous courtroom appearance, the Society for the Prevention of Cruelty to Children was formed and legislation designed to curb child abuse. The organization spread rapidly throughout the country, its many local chapters detailing the rescue of hundreds of victims of domestic abuse. For some thirty years Gerry wielded power, supported by social, political, and religious leaders and by prestigious newspapers, including the *New York Times*.[2]

Gerry certainly emerges as a rare figure cast in the heroic mold, but an obsession muddles his story, for both his and the society's energies were increasingly devoted to a much narrowed and far more questionable cause than the domestic and industrial abuse of children: a crusade to prevent children from performing on stage. The subsequent quarrel involving Gerry and stage children simmered and often raged well on into the twentieth century, actually having a sweeping impact on the theatrical art of the day and ultimately involving questions of aesthetics, public morals, religious beliefs and attitudes regarding children, the family, labor and industry as well as caste and gender. Gerry remained narrowly, immovably fixed on child performers, while resigning himself to the industrial abuse of children after the first attempt at state legislation failed. An examination of the conditions under which child performers worked, of their need for protection — especially when seen in the context of the abuses of industrial child labor at the time — and Gerry's own personal response to the presence of children on stage, will throw some light on the climate of opinion at the end of the century.

There is no denying that the abuse of children did exist in the entertainment field, but evidence shows that it was only in those fringe areas of show business like the circus. Memoirs of ex-performers reveal that life for those children who ran away or were given away to the circus was often a living hell. Even the popular child's book of the time, *Toby Tyler of the Circus*, an escapist-adventure novel includes accounts of the beating of children. In reality many cases were far worse than Toby's. These homeless waifs, or runaways, or poor children sold to circus personnel by their parents or guardians were paid starvation wages, if they were paid at all. They were habitually beaten for failure to hide their fear while attempting life-endangering stunts, often on the high wire or without safety nets. One case which strengthened support for the Gerry law against all exhibitions was

Church and Stage

the Society's discovery of "Little Prince Leo," a small boy who had been purchased and forced, with frequent beatings, to perform dangerous, even terrifying acrobatic feats.[3] His was not an isolated instance. In his memoir, actor Fred Andrew Stone recalls a few childhood months in the 1870s spent touring with a circus in the Midwest. His was such a glaring case of neglect that a local sheriff departed from his usual custom of looking the other way and instead put him on a train for home to the father who had turned him over to the circus in the first place.[4]

Although some girls, as well as boys, worked with circuses, most of them, for practical reasons, went on to the legitimate stage; circus boys were expendable and cheap. But little girls had more potential as stars and moneymakers. Sometimes a little girl was the sole moneymaker in the family. As a consequence, they were more often protected and cared for. The use of a talented young girl as "commodity" can be seen in the last decades of the nineteenth century in the case of Jessie Bond, a British singer who was tricked into marriage at age sixteen by a man who, having legal control, intended to use her, not merely as a mealticket, but as his personal gold mine.[5] Then there was Josephine DeMott, an American circus performer who as a young girl was kidnapped, drugged and forcibly married to one of her abductors in a scheme by grafters to collect profits from her equestrian act. Even after she escaped, the police ignored her protests, and for months she was pursued by the same men before they were finally caught and jailed.[6]

Obviously, in the circus and other peripheral areas of entertainment there existed the potential for inflicting real harm, but there is scant evidence of abusive conditions on the legitimate stage where the appearances of children were carefully overseen, almost to excess. But to the critics of Gerry it was a matter of priorities. The atmosphere of the stage at its worst was not ideal, but surely, in view of the terrible conditions under which children slaved out their lives in industrial sweatshops and factories and home-slum industries, there were better ways for the Society to spend its time than by removing little girls and boys from the stage. The theatre, by comparison with other institutions, emerges looking like paradise.

Within two years of the Society's formation, Gerry had brought about the first and, he thought, the most important law to combat child abuse: a ban on the use of children in "exhibitions." The Penal Code of the State of New York, Chapter 46, Section 292 read:

> A person who employs, or causes to be employed or who exhibits, uses or has in his custody for the purpose of exhibiting or employing any child

8. Children in Industry

> apparently or actually under the age of sixteen years, or who, having the care, custody or control of such a child as parent, relative, or guardian, employer or otherwise, sells, lets out, gives away or in any way procures or consents to the employment or exhibition of such a child ... as in any practice of exhibition, dangerous or injurious to the life, limb, health or morals of the child; is guilty of a misdemeanor.[7]

The original phrasing of the prohibition sounds reasonable. But subsequent interpretations of the exhibition went far beyond protecting children from physical or psychological abuse as the stress began to be placed on the danger to the "morals of the child," because Gerry and the Society regarded any exhibition as immoral. The banned "exhibitions" in the code came to be interpreted as any appearance of any kind on the stage, in any kind of part, "whether written or not, or whether or not impromptu...." Appendix 32 to the SPCC manual for 1882 makes this clear, further explaining that, even if a child stood on a stage or merely held a musical instrument without doing anything else, he or she came within the provision of the statute.[8] Furthermore, this law did not demand, as it did in domestic cases, that the Society treat each case individually and make recommendations based on specific evidence of cruelty. Just performing on stage was to establish guilt and, often, on no more evidence than that, children were taken off the stage and parents or managers were fined or sent to jail. Child actors on the legitimate stage were classed with street beggars, "acrobats," and children used in pornographic acts; there was thought to be something in the atmosphere, something inherent in the act itself, that destroyed both health and morality.

It is also significant that Gerry's law prohibiting exhibitions of children was enforced capriciously when few other child labor laws were enforced at all. It was not merely a lifeless statute passed as a sop and then forgotten, as was the case, for example, of an 1866 New York State law against the employment in factories of children under the age of thirteen, a law that Gerry had once tried to make effective, but without the resolve or commitment he brought to anti-exhibition laws. No manager, guardian, or child performer felt immune from investigation and prosecution. Daily newspapers and annual reports of the Society's chapters carried news of such actions, especially when singing and dancing were concerned. Child actresses were spirited in and out of New York like so much contraband whiskey. Something of the effect of all this is suggested by actress Elsie Janis' memory of her childhood encounters with the Society at the turn of the twentieth century. She made her debut in 1894:

Church and Stage

> I played Keith's Union Square and for some unknown reason escaped the eagle eye of the Gerry Society, better known as the Society for the Prevention of Cruelty to Children, whose Project it was and still is to prohibit children under sixteen from singing and dancing on the stage. Children can get a permit to play in drama, no matter how sexy or sordid, but they cannot sing and dance. I wouldn't know why. I only know that for eight years they stopped me from playing every time Mother would land what looked like a real opportunity, and for eight years Mother, undaunted, kept right on bringing me back to New York, only to be driven out again.[9]

Child professionals in the theatre evidently lived in mortal fear of Gerry, who became something of a devil in their minds, dedicated, they thought, to taking them away from their parents and putting them in orphanages. But social reformers of the Jane Addams School in Chicago in 1912 were fighting against any modifications of the Gerry laws. As late as 1932, the year Janis' memoirs were published, derivations of the Gerry laws were still in force and still controversial.

A brief glance at children's labor in the same period — the last three decades of the century — puts Gerry's crusade in context. In 1870, one of every eight children held a full-time job and, by 1900, the figure was one in six — or 1,750,000 laboring children. The 1890 census speculated that over 65,000 vagrant children under sixteen, most of them girls and most with no schooling, tried to eke out a living on the streets of New York City. In 1901, four-year-old girls were at work in canning factories in New York State and five- and six-year-old girls were working all day and some nights in cotton mills. In 1903, 80,000 children, mostly girls under fourteen, were employed in cotton mills. Girls under the age of thirteen, some of whom were only four, constituted about one-third of the working force in all cloth industries, carpet mills, and paper trades, the cigar industries, the garment trades, canning factories, match factories and candy factories. They made up a large proportion of cash runners in department stores, and the working force of sweatshops, oyster-shucking industries and farms.[10]

The conditions under which they worked during the years of Gerry's theatre crusade constitute a familiar chapter in American history that seems more, rather than less, terrible with retelling. John Spargo in his famous exposé, *Bitter Cry of the Children,* summarizes from firsthand observation:

> It is a sorry but indisputable fact that when children are employed, the most unhealthful work is generally given them. In the spinning and carding rooms of cotton and woolen mills, where large numbers of children are employed, clouds of lint-dust fill the lungs, and menace the health....

8. Children in Industry

Factories, including the textile mill pictured here, hired both boys and girls who worked fourteen hours a day under perilous conditions.

In bottle factories, and other branches of glass manufacture, the atmosphere is constantly charged with microscopic particles of glass.... In the manufacture of felt hats, little girls are often employed at the machines which tear the fur from the skins of rabbits and other animals. Recently I stood and watched a young girl working at such a machine. She wore a newspaper pinned over her head and a handkerchief tied over her mouth. She was white with dust from head to feet, and when she stopped to pick anything from the floor the dust would fall from her paper head covering in little heaps.

In some occupations, such as silk-winding, flaxspinning, and various processes in the manufacture of felt hats, it is necessary, or believed to be necessary, to keep the atmosphere quite moist. The result of working in a close, heated factory, where the air is artificially moistened in summer time, can be better imagined than described. So long as enough girls can be kept working and only a few of them faint, the mills are kept going; but when faintings are so many and so frequent that it does not pay to keep them going, the mills are closed. The children who work in the dye rooms and print-shops of textile factories, and the color looms of factories where the materials for making artificial flowers are manufactured are subject to contact with poisonous dyes, and the results are often terrible.... The children who are employed in the manufacture of wall papers and poisonous paints suffer from slow poisoning. The naphtha fumes in the manufacture of rubber goods produce paralysis and premature decay. The little boys who make matches, and the little girls who pack them in boxes, suffer from phosphorous necrosis, or "phossy-jaw," a gangrene of the lower jaw due to phosphorous poisoning.... Little girls who work in the hosiery mills and carry heavy baskets from one floor to another, and their sisters who run machines by foot power, suffer all through their life as a result of their employment.[11]

The ancient connection between child labor and the accumulation of capital became more vital than ever with the industrial boom that followed the Civil War. As Walter Trattner writes in his history of the National Labor Committee, *Crusade for Children:*

Not only the entrepreneur but society at large, in fact, sought to reap the economic benefits of using child operatives. Many Americans, not heartless in their grasp for money and power, were caught up in enormous opportunities for personal gain. Neither the dominant laissez-faire economic ethic nor prevailing social attitudes restrained such social practices.[12]

Jeremy Felt wrote that child labor supported the industrial North:

At the turn of the last century New York was the leading industrial state in the nation.... Children helped New York attain this preeminence, though in the course of their labors some fell down elevator shafts, burned to death, were mangled by machinery, worked standing in several inches of water, delivered messages to houses of prostitution, stood on their feet for twelve hours a day, sold newspapers at two o'clock in the morning, or froze to death in delivery wagons.[13]

Clergymen continued to bless the fortunes made for Northern capitalists through child labor, and both Northern and Southern capital was founded on child labor in Southern textile mills. Alabama reformer Edgar Murphy observed that those who fought controls of child labor implied "that there is some inherent and essential connection between the prosperity of the South and the labor of little children."[14] As Southern historian C. Vann Woodward writes, child labor was "an entrenched interest, a growing evil that had become ... the foundation of fortunes."[15] Wages for this kind of terrible, day-long work ranged from ten cents to one dollar a day.

In view of this reality in the world of nineteenth-century child labor, Gerry's and the Society's single-minded focus on antitheatrical laws seems

8. Children in Industry

even more puzzling. Was the enactment and the scrupulous enforcement of this law a rational, humane reaction to a real need, or merely another reflection of the still-religious public's wholesale fear of "theatre"?

For a picture of the situation of children on stage one must depend primarily upon the accounts of theatre folk who witnessed child performers up close. These memoirs and the theatre's aggressive denials at the time are, at least, convincing. Otis Skinner who, incidentally, hated working with child actors, David Belasco, who enjoyed training them, and many adult performers who had themselves been on stage as children, asserted that child performers were extremely well cared for. Most agreed with Belasco that any threat to their well-being came not from cruelty, but from "being spoiled by so much attention and petting."[16] Phyllis Dare, who made her debut on stage at the age of ten, declared, "I have met hundreds and hundreds of child actors and actresses, or rather perhaps I should say would-be actors and actresses. In not a single case, however, can I truly say that I have ever known of a child deteriorating through the profession."[17] Those who knew the theatre well argued further that most children on the American stage had far, far better lives as actors than they would have had otherwise. Belasco accurately observed that the young actor in America usually came from the "humble class"; and "those who knew most about its work and the influences around it agree that, relatively, it is better off in the theatre than under the conditions and influences from which more than 90% of young stage children are drawn."[18] Of course, one reason for this was that, unlike their contemporaries in factories and shops, stage children were well paid; care was taken to limit their hours in rehearsal and performance and to see that they received proper schooling. Fanny Davenport, in an 1892 *New York Times* interview provoked by Gerry's actions, declared that neither she nor her mother nor her grandmother, in all their many years as actresses, had ever seen misuse or immorality touch young girls on stage."[19]

Another persuasive argument offered in defense of acting for children was their obvious love for their work. Eleanor Robeson declared that she had "never seen any unhappy children" on stage,[20] and Phyllis Dare wrote, "Thus, in my own case, all the time I was playing in that first pantomime I used to work hard at lessons all day, so that really acting at night did not seem work at all, but came rather as a sort of playtime."[21] Speaking for the profession, a New York newspaper called the *Theatre* argued that "what will be work to them when they become older, is now only play, and it is a very narrow spirit which forbids them to play to their profit."[22]

The profession was so confident of its stand on this matter that in 1893 the *New York Dramatic News* challenged Gerry and the Society to furnish for print any list of children who had come to grief through employment in the theatre.[23] In the same year theatre folk took a very public anti–Gerry stance with the creation of two organizations designed to ridicule Gerry and publicize their own version of the truth: the "Anti-Gerry Society," composed of child actors who marched on the legislature on their own behalf; and "The Society to Protect Stage Children," an organization supported by Joseph Jefferson, who had been a child on stage himself.[24] Clearly, the testimony of theatre professionals supports a supreme irony: in a century that subsisted overwhelmingly on child labor, the theatre seems to have been one of the few workplaces where a child was treated decently. As early as 1881, the *Times* had felt compelled to ask the same nagging question: In the light of appalling abuses in business and industry, why had Gerry so wholly pursued the cause of child labor in the theatre to the neglect of children in factories?

> It is certain, at any rate, that his interference and protection is called for more urgently by thousands of cases in the City, where children are made to undergo cruel drudgery by their parents. In many factories and large stores can be found little girls who are employed as "cash girls," and at other occupations ... who are on their feet the live long day.[25]

In the face of increasing criticism, even from friends and supporters, Gerry not only persisted; he became more defensive, more aggressive. In 1883, the *New York Dramatic News*, a journal that praised Gerry very highly for his other reforms, now charged that "childhood on stage is Gerry's bogey ... his Banquo."[26] An editorial in the *Theatre* a few months earlier was even stronger: "The course which is invariably pursued by Mr. Gerry is a last vestige of the old time bigotry respecting the stage." The charge was also made that Gerry "persecuted" managers because of a "pronounced prejudice of his own."[27] By 1889 even the *New York Times*, which had supported Gerry from the start with many columns of favorable publicity, including appeals for funds and annual Society reports, charged that the Society was "wasting its efforts on a class of cases in which the children were subjected to no hardships nor immoral influences."[28] Six months later, the *Times*, while still insisting that the Society needed some discretion in the trying of cases, conceded "that discretion has been abused."[29]

As voices of protest rose, Gerry's fervor increased. His actions gave credence to charges of irrationality and fanaticism continued into the twentieth century. In 1907, a *Times* editorial of general praise contained distinctly

8. Children in Industry

jarring notes: Gerry, it was observed, had refused to allow a sixteen-year-old prodigy to play the piano; refused to allow two infants to be carried on stage in a production of *Madame Butterfly*; refused to allow a group of children to sing on stage. No one of these "performances," it should be noted, was ever intended to last more than ten minutes.[30]

More importantly, perhaps, Gerry is damned by his own words, above all by his one major statement of the conditions he hoped to improve. In an 1883 article in the *North American Review*, Gerry acknowledged that in industry 1,188,356 children between the ages of ten and fifteen frequently worked over ten hours a day under conditions that caused thousands of them to die yearly from disease and mutilation. His description of this abomination was *one and a half pages long*. Then, he gives in to the industrialists by noting that laws were ineffectual in preventing industrial abuse of children. He goes on to devote almost twice as much space to child labor in the theatre, calling theatres "equally injurious" to children, "yet more deadly in their results upon the moral and physical health of the child than any of the evils already enumerated," observing:

> [T]he very moment the curtain rises at the theatre, a draft of hot air blows from the audience on the stage, frequently paralyzing temporarily the vocal chords of the actors. When the curtain falls the cold air from the flies descends with equal rapidity and the children, who a moment before were exposed half-naked in the performance of some act of physical exertion, are chilled to the bone before they have a chance to recover from the sudden change resulting from this alteration of the temperature.[31]

Twelve years later, in 1895, still sensitive to children's exposure to changes in temperature, he maintained that a young girl be forbidden to act in a play because it was too hot.[32] At the same time, thousands of children were having heat strokes and sweltering in Southern fields scorched by the sun and in Northern factories made into ovens by hot machinery. Gerry seemingly continued to believe that the drafts and the irregular schedules in the theatre were "more deadly in their results upon ... the physical health of the child" performer than were the thousands of mutilations and diseases which he had just admitted were visited upon the factory child.[33] In his 1883 article, Gerry cites only one case of a child performer dying, yet he finds the stage more dangerous to the health of children than the factory, where child employees (as he noted) die by the thousands from job-related causes. The child-actor who performs "night after night" upon the stage "with apparent little effort" is more endangered physically than the factory children he had described as working over ten hours a day at heavy labor.

His language also gives him away, revealing a narrow morality, prejudice and class bias. The words *evil* and *vice* appear eleven times in five pages, in addition to such loaded terms as *votaries, beguiled, allurements, vicious, immoral, disease, decay, vanity, dissipation, insidious, false, temptation*, and *ruinous*, all used in reference to the theatre. One wonders why the slow death of all those other thousands was not equally evil. Clearly, however, the double demons of prostitution and popular arts, like the gates of hell, awaited the daughters and sons of working-class parents: "Girls ceasing to be children and becoming women fall into vice before they really know what vice is." "Boys with originally good instincts are beguiled, through allurements of dime novels and of blood-and-thunder dramas at cheap theatres...." The fault, Gerry contends, lay with laboring-class parents who, because they had to work, left their children unsupervised. Thus, children on stage were doubly in danger of that moral degeneracy to which low birth subjects its members, first, in being, as Gerry observes, the offspring of laboring, uneducated parents, and second, in choosing a vocation in a field frequently regarded as too low even to be classified.[34]

In the long run, Gerry's dogged attempt to convince the public failed. Realizing in 1887 that his attempt to prove physical abuse in connection with a minstrel show could only backfire, he shifted once more to the question of moral injury. The *New York Times* on December 17, 1887, quotes him as saying:

> The chief objectionable feature in Mr. Dockstader's performance is the song and dance business which is expressly prohibited by statute, on account of its pernicious effect on the boys themselves, who when once they acquire a fondness for that sort of life usually end as performers in the lowest dens and concert saloons in the city.[35]

Gerry further contended in a letter to Col. E. H. Beck in 1883, published by the *New York Dramatic News*, that girls, even on the legitimate stage, usually ended up as prostitutes:

> The very fact that money can easily be made by these children, with but little effort and with the surroundings of excitement and applause attending performance in a theatre before a crowded audience induces the girls, at an early age, to enter a life of splendid sin....[36]

Ten years later he was still arguing that allowing girls to sing and dance "simply means the education of female children for eventual lives of prostitution."[37]

8. Children in Industry

The case of "Little Corinne" was one of Gerry's greatest challenges. In 1881 he and the Society had the father of a nine-year-old actress, Corinne, arrested and sentenced to four months in jail for defying an order that his daughter refrain from appearing as an actress on the legitimate stage. She was known to be a protégé of the highly respectable actress and writer, Clara Morris. At first, Gerry argued, in attempting to have her mother arrested as well, that the girl's singing, dancing and committing to memory of long sections of the play were detrimental to her physical and mental health. In the courtroom, however, it became obvious that the child lived in luxury, was dressed extravagantly well, and even had her own carriage and servant. Moreover, a court physician found her to be in excellent health. The court was convinced that she was happy, loved her work, and was reasonably well educated by private tutors. Gerry's influence was such, however, that the terrified Corinne was taken from her mother pending further hearings. Even the *Times* was outraged and argued, as many had done before, that to crucify a family because its little girl appeared on the stage was beyond all reason.[38] In answer to the *Times*, Gerry replied that the real "evidence" against Corinne's parents was yet to be revealed.[39]

Once again, having failed to prove physical neglect or abuse, he turned to the moral argument, contending that, although Corinne had been told of the existence of a deity and been taught to say her prayers each night, she had been instructed neither in the Bible nor about Jesus Christ. The case against Corinne was one of the few that Gerry lost. The judge ruled that the prosecutor's entire argument rested on the little girl's being ignorant of a particular religion, and that the state had no business directing religious beliefs.[40]

The records show that in the last ten years of his career as president of the Society, Gerry became increasingly capricious and irrational, at one time commencing to shriek in the courtroom after one opposing lawyer dared to describe him as "whimsical."[41] In 1887, he forbade a ten-year-old pianist from, as the *Times* described it, "hammering his bread out of a piano when the operation would take only about five minutes each night."[42] Gerry's answer was that if this young classical pianist were allowed to perform he would likely end his career playing in a saloon. In 1889 he tried to forbid a seven-year-old to sing on stage for ten minutes a night.[43] When a theatre offered to cut the singing time of a group of children in half, to five minutes, and allow only one song, Gerry again refused permission.[44]

One is forced at last to the conclusion that like so many other nineteenth-century reformers who provided the age with its finest hours,

Gerry missed the mark ultimately because he fought not the causes of the social ills he so deplored but rather a phantom of innate depravity. His theatre laws, testaments to Victorian hypocrisy and Calvinistic cynicism, emerge as a way to keep his reputation as a reformer without confronting those with power.

The implication in Gerry's words and works is that the theatre laws were a convenient means of avoiding a confrontation with rampant industrialism, a battle that he was bound to lose. They afforded the reform-minded public an opportunity to take a stand against the labor of children without threatening or diminishing the fruits of capitalism. There was less risk of any dangerous counterattack in crusading against the theatre's use of children than in objecting to their use by more powerful segments of society, namely industry. At a time when the subsistence and expansion of industry was made possible to no small degree by massive amounts of cheap child labor, to fight effective child labor laws in other areas as rigidly as they were enforced in the theatre was a perverse exercise in self-destruction, not to mention futility.

Another Victorian attitude which seems to have led the theatre to be a target was the view that hidden evil was not as bad as public evil. The Gerryites concluded that children who suffered infinitely more and in far greater numbers in factories than in theatres were of less consequence because they were hidden from view behind the walls of sweatshops and cotton mills. But the labor of children in the theatre was intolerable because it was an unavoidably open display. Unlike industry, the theatre was a safe, even a popular, target. By concentrating efforts where there was little public approval, one could remove an apparent social stigma — a child doing adult work — and diminish one's personal shame without striking at the foundations of capitalism. Thus the all-important appearance of virtue was maintained, and the reformer and his followers could say, with the narrator of Herman Melville's "Bartleby the Scrivener," "Here I can cheaply purchase a delicious self-approval" costing "little or nothing, while I lay up in my soul what will eventually prove a sweet morsel for my conscience."[45]

Gerry's choice of the theatre as a target may also be attributable to a combination of upper-class and Calvinistic cynicism. At the same time that his heart went out to the dispossessed, he shared with others in his age the suspicion that the poor, the lower classes, women, and children were especially and dangerously subject to depravity and were saved from moral oblivion only by the strictest adherence to form and place. Civilization, rules, schedules, and caste kept the darker elements within people of these

8. Children in Industry

ranks hidden and within bounds. The Victorian, God-decreed chain of being required that man should be the provider, the household's link with a world which belonged to men. Woman's place, distinct from man's world, was in the home and the church. It was the child's place to work at being neither seen nor heard. Within the model household, they belonged in the nursery, neither playing nor eating with adults. And by the maintenance of these proper roles, order and moderation were served.

In an attitudinal climate such as this, children who went into the theatre naturally would be seen as posing a danger both to themselves and to society. For within the walls of the theatre, the religious checks—intended to keep in check the wild propensities of children, especially working-class children—were turned inside out. There, children did not stay in their proper places. They came out of the nursery, worked with adults, and were paid adult wages to be seen and heard; at times they were the center of attention. They were seen as being subjected to the same perversity in the theatre that took women out of their natural places in the home to work in public side by side with men, to assume male roles on stage and male functions as breadwinners and managers offstage. It was almost impossible for the child actor to maintain the moral schedule of the model home. Note Gerry's language:

> Night after night they are subjected to these changes. During the day they sleep as best they can. Their nervous systems soon become disorganized, digestion is rapidly impaired; late work necessitates late suppers, and the associations into which they are brought very soon leads to loss of modesty on the part of the girls.[46]

In 1892, he shamelessly confesses outright (what he had always implied) that he believes restrictions on child performers are more necessary than restrictions on child labor in factories. Speaking of the legislative attempt to ease restrictions on theatrical performance, he writes:

> It is worse than the factory bill for that permits the slavery of children during the day, to the exclusion of their schooling, for which the state pays. But this bill permits them to be employed by night in performing and getting tuition in vice, and by day in rehearsing for the night.[47]

Gerry's paradoxical mixture of benevolence, hypocrisy and cynicism doubtless arose in large measure from a profound confusion about theatrical art and powerlessness. In his heart there simmered an atavistic fear that public entertainment was inevitably synonymous with the unscrupulous exploitation of those without power. He saw the entertainer as the defenseless, exposed tool. Singing or dancing was a means of abasement, a validation of the heartless manipulation from the wings of one of God's creatures—the old black man dancing at the order of his white master, the reluctant prostitute dancing at the command of the sultan, the slavish song of Svengali's mesmerized Trilby. Gerry and his supporters reinforced this intensely felt obsession in their erratic reactions to any young girl's stage performance.

To restate, the law in New York City, which was ambiguous about acting, clearly forbade children to sing or dance on stage, but much depended on how Gerry personally decided that the law should be enforced on the moment. He sometimes allowed children to sing but not dance, sometimes to act but not sing or dance. Sometimes only performances on wind instruments were forbidden; sometimes piano performances were also shut down. Gerry would allow a child to appear in a major dramatic role night after night but would go to court repeatedly to keep a child from singing or playing the piano for five minutes an evening. In his last case before an amendment of the Gerry law was passed, taking away much of his authority, he suggests the heart of the problem (paraphrased by the *Times*): "It was the exhibition of the child as a dancer and not the simple dance that was prohibited."[48]

Perhaps Gerry expended much more energy and publicity on child actors than on four-year-old cotton mill hands because he gave the cotton mill no moral definition, no sexual connotation as he did the theatre. Because parts of the theatre had been gathering places of prostitution in America as late as the 1860s, many misguided individuals of the 1880s and 1890s were convinced that prostitutes and pimps still dominated the territory both before and behind the curtain of every place of entertainment. Though Gerry insisted on occasion that he had no quarrel with legitimate drama, quite inconsistently, he would also sometimes insist that most adult female entertainers were prostitutes and would voice his worst fears that young girls who danced and sang in the most reputable theatres would inevitably end up appearing in low-life variety halls and become prostitutes. The point was often made by a few religious leaders that the theatre still encouraged and subsisted from an alliance with prostitution—quite literally. More often toward the end of the century, however, the charge was intended to be metaphoric rather than literal. Behind every argument lurked the not-quite expressed conviction that, even if the stage were not the first step toward that ultimate degradation (as Gerry said it was), the mere fact

8. Children in Industry

of such "exhibition," however innocently intended, was itself figurative prostitution, with the young actor's parents and theatre manager assuming the roles of pimps. In the cotton mills they merely died; in the theatre they sinned.

Elbridge T. Gerry deepens our understanding of the complex spirit of the nineteenth century and the religious moralist's war against the stage. His extraordinary obsession with children on stage allows us a valuable perspective from which to view with greater precision the intensity and source of attacks on the theatre in the context of public morals and industrial labor. It is clear that Gerry, genuinely wrenched by suffering, was driven to take action on behalf of the dispossessed, and he maintained passion to the end; but his humane instincts were incapable of carrying him beyond the narrowness of antitheatrical bias.

9

Prostitutes and the Bar

That dark, horrible, guilty "third tier"
— Olive Logan

Despite the clergy's overwrought and misguided rhetoric, there was one charge against which the stage had no defense: the presence in the theatre of a bar and a third tier devoted to prostitutes, a clientele not only tolerated but invited there by theatrical management to attract male members of the audience and swell the nightly take of the house. No circumstance presented the public with such a dark underside of the theatre as did its persistence in maintaining an upper row of seats for the cities' prostitutes, a practice which affected every aspect of the nineteenth-century theatre.[1] Even so, the acknowledgment of its existence by most theatre historians has been cursory — even as critical as the third tier was to the economy, public relations, physical design, play selection, and acceptability of the theatre, and as fully as it has been documented in the press of the times, in religious objections, and in memoirs of managers, players, and playgoers alike. It is true that no part of the theatre (and its neighborhoods) was completely free of prostitutes for most of the nineteenth century. But the third tier was the sanctioned, official place in the house reserved primarily for prostitutes and their clientele. Here, officially tucked away in an upper balcony, was the epitome of all that the church and genteel religious society feared and denied — unabashed sexuality. The third tier was the converse of everything that capitalist society held dear. It was noisy and disorderly; it was a temptation to idleness and excess rather than industry and moderation, especially for the young men on whom the future of the economic enterprise rested; and it was an uncontrolled and turbulent display of ungodly rather than holy

9. Prostitutes and the Bar

passion. In those moments when the laughter and shouts from the third tier spilled over to drown out the dialogue on stage in profane anthems and when, looking up, a patron or an actor glimpsed, not a choir of scrubbed white, angelic faces, but the painted faces in the dark, the upstanding Victorian patron found it easy to endorse the moral crusader's damnation of the theatre as the devil's church. Many theatre supporters, including actors and managers, saw the inversion of heaven as they looked into the third tier. *Pandemonium*, the Miltonic term for heaven's inversion, came to actress Olive Logan's mind as she gazed on "the brutal exhibition of faces" from her place on stage.[2] Logan labeled the upper row above the dress and family circles that was set aside for the sole use of prostitutes as "that dark, horrible, guilty 'third tier'" (pp. 33–35). The playgoer, as well as the performer, could observe in the top row of boxes what one person described as "the hard-visaged, the ill-behaved, the boisterous, the indecent."[3] The third tier was a frustrating, maddening reality to those who worked for the survival of the theatre. Of all the accusations hurled at the theatre by its enemies, the charge that theatre managers allowed, even invited, prostitutes to occupy the third tier was the strongest, least refuted argument advanced by enemies of the stage. In short, the third tier was the most powerful ammunition in the church's arsenal against the theatre. The third tier had a great influence on American culture and was a pivotal and frequent subject of discussion, a theatrical fact of life that was at the center of the church's war on the stage. The third tier alone prevented acceptance of the theatre by many who might have supported it otherwise.

Many early theatre historians seem to have felt duty bound to keep secret this unsavory truth of stage life, deciding to leave it unrecorded and undiscussed. It was a distinct embarrassment that no friend of the theatre enjoyed talking about. To learn about the third tier, the modern student must consult the editorial pages of urban newspapers of the day, contemporary treatises attacking or defending the theatre and a few theatrical memoirs. William Dunlap, playwright, theatre manager, and one of the first chroniclers of the American stage, is one theatre historian who throws the dirty linen of his profession out for all to see. Moreover, Dunlap considered the presence of the third tier of sufficient importance to conclude his *The History of the American Theatre* (1797) with a description of the grave problems posed by the third tier.

Dunlap's record establishes the existence of the third tier in American theatres in the mid–eighteenth century. In his words, it was "a distinct portion of the proscenium" allocated to "those unfortunate females who have been the victims of seduction." From the beginning it was "a separate place," "set apart," which could "present to the gaze of the matron and virgin the unabashed votaries of vice" and "tempt the yet unsullied youth, by the example of the false face which depravity assumes for the purpose of enticing to guilt."[4] In a nation, established as a City on a Hill to right Old World wrongs, the theatre, observed Dunlap, remained the repository of an unreformed, abusive custom. The tier's genesis, according to Dunlap, may have been British. Dunlap is one of numerous managers throughout the country that called for reform by first ridding the theatre of third tier practices:

> The evil we mean, and shall protest against, is that which arises from the English and American regulation of the theatres, which allots a distinct portion of the proscenium to those unfortunate females who have been the victims of seduction.
> If a regulation was enforced, that no female should come to a theatre unattended by a protector of the other sex, except such whose standing in society is a passport to every place, the evil would be effectually remedied.
> The improper, indecent, and scandalous practice of setting apart a portion of the boxes for this most disgusting display of shameless vice, has no connexion with the question of the utility of theatres.
> It is to be lamented that when the people of Massachusetts introduced the theatre in their capital, having the experience of the world before them, they had not set an example to their fellow citizens by purifying the dramatic establishment and abolishing this evil. They appear to have noticed it, but instead of remedying, they, if possible, made it worse....The new theatre of Philadelphia gave an opportunity for reform, as did that of New York; but these opportunities were neglected.[5]

Many firsthand references to the third tier in eighteenth-century America delineate its true nature as an other-worldly, noisy, and unruly area to which are relegated a population unacceptable to the religious mainstream. A 1794 description of the Chestnut Theatre in Philadelphia by a French traveler, Moreau de Saint-Mercy, noted, "Women as well as men sit in the pit, though not a woman of fashion. There are women also in the gallery and the Negroes have no other place."[6] Whether this meant that the women in the gallery were prostitutes is left unsaid, but the fact that they were segregated in an area with blacks suggests that the writer is speaking of the same women whom Dunlap describes as prostitutes. Washington Irving's Jonathan Oldstyle letters note that the third tier is kept "in *excellent* order by the constables," but later recommends that the upper tier have "less grog and better constables."[7] Again, there is no clear mention of any place being given over to prostitutes and their customers, but obviously it was sufficiently rowdy to demand policing, again suggesting that Irving left unsaid what Dunlap acknowledges—that the third tier was the domain of prostitutes.

By the nineteenth century the third tier had become an understood theatrical appendage. *Femmes du pave*, as they were euphemistically called, were welcomed into the third tier of New York's high-class Park Theatre from the time of its opening in the late eighteenth century. Its lower-class counterpart, the Bowery, opened in 1826, reserving an upper row of boxes for the same clientele. By the 1830s and 1840s, the relinquishing of the third tier to prostitutes had become an established national tradition, not only in New York, but in most large cities, including Boston, Chicago, Philadelphia, St. Louis, Cincinnati, Mobile, and New Orleans, among others.[8] Theatrical manager Francis Courtney Wemyss notes the existence of the third tier in Philadelphia's Chestnut Street Theatre when he complains of the effect of the new chandeliers in the house which, lighted up the third tier in 1822:

> [A]nd another objection to this mode of lighting the theatre, is, that it exposesd to view, that very portion which has contributed more to the downfall of the drama, than all the other causes put together; I allude to the third tier of boxes, where licentiousness prevails in the worst form.[9]

Noah Ludlow confirms the continuing practice in St. Louis in 1835 when the design of a newly constructed theatre originally included separate doors in the side and the back for pit and third-tier clientele.[10] Without much certitude, Solomon Smith supposes that prostitutes in the third tier had been replaced by "colored people" in St. Louis theatres since 1838: "If I am right in this assumption, it is sufficient to say that *here* in St. Louis, there has been no saloon or bar-room carried on in the theatre for ten years, and that the third tier is frequented by as honest and virtuous a set of auditors, male and female, as can be found in any community—of colored people."[11]

The third tier may have closed in St. Louis in 1832, but, according to reporter George G. Foster, a chronicler of the dark side of New York, the third tier was still very much alive in most New York theatres in the 1840s. Only Niblo's Theatre had a rule that "no woman is admitted at this house, under any pretext, unless accompanied by a gentleman."[12]

While the nineteenth-century church was considered a place of conversion from sin to morality, the third tier was regarded as a place of conversion from innocence to immorality. The rituals of the gallery were apparently simple: The entire inhabitants of houses of prostitution would customarily descend on the theatre in a body, entering by a separate stairway, designed for their use alone, an hour or two before the rest of the house was opened. The higher-class prostitutes sat throughout the theatre, usually meeting customers there by pre-arrangement through such means as newspaper advertisement. But the lower-class prostitutes made initial contacts with their customers in the third tier or met their customers of long standing there. Other men were introduced to the theatre's prostitutes when mutual friends took them up to the third tier from other parts of the house. A bar was located nearby, contributing to the rowdy behavior which was a constant disturbance to the rest of the house, not to mention the actors.[13] At times women would even leave the third tier and solicit customers in other parts of the house. In 1837 the Reverend Robert Turnbull seems to concede prostitutes their place in the theatre, being less indignant about their being in the theatre at all than about their being allowed "to leave their appropriate place and invade the pit."[14] The primary business of the third tier was not to watch the play but to make arrangements for the rest of the evening. Having met there, they and their customers might go directly to a house of ill repute. Others might lengthen the evening's activities, as did the higher-class prostitutes whom John J. Jennings describes in St Louis: They proceeded with their customers to a

> quiet restaurant of the most questionable reputation and took one of the private supper-rooms, which are at the disposal of people whose visit to the establishment is not by any means for the sole purpose of drinking and eating, but has a broad and very unmistakable suggestion of immorality in it.[15]

John Murtagh and Sara Harris, writing on the history of New York prostitution, found that for many prostitutes the upper tiers and galleries of the Bowery Theatre were not just meeting places, but convenient spots for completion of their business: "They swarmed the galleries, using them not only for purposes of pickup, but also as places where their relations with unfinicky customers could be consummated."[16]

As early as 1837, Noah Ludlow, prominent theatrical manager, had made the revolutionary decision to close his Mobile theatre, including the third tier, to "women of the *pave.*" Eventually he would spread this practice to theatres in St. Louis and other cities where his traveling company played. His description, nevertheless, illustrates the degree to which the tier had become entrenched. It also shows that the decision to abandon the prac-

9. Prostitutes and the Bar

tice often called for a certain amount of courage on the part of theatrical managers like himself:

> On the opening of this house I made a beginning of a reform which I adhered to and carried forward in after years in all the theatres under my management. This was to refuse admission to any female to the performance who did not come attended by a gentleman, or some one having the appearance of a man of respectability, not even in the third tier, and women notoriously of the *pave* were never, under any conditions, admitted. The result of these rigid measures was that the third tier in our theatres was as quiet and orderly as any portion of the house.
>
> ...I had a hard struggle for this scheme of reformation. There were several attempts made by lewd women and their bullies to pass door-keepers having obtained tickets by sending boys and servants for them under the names of respectable citizens. However, I foiled their stratagems through the vigilance of a private policeman, well acquainted with such kind of persons by sight, and who knew how to deal with them. From time to time, for some two or three years following my management in St. Louis and Mobile, and in subsequent years in New Orleans, I had sent to me through the post-office threatening missives, such as "cow-hidings," "fisticuffings," and "shooting" and the like, for refusing admission to these filles de joie; but I persisted in my course, and finally gained my point.[17]

The manager of the Park Theatre in New York City summoned the courage to try closing the third tier in 1842. In this landmark experiment, one finds language which places the theatre, because of its association with prostitutes, in direct opposition to the church. The prominence of prostitutes is underscored by the language of the reportage that brands the theatre as a "temple" of the harlot. The experiment began when Edmund Simpson, the Park's manager, attempted to meet the objection of critics of theatre immorality by producing a religious play, "The Israelites in Egypt, or the Passage of the Red Sea." But a letter writer to the *New York Herald* in November of 1842 drew Simpson's attention to the fact that the Park's continuation of the third tier made any other attempts at moral reform somewhat ludicrous: "Look at the inconsistency of the production of sacred drama in a temple devoted to the harlot." As a result, Simpson closed the third tier and was congratulated by the *Herald* for his courage in "purifying the third tier," by excluding "the frail women who frequented that quarter." But Simpson's courage failed; before the end of the play's eighteen-night run, the prostitutes were back in the Park's third tier.[18] Another milestone in the third tier's dwindling existence was recorded by *The Spirit of the Times*, which lauded manager J. H. Hackett for thwarting the corruption of the innocent when he reopened the Howard Athenaeum in 1846: "We understand that the great objectionable features of theatrical representation are to be excluded from the Athenaeum — the 'third row' and 'the bar' which have proved the ruin of so many young men."[19]

In 1857, however, a clergyman named Agnew, obviously a hostile observer, claimed that the third tier was still the "resort of lewd women" who went there "to attract attention" and continued to make the theatre "the house of the harlot" where "she holds her court."[20] Even as late as 1875, the Reverend Talmage insisted that prostitutes still sat in the third tier.[21] By the 1880s, however, writers sympathetic with, as well as those antagonistic to, the stage agreed that the third tiers of legitimate theatres had finally closed.[22]

Had the practice of maintaining a third tier been a short-lived, isolated episode, the subject would deserve no more than the passing reference it has received. But such was not the case: Records indicate that this widespread, peculiar relationship between the America theatre and prostitutes colored stage policy for fifty years or more.

The third tier affected theatre design and practices. For instance, the theatre's design allowed prostitutes and their customers to arrive into an unholy choir loft with as little fanfare as possible. In true Victorian fashion, every effort was made to keep their customers out of sight. They were not only tucked away in their own gallery, they entered by a separate entrance onto a side street which led to a separate stairway. Patrons of the rest of the house used a front entrance and a central stairway. This arrangement reminds one of the separate balcony, stairways and entrances in movie houses once designed for blacks in the segregated South. Dunlap describes the circumstance as it existed in Boston in the eighteenth century:

> [T]he Federal Street Theatre provided a separate entrance for those who came for the express purpose of alluring to vice. The boxes displayed the same row of miserable victims, decked in smiles and borrowed finery, and the entrance could only, by its separation from those appropriated to the residue of the audience, become a screen inviting to secret guilt.[23]

Somewhat later, in the nineteenth century, St. Louis theatres had a similar design: There were three tiers or galleries of seats and a so-called "parquet," which term came into use after 1850. The first tier was called the dress circle; the second included a bar and the family circle; and the third, the gallery. The entrance to the third tier or gallery was from outside the building by a "flight of winding stairs having no connection with the

9. Prostitutes and the Bar

other entrances."[24] In a theatre in New York, the separate stairway onto a different street was only later provided for prostitutes. This move was called "a laudable effort to reduce to less prominence the disgusting feature of the stage." The manager of this theatre was less successful in erecting a partition to shut off the prostitutes from other patrons altogether: "He soon yielded to the dreadful necessity of the stage, and the protest of this class, and removed the partition."[25] Foster, in 1850, makes reference to the physical design of New York theatres intended to accommodate prostitutes and their effect on the rest of the house:

> It is true that thick walls and wide stair-cases separate the public entrance from that for abandoned women: yet it is nevertheless true that one-quarter of the entire house is set apart exclusively for the use of the latter, in which they nightly and publicly drive their sickening trade.[26]

Another policy of the theatre seems to have been intended to hide the third tier from the more respectable public and to further the ends for which the separate stairway and partition were designed: Public announcements indicated that the gallery was open to the public much earlier in the evening (sometimes by as much as two hours) than were other parts of the house.[27] This policy kept third-tier patrons off the adjacent street and out of sight well before other "respectable" theatregoers arrived at the front entrance of the theatre, hiding and denying a custom that even many theatre folk deplored.

No picture of the economics of theatre management in nineteenth-century America is complete without taking the third tier into account. Everts correctly charges that many managers argued that profits from the third tier actually kept their theatres operating. One manager, in answer to an inquiry, declared that his theatre's bar would never be closed because the third tier supported the theatre and the bar supported the third tier.[28] To fill the third tier was a guarantee of a good house in many theatres in which the gallery held more people than any other tier. Ludlow, for example, describes the gallery of his St. Louis theatre as holding three hundred and fifty patrons.[29]

In the earlier days of the nineteenth century, managers were content merely to make the third tier available for prostitutes in exchange for a good house. However, as the century wore on, they aggressively courted them with free tickets. When receipts were poor, managers often went so far as to send messengers to houses of prostitution with blocks of free gallery tickets to attract the women and their clientele to the theatre.[30] In 1866

Church and Stage

Everts claimed: "In some instances in Eastern cities, in addition to free admissions, messengers have been sent to the haunts of vile women, to invite their attendance as the necessary attraction of a large and indispensable portion of the patrons of the stage."[31] Actress Olive Logan reported that when public pressure led managers to close the third tier, profits usually fell off so miserably that they were forced to change their minds and redouble their solicitation of prostitutes.[32]

The Tremont Theatre in Boston was frequently cited as an example of how the closing of the third tier had destroyed a theatre. Speaking of the theatre's prostitutes, William Everts believed: "The neglect of provision for this class would probably be fatal to the prosperity of any theatre. The experiment has been partially tried in different cities without success. In one instance, the night after their interdiction, scarcely fifty persons were present and the third tier was again opened as usual."[33] The Reverends Henry Ward Beecher and John Angell James both gloat over the inability of the Tremont Theatre to separate itself from the bar and prostitutes in the third tier.[34] James quotes an article written by "a Boston correspondent" which appeared in the *New York Observer* of June 29, 1839:

> The Tremont theatre is in trouble. It proves to be a losing concern, and there appears to be no way to make it profitable. It was built with the avowed intention of raising the respectability of the drama; and I believe the manager has honestly done his best to meet, at once, the demands of those who love theatres and those who love good morals. Several years since, he abolished his bar for the sale of intoxicating liquors; in consideration of which he solicited and obtained a license for his theatre, without paying the usual tax. He afterwards attempted another reform, which he delicately announced by a notice that no *lady* would be admitted to any part of the theatre unless accompanied by a gentleman, thus excluding all "ladies" in whose company no gentleman would be willing to be seen. This was necessary, because so many of both sexes utterly refused to attend a place of amusement where it is known that such "ladies" form a part of the company. But the loss of the patronage of such "ladies," and of those who stayed away when they were excluded, was more than the manager's purse could bear, and in a few weeks the rule was suffered to fall into disuse. Of late, there has been an investigation of the affairs of the company, and a report has been published, from which it appears, that even if the manager had the building rent-free, the receipts would fall considerably short of meeting the other expenses.[35]

The managers were caught in an almost impossible situation. They could, by continuing to keep the third tier open, find themselves condemned in

9. Prostitutes and the Bar

the press and avoided by many "respectable" patrons, or they could close the tier and face sudden financial ruin.

On the other hand, some people had come to the startling conclusion that managers, by closing their third tiers, would eventually attract a wider clientele. Dunlap came to such a view at the turn of the nineteenth century: "the prohibition of the immoral display would remove a just stigma from the theatre, and would further the views of managers by increasing their receipts."[36] P. T. Barnum took this approach when he turned the prostitutes out of his theatre and began appealing to family audiences with his "museums." And the writer of a lengthy article on the matter in the *Cincinnati Daily Enquirer*, quoted by Logan, suggests that the presence of prostitutes repelled so many theatregoers, especially decent women, that when the third tier was abolished and single women refused admission to the theatre, attendance at plays would go up.[37]

The continual clerical battle against the stage, fired by its alliance with prostitutes, ate away potential support. Those who disapproved on principle argued that vice was endemic to the theatre. It was clear and irrefutable evidence of this, they contended, because without it the stage would disappear. Writing in 1837, the Reverend Turnbull was convinced that the third tier continued to be open to prostitutes because "that class of persons know that it (the theatre) is a favorite amusement of those who are most easily tempted to sin. Besides, they find there much in accordance with their habits and feelings."[38] One of Turnbull's melodramatic stories, offered as proof of this charge, was told many times by others as well: A once-innocent young man is dying from pneumonia after having fallen into a canal while in pursuit of a prostitute named Emily. On his deathbed he gasps out the story of his ruin, which supposedly appeared in numerous newspapers:

> It would tire you to relate how I was first enticed to go up stairs into the splendid saloon, then to the third tier where the prostitutes are allotted a place. One night, the most fascinating amongst them, Emily was her name, came up to me, and took my arm. I had not the power to resist the tempter, and was persuaded to accompany her to her brothel.[39]

Some thirty years later, in 1866, the rhetoric is still as heated, as another minister, Robert Hatfield, stated that:

> The theatre has been a moral pest all of its life of two thousand, five hundred years.... [It] has affinities with crime and destroys neighborhoods.... The private house is turned into a bagnio; the shop of honest trade into

the faro saloon or barroom, and the playhouse stands as a spectacle of vice, supported by its congenial aids of rowdyism, gambling, drunkenness and prostitution.... The theatre leans upon them and supports them, and is supported by these places.[40]

The rhetoric of the theatre's critics rarely masked their ignorance of their subject, but the reality of the third tier and what went on there was not denied and only occasionally defended by theatre supporters. It proved to be the theatre's one truly vulnerable spot. Whenever financial collapse followed the closing of a third tier, critics had "proof" that theatres and vice were inseparably linked, that the theatre could not be reformed. Friends of the theatre, on the other hand, were encouraged by the closing of third tiers and could, in the late 1800s, at last point to a dramatic establishment in the country, free of any open, formal alliance with prostitution. The clerical practical stand against the stage, based so solidly on the theatre's relationship with prostitutes, kept many would-be theatregoers away and prevented any significant broad-based support from developing. Furthermore, many patrons were driven away by disagreeable firsthand experiences and by the location nearby of houses of prostitution.

The third tier practice raises literary and cultural questions not so readily resolved in nineteenth-century documents. For instance, to what extent did having a large group of prostitutes in the audience affect the types of plays written for and performed on the American stage? Was there a relationship between the third tier and the "leg shows" which followed in the tier's demise? What were the extra-financial motives behind this remarkable custom? Was there a significant relationship between the tier and acting companies?

The existence of the third tier has to be seen in the context of the times. As we see, for example, in Foster's reportage, in the account of Sara Harris and John M. Murtagh (identified as the chief magistrate of the city of New York), and in the report of reformer William Sanger, prostitution raged throughout the city, not just in the third tier of theatres.[41] In the neighborhoods around the Bowery, Five Points, 24th to 40th streets between 5th and 7th, known as Satan's Circus, scarcely a structure did not serve as a house of prostitution. In the most infamous, the Bowery, poverty-stricken mothers and daughters plied their trade even in tiny rooms occupied by entire families. Not until 1892 with the reforms of the Reverend Charles H. Pankhurst was significant progress made in cleaning up areas of abject poverty that fostered prostitution and calling to account politicians and members of law enforcement who thrived on vice. Pankhurst's congrega-

9. Prostitutes and the Bar

tions and other audiences found his persistent work toward reform to be embarrassing, vulgar, and disrespectful of the city's leaders, but no one, including the city's newspapers, was successful in shutting him up.

The question arises, why, with prostitutes swarming the streets of New York's underground, was the third tier singled out by the clergy for special excoriation and why was the stage blamed for attracting houses of prostitution to its neighborhoods? Foster, for example, not a cleric but a reporter, implies that the third tier of the Broadway Theatre is the worst of all the lurid scenes he has described of New York's night life:

> Within a few feet and under the same roof where our virtuous matrons with their tender offspring are seated, are momently enacting scenes of cold-blooded depravity enough to make the heart of humanity shudder. Painted, diseased, drunken women, bargaining themselves away to obscene and foul-faced ruffians, for so much an hour — drinking, blasphemy, fighting, rioting — such are the accompaniments, the antithesis, would we might add, to what is transpiring on the stage. This is the greatest and most obstinately-persisted-in outrage to public sense and public decency of which the age furnishes any example.[42]

The answer has to lie in the tier's violation of the supreme Victorian value of concealment. Grinding poverty, prostitution, gambling, and alcoholism were successfully covered up and isolated in the neighborhoods and slums where polite society never saw them. But cultured people who did attend the theatre came face-to-face with the dark side of society in the third tier. What should have been and ordinarily was, suppressed was exposed here as an undeniable and ugly reality.

The history of the third tier is paradigmatic of the cultural history of Victorian America. Two struggles are going on here: a secular art form struggling for legitimacy against long-standing religious disapproval, and a stricter moral code struggling against customary vice.

The theatre's bar also violated every moral precept of the Christian church. It was disorderly, loud, out-of-control, vulgar, and excessive. Ministers usually objected to the bar maintained by the theatre in the same breath with their objection to the third tier. Bar and theatre were, they claimed, inevitably connected. Veteran third-tier johns required access to alcohol, usually located on the tier below, and novices were plied with alcohol from the bar before being introduced to the third tier. The bar was invariably described as a noisy riotous place where deafening arguments and fights took place, often drowning out the lines of the actors. Slightly different versions of the often repeated story of the corruption, death, and damnation of once innocent youth begin in the bar of the theatre. Again, as with the third tier, managers feared that the theatre would close without the bar.

Another related problem confirmed by actors and managers, and exacerbated by the theatre's maintenance of the bar, was the problem of alcoholism among actors. The theatrical genius, Junius Brutus Booth, was as well known for his heavy drinking as he was for his brilliance as an actor. The stories about the extremes to which alcohol led him are legend. Harry Watkins records numerous fellow players who were more often drunk than sober: Junius Brutus Booth, whose drunkenness caused him to refuse to die as he was supposed to in a fencing scene and drove his opponent out the stage door and into the street; Frank Drew, whose family renamed him Drank Few; Joseph Dunn and an actor named Linden, who both developed delirium tremens. All this led Watkins to declare that the two impediments to stage ambition were consumption and drink — "Oh, this curse of drunkenness in my profession."[43] Solomon Smith also regrets the ravages of alcohol on Booth, regarded by many as the greatest actor of his time. "When I first knew him (in 1827) he was a truly great actor, and continued so to be until he fell into bad company in New Orleans, and took to hard drink. Then he became undependable, and 'putting an antic disposition on' made many believe he was crazy. *I* never believed him to be a crazy man except when he was excited by liquor, and that was pretty often — nearly all the time, in fact."[44]

Francis Courtney Wemyss adds another anecdote about a fellow actor named Webb:

> Mr. Webb, an actor of some repute, who was to have been the representative of Votimar, had been studying ancient history too closely, and came to the conclusion, taking Shakespeare for his authority, that the Danes were powerful drinkers, and therefore, appeared upon the stage so perfectly undisguised in liquor, that the audience thought proper to hiss, which he resented, by walking out of the theatre.[45]

Many managers admitted the problem of drunkenness among actors and some were serious about effecting reforms. William Wood stresses the need for theatres to be respectable throughout his memoir. One version was issued with a publication entitled "Who Slew All These?," printed by the American Tract Society about the ruinous effects of alcohol on a family of actors.[46]

Actors Otis and Maud Skinner wrote, in their edition of Watkin's mem-

9. Prostitutes and the Bar

oirs, that drunkenness and alcoholism were serious problems among actors at mid-century, even those of considerable standing:

> The blight of drunkenness fell upon far too many of these mid-century stars. The social glass became a necessity to carry them through long bills and tremendous exertions. Finding in alcohol a release from their inhibitions and their weariness they often relied upon it for their most cherished effects on stage.
>
> Draughty, unheated theatres, inferior hotels and bad food in the lesser towns, devastating journeys by steamboat and unsanitary cars could be forgotten when the easily procured stimulants set their veins on fire. For the poorly paid supporting actors temptation lurked on every side, and when the saloon was always next door it required a Spartan will to resist the call.[47]

On the testimony of Solomon Smith, we can deduce that drunkenness was a problem among theatrical companies, but whether it was greater than in other segments of society is doubtful. Sol's advice to male actors:

> Shun the bottle, your worst enemy — not *yours* only, but the enemy and cause of ruin of many of the wisest and best of *all* professions.[48]

C. A. Logan, in his defense of the stage, tries to put the theatre's bar in perspective:

> ... I would say, that if men will drink in despite of Temperance Societies, it matters but little where they get the liquor. If there were no bars within the house, the thirsty would most certainly find the stimulant out of doors. And yet bars are no more necessary to the theatre than to the pulpit. I am old enough to remember the time when men would assemble at the tavern nearest the church as soon as the service was over, and there discuss the merits of the sermon and of brandy and water at the same time. The Temperance movement, however, wrought wonders, and I believe the same men do not drink now — at least not until they reach home.[49]

Throughout the century, alcoholism was rampant among young single men of the upper and middle classes but primarily among the working poor. Sean Wilentz's examination of the problem in *Chants Democratic* concludes, of the working-class culture in the first half of the century, that "its centerpiece was alcohol." Wilentz describes the incredible extent of drinking:

Church and Stage

> [A]t all times, in and out of the shops, New York's journeymen could be expected to drink. By the 1820s, workingmen's saloon and grocery-grog shops had achieved a separate identity within New York's renowned barroom culture.... Some of these drinking places served as informal labor exchanges, where employers from outside of the state set up temporary hiring hall.... At work, meanwhile, prodigious amounts of alcohol appeared at the very benches of the trades as a sort of sacrament....[50]

As with prostitution in the theatre, so with drinking—both seemed worse in the theatre because they fed on one another there and openly announced themselves to audiences accustomed to the concealment of the underside of Victorian society.

The sanctioned presence of the bar and prostitutes in the third tier buttressed the church's denunciation against the theatre and set it apart from mainstream society as nothing else did, turning customs and values, fundamental to "acceptable" Victorian society, upside down and, ironically, necessitating typical Victorian secrecy and hypocrisy to maintain this maverick subculture within society's boundaries.

By the 1880s, the contest between the theatre and the religious public began to be resolved. When this happened, a change began to come about in American public opinion, a change that was only possible when the theatre broke its historical ties with prostitution and the bar.

10

Violence in the Audience, Irreverence on the Stage

> *Discontented and Ignorant Rabble*
> — Timothy Dwight

The church's warning that naïve playgoers might encounter violence in the audience and mockery from the stage did alarm the public, especially women and children. And the truth was that violence did occasionally break out even in the most respectable theatre, and was to be expected on a regular basis in New York City's working-class theatres. But the church's greatest fear was not so much that innocent people would be hurt physically in the theatre, but that a class struggle was erupting in these theatres that threatened to undermine the very foundation of the society built by the church-business partnership. At the same time that worker discontent was growing and union activity was escalating, laborers in the city were finding their homes and gathering places in certain theatres. The poor who were welcomed into these theatres initially were able to give focus and voice to their personal grievances through the nationalistic and class war that had been part of the theatrical scene from the turn of the nineteenth century. And fueling that disruption of a quiet, well-oiled industrial system were the theatres' outrageous parodies of Shakespeare, which ridiculed the British, upper-class American Anglophiles, and powerful politicians. George C. D. Odell called them, appropriately, the working-class man's "light artillery." In short, in the theatres of the poor, literary violence was intertwined with political violence.

In the background is always the church's advancement of the Protestant

Ethic, which it was pleased to see big business use to its advantage, as was discussed in chapter 2: the disapproval of Americans who adopted behavior inappropriate to their stations. The ruling class had the God-given instincts and rights to govern while the lower classes were to work quietly in the stations where God had placed them. The rabble-rouser, the union organizer, the striking worker, the rebel, the loudmouth — all were challenging the God-decreed system of callings. A typical example of the admonition to remain quietly in one's place is the Reverend Bushnell's 1875 address, entitled "Every Man's Life a Plan of God." The following excerpt lays out his argument:

> In this view also you are never to complain of your birth, your training, your employments, your hardships; never to fancy you could be something if only you had a different lot and sphere assigned you. God understands His own plan, and He knows what you want a great deal better than you do.... Hence it was that an apostle required his converts to abide each one in that calling wherein he was called, to fill his place till he by filling it opens a way to some other; the bondsman to fill his house of bondage with love and duty, the laborer to labor, the woman to be a woman, the men to show themselves men — all to acknowledge God's hand in their lot, and seek to co-operate with that good design which He most assuredly cherishes for them.[1]

Bushnell and other ministers, in disparaging the poor and their attempts to better their lot, were speaking of the very people who had found a home in working-class theatres. The armies in the war between democracy and rampant capitalism were gathering on the battlefield. And it was played out intensely and passionately in the smaller world of the working-class theatre where the "vicious" poor dared to launch riot after riot, thereby violating another one of the most significant dictates preached by advocates of the Protestant Ethic outlined by Bushnell — that one should remain quietly acquiescent in one's station or place. What did the clergy blame for the defiance and violence of the working-class audience? As Timothy Dwight confidently preaches, it is the theatrical companies and the plays they produce that corrupt the weak-minded workers who attend such exhibitions. The companies encourage disrespect for authority with their coarse burlesques of everything sacred. Furthermore, the plays chosen by the companies show young audiences the unacceptability of their poor lives, the reasons behind it, and ways to protest it.

> The discontented and ignorant rabble, thus led into imaginary evils, and distress ... have been driven to outrage and to bloodshed.

10. Violence in the Audience, Irreverence on the Stage

> While the miseries of their lot have been exhibited to the discontented and the poor.[2]

As the laborers (who made up the audiences of the vigorous working-class theatres like New York's Bowery, Chatham and Olympic) began to assert themselves, the Protestant mainstream had further reason to denounce the theatres in which political battles were pitched. On the surface, the unruliness and the growing violence in theatres, often of an anti–English, anti-aristocratic kind of nationalism, underscored the old religious arguments against the theatre. It also played into basic animosities. These audiences were not part of the Victorian establishment. Many were Irish, Roman Catholic immigrants, struggling to survive in an Anglicized Protestant culture that discriminated against them and despised them for taking jobs away from natives. National pride took many forms in the 1830s and 1840s. In 1834 the Protestant Association was formed; in 1835 the Loco-focos and Native American Democratic Association came into being; in 1845 the Native American Party and the Patriotic Order of Sons of America arose. Many members of these groups eventually found a common home in the Know-Nothing Party, led by Ned Buntline. Despite their rivalry over jobs, these working-class young people were linked to the Irish, at least in their hatred of privileged Americans. Young people made up a variety of gangs, including the colorful, famous Bowery B'hoys and G'hals who were comprised primarily of natives, but actually welcomed a variety of nationalities including some Irish. The mythical Mose, a kind of Paul Bunyan of the Bowery and the main character in a popular play, was a volunteer fireman, like many of these young people. They took on the most degrading jobs available, were paid starvation wages, and survived in the most horrifying slums imaginable. According to Bruce McConachie, these young people found a rallying place in the theatres, poked fun at everything respectable, everything that could be classified as normal social behavior.[3]

A typical patriotic playgoer attended William Mitchell's Olympic Theatre, one of several which catered to the working class by setting its prices to oblige the modest wage-earner. A seat in the pit, one of the cheaper portions of many houses, cost twelve and a half cents. Indeed, the real heart of the Olympic was its pit, largely reserved for the city's fire "B'hoys" and newsboys.[4] Mitchell, who ran the theatre, played especially to the pit of fiercely loyal rowdies whose disruptions would often necessitate his appearance in front of the curtain with a warning: "Boys, if you don't behave, I'll raise the price to a quarter as sure as you live."[5]

Church and Stage

It was scarcely surprising that some theatres, which, incidentally, had lured women out of their proper stations into the public arena, would collaborate with and encourage defiance of what the upper- and middle-class religious public regarded as a divinely sanctioned socioeconomic system. Upper-class, Anglophilic arenas, like the Astor Place Opera House and the Park, were bad enough in the eyes of the religious public, but working-class theatres were even worse in enthusiastically serving as a rallying point for those who noisily resented a world where a few lived in opulence and ease while so many eked out a miserable existence in the city's slums. The individuals in these audiences were not content to remain quietly in the stations to which they were born.

Washington Irving was one of the earliest recorders of the excessive disorder in American theatres. Just after the turn of the century, he wrote of Jonathan Oldstyle being hit in the head with "a rotten pippin" thrown from the gallery and of a stranger near him being hit with an apple.[6] George C. D. Odell recorded numerous instances in New York in the 1820s when the stage was bombarded with food, and Judge Charles H. Haswell, another firsthand observer of New York theatres between 1816 and 1860, remembered that, after suppers were consumed in the upper circles of theatres, the leavings were usually aimed at the heads of the patrons in the pit.[7] Mrs. Trollope, the most graphic exposer of American behavior in the theatre, was repulsed by the constant yelling, throwing, and spitting even in fashionable parts of midwestern and eastern theatres. On one occasion she was shocked beyond belief to see a man have a violent fit of vomiting in the theatre and even more amazed to observe that the other members of the audience treated it as a normal occurrence.[8] Conditions among southern audiences seem to have been much the same. W. Stanley Hoole, in his *The Antebellum Charleston Theatre*, mentioned constant complaints from the public about the yelling, spitting, picking of pockets, drunkenness, and brawls in the audiences.[9] What Maria Child observed in the Bowery was representative of many theatre nights all over the country: the pit patrons, she writes, "get up a gratuitous battle, more lively than those on stage."[10]

The violence that erupted in the theatre was almost inevitably politicized, involving rivalries and bad blood between people of different nationalities, especially between competing English and American actors. An instigator of much of working-class theatre's violence was the humiliation of the American actor by Anglophiles, interpreted as a slur on America in general, and specifically the American artist, who suffered through the

10. Violence in the Audience, Irreverence on the Stage

actions and attitudes of the English and American privileged classes. Americans were obviously English cast-offs, bumpkins who could never equal the talent of the mother country's composers, painters or writers, and who could point with pride to Shakespeare, Milton, Samuel Johnson, and to the magnificent actors, David Garrick and John Phillip Kemble. The war for independence from England, which it was thought had never been won on the social, economic and cultural fronts, had gathered considerable steam in the 1830s and 1840s. Newspapers of the day substantiate the claim that the red-blooded super patriot also considered himself in a class war perceived in national terms: the English successfully manipulating, fostering and underwriting an adoring American aristocracy.

Political and social nationalism ran parallel to support for cultural independence. Emerson's Phi Beta Kappa address of 1837, "The American Scholar," is probably the most famous of many appeals for a culture based on nature, not shackled to the English. In his first paragraph, he states hopefully: "Our day of dependence, our long apprenticeship to the earning of other lands, draws to a close. The millions that around us are rushing into life, cannot always be fed on the sere remains of foreign harvests." He closes, in the last paragraph, with: "We have listened too long to the courtly mass of Europe. The spirit of the American freeman is already suspected to be timid, imitative, tame."[12] To facilitate American independence, theatre managers were encouraged to stage plays written by Americans.

The collision between American actors, admired by the lower-class theatregoers, and English stars, held in awe by the upper class, sparked the class war that had its base in the theatre. American actor Edwin Forrest, according to Noah Ludlow, was a victim of the prejudice against Americans, snidely assigned to a rank lower than English actors. Ludlow writes of the reaction to Forrest's appearance in Caldwell's company in New Orleans:

> With the public of New Orleans Mr. Edwin Forrest made a very favorable impression on his first night of performance; but the members of the company were decidedly of the opinion that he evinced very little, if any talent, and that little they considered of the roughest and most unpolished kind.... The fact of the matter was that the most of the leading members were of English birth, and in those days there were many well-meaning persons, on and off the "stage," who imagined there was no dramatic talent to be found that was not of English growth. My estimate of the abilities of Mr. Forrest was attributed to the fact that we were both *Western actors*.[13]

At the same time, Ludlow points out that Forrest eventually became an icon to the working-class playgoers:

> We are inclined to believe that Mr. Forrest is not to be judged by the ordinary canonical standards of criticism, at least on his native soil. He has created a school in his art, strictly American, and he stands forth as the very embodiment, as it were, of *the masses* of American character. Hence his peculiarities. Hence his amazing success. And further, Mr. Forrest in his acting is not merely the embodiment of a national character, but he is the *beau ideal* of a peculiar phase of that character, — its *democratic idiosyncrasy*. Of this, both physically and in his artistical execution, he is a complete living illustration.[14]

Conversely, for these politically conscious citizens, no single figure was so clearly representative of upper-class culture as many an English actor, an imposing figure of polished manners and speech who could properly place himself in a long and grand theatrical tradition, and could, with justification, be haughty and disdainful when he came to perform on American soil. And the faithful working-class theatregoers found every reason to despise him.

Actor Edwin Forrest, symbolic of the democratic American, played a crucial role in the Astor Place Riots.

Nationalist issues surfaced in a case of violence in 1811 in the Philadelphia theatre managed by Englishman William Wood. He chronicles a story of a Scottish actor, named McKenzie, who was found to have manipulated national rivalries after ignoring his engagement with Wood to perform in another company. The managers issued a playbill before the performance, explaining that McKenzie had embarrassed the company by withdrawing himself without giving them any explanation, and that someone else would be taking the role of Mordant which McKenzie had been contracted to play. In defense, McKenzie

10. Violence in the Audience, Irreverence on the Stage

decided to incense the Scottish population by leading them to believe that the Philadelphia House routinely humiliated Scots. So the reaction to the playbill, later seen as incited by McKenzie, was violent. On the night, of the performance, when another actor took on the role McKenzie had been contracted to play, the house was packed:

> The cries "Kill him! Drive him from his stage! Kill him!" were repeated in the hearing of numbers.... Dwyer, who was playing with me, was excessively mortified, and pronounced it a more ferocious riot than he had ever witnessed in the rudest Irish theatres.[15]

On the next night when the company offered *Romeo and Juliet*, there were few women in the audience and the reaction from the organized groups in the audience was more belligerent:

> In the last act, where Romeo brought forward the awakened Juliet from her tomb, the lady (my wife acting this part) received a violent blow on the arm from a musket ball, thrown from an upper box near the stage.[16]

The disruption continued on- and offstage for the following nights, resulting in a full-scale riot in the streets. Friends of the Philadelphia House suggested calling in military force. Finally, the community got to the bottom of the riot. McKenzie, so afraid that the company was going to sue him for breach of contract, had rallied a large group of rowdies by spreading a rumor that "'the manager habitually indulged publicly and privately in most insulting attacks upon the Scotch portion of our citizens, as well as upon mechanics in masses.'"[17]

Additionally, William Clapp records two instances of audience disruption in Boston. One notorious event set the stage for violence in numerous American theatres on the occasion of English actor Edmund Kean's appearances. Kean had made few friends in America because of his English arrogance and scorn for Americans as little more than country bumpkins. The action that provoked riotous objections to him among playgoers began in the Boston Theatre in 1821 when, early on the evening of his performance, he was displeased to see too few people in the audience. He declared immediately that he would not perform and left the theatre. A few minutes later, the managers called on him in his lodgings to report that the theatre now held a respectable number of customers and urged him to return. But Kean haughtily refused. Next day, to show their displeasure, the playgoing public tried to find him, and students broke the windows and benches in the theatre in protest, but Kean had safely gotten out of town. However, he was scarcely safer in New York City than he had been in Boston. Both Kean and the New York theatres had good reason to believe that a full-scale riot would erupt if he appeared, so he cut his American tour short and sailed back to Liverpool.[18]

In 1825, Kean again returned to play in American theatres. In New York City he was subjected to hisses and shouts from the audience. Then he went to Boston where the playgoing public had not forgotten his earlier insult. On the first night, the theatre was crammed with men from top to bottom but without a woman in sight — a sure sign that trouble was brewing. It was no surprise that he was pelted off the stage. On his second night a full-scale riot ensued. Inside, the play had to be performed in dumb show because of the deafening taunts and threats from the audience. Outside the scene was truly scary:

> In the meantime, the mob without had become excited to phrenzy, and made several assaults upon the house; and the audience within began to think not so much of Kean as of their own preservation from danger. The rabble began to assail the lamps, the windows, and the entrances to the boxes, gallery, and pit.... The few police officers were soon overpowered....
> The audience, who were in the second tier of boxes, found themselves in a most trying situation. The fierce conflict with brick-bats, clubs, etc., at the stairs and doors, effectively shut out their means of retreat, and they were compelled to await in anxiety, and witness the increasing outrages, and approach of the immense mob without, expecting every instant when the internal resistance would be cloven down, and the thronging rabble precipitate them into the pit, or maim them with deadly missiles, or crush them to death in the lobbies.[19]

In 1825, Kean was extended an invitation to play in Philadelphia, over the objections of manager Francis Wemyss who believed that Kean's life would be in danger if he appeared in the city. True to Wemyss's predictions, when Kean walked on stage for his first night's performance, he was drowned out by objections from the audience. "The row which followed was a serious affair — the outrages perpetrated disgraceful to a civilized community. Rotten eggs, children's bullet buttons, and other small missiles, were thrown upon the stage in countless numbers."[20]

In the next year, rioting against Kean broke out in Baltimore, where Kean's friends foolishly goaded the general public. As a result "a brickbat thrown at the windows of the theatre's saloon, was followed by a rush towards the door. The theatre was saved from destruction by the spirited

10. Violence in the Audience, Irreverence on the Stage

conduct of Mr. Montgomery, the mayor of the city...,"[21] and Kean was rushed out of town while his enemies searched every carriage to find him.

At about the same time, another politicized threat surfaced after Wood's theatre on Chestnut Street in Philadelphia had been refurbished, providing a separate entrance on Sixth Street for the pit (and a separate one for the gallery). This was perceived to be a slap at the working-class Philadelphians who frequented the pit. The reaction was an inflammatory handbill entitled, "Equality, or the New Theatre As It Should Be."

> You, citizens, whose patronage the drama is proud to acknowledge, and whose inclination, taste, or means may lead to the Pit or Gallery, why subject you to an entrance comparatively less respectable than what has been assigned to those whose *assumed* superiority has led to distinctions wherein *no* distinctions are at all justifiable?
>
> The national spirit of America has triumphed over the pride of European armies; shall that spirit slumber under the degradation of European distinctions?[22]

Wood responded by providing a pit door opening onto Chestnut Street.

Further nationalistic tensions erupted in Philadelphia in 1828 when a Dr. James McHenry provoked the Chestnut Street audience. As Wemyss recounts:

> The old story of slighting native talent, (native talent, in this instance, at least, born in Ireland,) and treating America with disrespect, was revived; some persons carrying their malignity so far as to accuse me of having forbidden the orchestra to play the national airs, nightly called for by the audience.[23]

Wemyss, who was English-born and thought by Ludlow to be anti–American, was obliged to object in a public playbill that the charge was untrue and wrote, "Much as I have suffered from willful misrepresentation, I admire that feeling of patriotism, which will not brook even a breath of insult from the lips of a foreigner. I have always regarded the institutions of America with pride, while I never shrink from defending my native England, when unjustly assailed."[24]

Obviously, working-class audiences were easily insulted by English actors. Clapp records another riot in Boston in 1831 when an English actor named Anderson, who had been rumored to have insulted Americans on his ship from England, was driven from the stage and incited rioters who invaded the theatre.

Church and Stage

In 1832, the English actor Hamblin, playing at the Walnut Street Theatre in Philadelphia, suffered an asthma attack in the middle of a performance of *Richard III* and was forced to withdraw. When the manager did not finish the play, but instead performed other light fare, the audience became infuriated and "some gentleman blackguard, (aside) threw a large piece of plaster, extracted from the roof of the pit passage, with some force upon the stage." It barely missed the actress, Mrs. Charles Green. Her husband, playing on stage with her;

> hurled it back upon the audience with the emphatic phrase, that the man that threw it was a blackguard and a coward. A general row ensued, in which stoves were overturned, no coals distributed, and the melee ended by leaving actors and audience in the dark, the lights being rapidly extinguished. How many black eyes, and how many useless threats were uttered, I stop not to detail.[25]

In many cities, disruption, which began in a theatre as an expression of nationalism, shortly connected with a variety of other groups with political agendas, swelling the disturbance and intensifying the violence. One such case occurred in 1834 in the Bowery Theatre of New York City when the troublesome McHenry refused to accept a fine for a violation of the theatre's rules. As a result his English managers, George Farren and Thomas S. Hamblin, fired him. A large group of rowdies came to McHenry's defense, and a brouhaha broke out in the press. Matters escalated when Farren was heard to say, "Damn the Yankees; they are a damn set of jackasses and fit to be gulled!"[26] One thousand rioters appeared in the theatre on the occasion of Farren's benefit, taking the opportunity to tear the house apart and terrorize the actors. The police herded them out, without pressing charges, and they moved on to join other groups in revolt, swelling the number to 5,000. The largest among them was an anti-abolitionist group that beat up African-Americans and torched the home of abolitionist Lewis Tappan.

One essential cache of ammunition used in the warfare waged by New York's poor against their "bettors" was the burlesque of William Shakespeare, the indisputable English literary master. Ironically, Shakespeare, whose heroes were noblemen, was disparaged by the church and parodied by the working-class theatre. The church considered Shakespeare diabolical and obscene. He had such a bad reputation that theatre people claimed that ministers would often quote Shakespeare but without identifying their source. Even some theatre lovers were convinced that Shakespeare should be edited carefully before his plays were performed. But while all audiences

10. Violence in the Audience, Irreverence on the Stage

took pleasure in Shakespeare's plays, the working class also scoffed at the playwright as an upholder of kingship and nobility, the diametric opposite of democracy. This opinion is illustrated in 1837 by William Leggett, one of the foremost American reformers and journalists of the 1830s and 1840s:

> The two divinest bards, that ever addressed their strains of undying harmony to the enraptured ears of mortals, were the flatterers and the upholders of aristocratic pride, and the scoffers of the rights of the people.[27]

Walt Whitman, who certainly revered Shakespeare and frequently acknowledged Shakespeare's influence on his own work, nevertheless regarded his work as "poisonous to the idea of the pride and dignity of the common people, the life blood of democracy."[28] Whitman's and Leggett's pronouncements are typical of the simultaneous admiration and disapproval with which many other democrats in an emerging American culture approached Shakespeare in the nineteenth century. In their eyes, he was both "the divinest bard" and a potent spokesman for every aristocratic ideology endangering not only the development of national literary confidence, but the very egalitarian values underpinning a true democracy.[29] There was, in the minds of many Americans, an association of "English" with "aristocratic," and the despised UN-AMERICAN refinement and privilege characteristic of both were vividly delineated in Shakespeare's characters and in the English actors who portrayed them.

The way in which national and class enmity manifested itself in theatres is phenomenal. On stage, class rebellion betrayed itself in parodies of English masterworks, especially those of Shakespeare. Americans created their own burlesques while importing similar burlesques from the working-class English theatres. William Leggett and Walt Whitman were not alone in their suspicions of the political convictions seemingly recommended in Shakespeare's plays. Even the casual viewer had to be impressed by the refinements of class made attractive in the Shakespearean spectacle and in the aura of luxury surrounding the characters. The politically conscious, intellectual observer saw inherent in these plays a deep commitment to the ruling class, the abridgment of whose power always brought chaos in its wake. In short, Shakespeare's social convictions, as they were interpreted by Americans, would not strengthen and broaden the principles of a new democratic country.

The genre of Shakespearean burlesque began to flourish in the 1840s under the condition necessary for its existence: a climate of intimate famil-

Church and Stage

iarity with the masterworks. Two of the most successful New York theatres of the 1840s were William Mitchell's Olympic Theatre and William Burton's Chambers Street Theatre, both famous for their burlesques of classic literature, including the plays of Shakespeare. In the 1850s, burlesques of Shakespeare began to appear regularly in that most American of all stage entertainments, the minstrel show, where it proved successful for forty years. A number of historians, of New York in the 1840s, of the frontier theatre, and of the minstrel show, have written lively accounts of the nineteenth century's insatiable appetite for the burlesquing of every conceivable serious subject.

Violent labor unrest and parody began to come together in the 1840s with English actors as provocateurs. While Edwin Forrest was the symbol of the democratic American, the English Shakespearean actor, William Charles Macready, was representative of the arrogance and snobbery of the English and their upper-class admirers. Economics was an integral part of the culture wars. For example, while Macready was actually sympathetic with democratic causes, working-class audiences believed that he took more money away from America back to England than any of his contemporaries, and the lavish and expensive sets of Charles Kean (son of Edmund) were viewed as wasteful displays in a city of intense poverty. It is no surprise that one of the burlesques most popular with working-class audiences, W. K. Northall's *Macbeth Travestie* (1843), was designed to parody William Macready and his staging of *Macbeth*.[31]

While Edwin Forrest represented the democratic American, William Charles Macready was the epitome of the arrogant British performer who was pampered by the American upper class and took thousands of dollars back to England without contributing a dime to the U.S. economy. In attacking, the theatre audiences viewed themselves as attacking the unjust American class system.

The chief burlesques produced between 1840 and 1890

10. Violence in the Audience, Irreverence on the Stage

served to ridicule aristocratic tradition by taking Shakespeare's characters out of their pomp and purple and turning them out into ordinary streets like those in which the humblest American had to survive. No longer were they occupied by the intricacies of regal society, by important matters of state, or by profound philosophical questions. Instead their situations and activities were reduced to the mundane and the comic, their poetic dialogue replaced by the exaggerated crudities of Bowery B'hoys and blackface minstrels. In this way the aristocrat was stripped of his finery and thrown onto the streets of New York like a prince who has been made to exchange identities with a pauper, a pattern discernible in the few extant nineteenth-century American burlesques of Shakespeare.

As early as *The Macbeth Travestie* (1843), Dr. W. K. Northall placed his ambitious aristocrats in an urban American setting, and the witches who present Macbeth with the mystical prophecy became mere rag-pickers and "loafers' wives" from the slums of the city. They irreverently bid Macbeth farewell by thumbing their noses at him. Other prophecies are made not by the usual spirits and demons, but by a Yankee peddler and by Father William Miller, the Adventist, who had encouraged members of his flock to mount a hill in their white robes to await ascension into heaven as life on this earth ended. Other activities and comic action make the characters more ridiculous: King Duncan is concerned not with affairs of state but with a blue-bottle fly that insists on attacking his nose, and Macbeth's familiar imaginary dagger, visible to the audience in this case, repeatedly jumps and bobs out of his reach as he futilely stumbles forward in his attempts to secure it. In this play, as in others, food, drink and patent medicines replace the more profound spiritual sustenance. For example, the spirits that unsex Lady Macbeth are alcoholic. Later, she is driven mad by a longing for horehound candy, and Malcolm is brought to the breaking point by the memory of his mother's pickles:

> Stay, Macduff, stay; this passion for my sainted mother's pickles
> Causes this tear which down my cheek now trickles.

Even as early as the fall of 1843, on one of Macready's visits to America, the public began discussing the growing political implications in the Macready and Forrest feud, and Macready had already begun to inflame passions by making unflattering comparisons between himself and Forrest in the press and on the street. On October 31, Macready reported that the American press was speculating about what might be done to drive him from the stage. At precisely this time, October and November of 1843, the Olympic began offering burlesques of Shakespeare, including Northall's *The Macbeth Travestie*, one just four days before Macready's farewell performance at the Park. It ran simultaneously with the derision of Macready in the American press. Mitchell's bill, circulated on the same day that Macready was scheduled for a benefit, caricatured Macready's whole concurrent engagement at the Park, announcing a burlesque of Shakespeare intended to rival Macready's benefit:

> Mr. Mitchell
> Has much pleasure in announcing to the Public that
> he has, at an enormous expense, effected an
> engagement with himself for a few days, during which he
> will appear in a series of
> Shakespearian Characters,
> In the true Tragic-Comico-Illegitimate style.
> During this engagement he trusts he shall be
> able to induce himself to appear as
> *Hamlet!*
> With Comic Songs!
> Richard No. III!
> And
> Macbeth![32]

Even as the English tragedian opened in *Hamlet* on May 13, and throughout his engagement, which lasted until June 3, many Americans were publicly and privately declaring Forrest to be the more powerful Shakespearean. At the same time, during Macready's last week in New York City, two working-class theatres ran burlesques of Shakespeare. During Macready's benefit, Yankee Hill played the first of several performances of Charles Selby's *Kinge Richard Ye Third* (c. 1844). The momentum, seemingly arising from Macready's presence that spring, was sufficient to keep several burlesques of *Hamlet* and *Macbeth* going throughout the summer.

Anti-Park and anti–English sentiment emerged once again in burlesque during the 1845–1846 season when two other English actors, Mr. and Mrs. Charles Kean, arrived with extravagant fanfare at the Park, where productions of *Hamlet, Romeo and Juliet, Much Ado About Nothing, The Merchant of Venice* and *Twelfth Night* lasted on and off from September until mid–June. The high point of the Keans' engagement was a production of *Richard III* which played a record-breaking three-week run in January. Mitchell produced a *Hamlet Travestie* and a *Romeo and Juliet* burlesque of

10. Violence in the Audience, Irreverence on the Stage

obscure origin in December as counters to the Kean performances. Mitchell's tour de force, however, was what Odell calls a "killing burlesque," entitled *Richard Fit to Kill*. The travesty opened on January 26 and was played until mid–February, running simultaneously with Charles Kean's spectacular and serious *Richard III*. The real star of Kean's production had been the imported scenery, a sore point with Americans who saw the English reaping vast sums of money from theatricals which were produced in America and enjoyed by wealthy Americans without resulting in contributions to the American economy. The imported costumes, armor, and scenery cost ten thousand dollars and received considerable publicity and comment in the press. Mitchell's ridicule of the whole venture in a December advertisement was not intended to add to the English mystique:

> Mr. Bengough the Artist, has been engaged for nearly twenty minutes a day, during the past week, and the Costumer has not slept much except at night, during the same period....
> N.B. A roll of red flannel has been imported expressly for the occasion.
> The manager in announcing this great *Walcoterian Flare Up!* begs to insist upon the public understanding that he has been totally regardless of expense, because it hasn't amounted to anything.... The Scenery is so far beyond description that it would be tempting a state of lunacy to detail it.[33]

The Keans were again the subject of parody later in the season when they staged an elaborate production of *King John* costing twelve thousand dollars. The play opened on November 16 and ran for three weeks. It was, incidentally, followed by another foreign group, the Viennoise children. True to fashion, Mitchell, on December 14, made fun of Kean's extravagance with a Shakespearean burlesque, *King John and the Very Nice Children*. The Bowery, the Chambers Street and The Chatham continued occasional burlesques of Shakespeare throughout the year.

Two years later the public eye was turned from the Keans back to Macready as he began what would be a disastrous 1848–1849 tour of the United States. Macready and the American Forrest had kept their animosity politely suppressed until 1848, when Forrest invaded Macready's territory to perform in London. During his performance he was hissed, and decided that the insults came from Macready's henchmen. Forrest responded by traveling to Edinburgh to attend a performance of Macready and hissed him himself. Afterward, he continually justified himself by claiming that he had taken umbrage at a weird dance Macready had performed in the role of Hamlet and just wanted to improve his acting. A nervous Macready took the chance of accepting offers in the United States in 1848. Tensions mounted when both actors ended up in different theatres in Philadelphia playing the same role — Macbeth — at the same time. Macready was pelted with rotten eggs. And each actor tried to excuse himself and blame the other in the press and in speeches. Many believed that the several speeches Macready made before the curtain at various performances were insulting to Americans and had much to do with inciting the working-class mobs, especially a speech he made at the Astor Place on October 25.[34] That same fall Macready also played Macbeth at the Astor Place Opera House in New York, a decidedly Anglophilic hall. On the night of his opening, the National Theatre added a burlesque of Shakespeare to its usual magazine of nativist gunpowder. *Mr. Macgreedy, Or A Star at The Opera House*, which included Lady Macbeth and Hamlet, and was, as its title suggests, intended to ridicule Macready. The performance brought out the most high-powered stars of the working-class theatre: Frank S. Chanfrau, famous for his Mose parts, was Mr. Hamlet, and Charles Burke played the title role. *Macgreedy*, continually drawing audiences for an impressively long run, was kept on the National program throughout William Macready's entire fall performance at the Astor Place, successfully helping to keep alive a favorite sport: fun at the expense of the upper-class Astor Place patrons and their English stars. In Odell's account of the September offerings at the National he writes:

> *Mr. Macgreedy, Or A Star At The Opera House*, satirized the great English temperamentalist in a way that must have galled him. In considering Macready's state of mind in the year that led up to the fatal riot of May 10th, we might justly consider the effect on his sensitive soul of the burlesque skits of this nature that served as light artillery in the trouble.[35]

When Macready returned from a tour of the country to read Shakespeare at New York's Stuyvesant Institute, from the fifth of December through the eighth, the Olympic had already been amusing its audiences with *Magreedy* for several days. The season's final thrust from the burlesque stage came in March, not long before Macready was expected to return to New York and shortly before an outbreak of violence, when the Chambers Street Theatre enjoyed a substantial run of the always popular burlesque intended to ridicule Macready, *The Macbeth Travestie*.

To reemphasize the relationship between the burlesques and the infamous riot of 1849, Odell mentions, in his account of another parody, the

10. Violence in the Audience, Irreverence on the Stage

Olympic's *Who's Got Macready?*, the effect not only on Macready but on the public as well:

> This skit — running contemporaneously with *Mr. Macgreedy* at the National — may not have been without its effect in the rising tide of anti–Macreadyism which culminated in the fatal riots of May 10, 1849.[36]

For several weeks before Macready's appearance, conspiracies were afoot in and around New York's working-class theatres, much of it under the direction of Ned Buntline and the Know-Nothings. Statements by political nativists in the 1840s make the connection between nationalistic sentiment and class struggle unmistakable. One is a frequently quoted bill distributed by Buntline just before the Astor Place Riot:

> WORKINGMEN
> SHALL
> AMERICANS OR ENGLISH RULE
> IN THIS CITY?
> The crew of the English steamer
> has threatened all Americans who
> shall dare to express their
> opinion this night at the English
> Aristocratic Opera House![37]

Another placard is quoted in Richard Moody's *The Astor Place Riot*:

> Americans!
> Arouse! The Great Crisis
> Has Come!!
> Decide now whether English
> Aristocrats!!
> And
> Foreign Rule!
> Shall triumph in this
> AMERICA'S METROPOLIS,
> Or whether her own
> Sons
> Whose father once compelled the base-born miscreants to
> succumb, shall meanly lick the hand that strikes, and
> allow themselves to be deprived of the liberty of
> opinion — so dear to every true American heart.
> AMERICANS!!
> Come out! And dare to own yourselves sons of the true hearts of '76![38]

Church and Stage

What happened during Macready's appearances led to one of the deadliest riots in U.S. history. Included here are two eye-witness accounts of the Astor Place Riot. One is by Harry Watkins, who was an actor on the scene in the mob outside the Astor Place Opera House and included his observations in his journal. Another is from Macready's own diary. The following is by Watkins:

> Monday 7th. Great row at the Astor Place Opera House. A plot to drive Mr. Macready off the stage. Apples, eggs, pennies, chairs were thrown at him. He got as far as the first scene of the third act, but the tumult increasing, he was obliged to leave the Theatre.
>
> Tuesday 8th.... The papers openly charge Forrest with being the getter-up of the row against Macready. He contradicts it in a letter published in *Courier* and *Enquirer*.
>
> Thursday 10th. A riot tonight at the Astor Place Opera House. Macready, who was driven from the stage on the 7th, appeared again, several leading men of the city having assured him protection. A large police force was in attendance. The House was filled early. The play commenced and when Macready appeared, he was greeted with applause mingled with hisses, but his friends were in the majority and the rioters were apprehended. On the outside ten thousand persons assembled, the greater portion drawn there by curiosity. The rioters commenced throwing stones at the windows, and endeavored to force the doors. After some time, two or three companies of horsemen and infantry soldiers came upon the ground, marched to the front of the House and formed a hollow square. They had hardly taken their positions when they fired upon the crowd. Everybody thought the cartridges were blank; it proved to be otherwise. Five persons were lying wounded and dying in one drug store. A man was brought into a barroom where I was with a musket ball through his breast above the heart. He died shortly after that. The Mayor (Woodhull) is to blame. His conduct incited the rioters to resistance to the law. The lessees of the theatre went to see him to ask if they should play. He told them to do so, and he would protect them. The military were not called out until the mob got under way. They assert that the Riot Act was read. I was in the crowd and heard nothing of it.[39]

The following is an excerpt from Macready who was experiencing the riot from within the walls of the theatre:

> My first, second, third scenes passed over rapidly and unheard, at the end of the fourth one of the officers gave a signal, the police rushed in at the two sides of the parquette, closed in upon the scoundrels occupying the center seats and furiously vociferating and gesticulating, and seemed to lift them or bundle them in a body out of the center of the house, amid

10. Violence in the Audience, Irreverence on the Stage

On May 10, 1849, rowdies from working-class theatres, who resented the arrogance of British performers and privileged Americans, stormed the upper-class Astor Place Opera House. Many rioters were shot by the National Guard.

> the cheers of the audience.... As well as I can remember, the bombardment outside now began. Stones were hurled against the windows in Eighth Street, smashing many; the work of destruction became then more systematic, the volleys of stones flew without intermission, battering and smashing all before them....
>
> Going to my room I began without loss of time to undress but with no feeling of fear or apprehension. When washed, and half dressed, persons came into my room consternation on the faces of some; fear, anxiety, and distress on those of others.... Suddenly we heard a volley of musketry: "Hark! What's that?" I asked. "The soldiers have fired." "My God!" I exclaimed. Another volley, and another ... News came that several were killed, and I was really insensible to the degree of danger in which I stood, and saw at once — there being no avoidance — there was nothing for it but to meet the worst with dignity, and so I stood prepared.[40]

Watkins shared the opinion of aristocrat and democrat alike in seeing the Astor Place Riot as part of a class war: "This will generate a hatred of the aristocracy by the lower classes that will be bound to show itself."[41] James Rees, in a biography of Forrest written fifteen years after the riot, provides several proofs that this was part of a class war. One of the chants heard throughout the streets was, "three groans for the codfish aristocracy!" The riot was, he writes, "Aristocracy and the English Clique *vs.* The Lower Classes."[42] Richard Moody, quotes from the *Philadelphia Public Ledger* of the day: "There is now in our country, in New York City, what every good patriot has hitherto considered it his duty to deny — a *high* class and a *low* class."[43]

Broad comedy, also present in the burlesques of the fifties, had the continued effect of belittling not only Shakespeare's high-born characters but the refined English actors who portrayed them. Alexander Do Mar's *Othello*, for example, first performed in Wood's Theatre in 1850, transformed the usual Shakespearean cast into a band of ragged, down-and-out minstrels who proceed to create Othello's great rage with a bar of soap — it is sufficient that he foam at the mouth by means of the prop.

The sixties and seventies saw an even greater demand for burlesques of Shakespeare, especially from the nation's minstrels. Burlesquers began heaping their plays with more and more topical references, subsequently defining their American settings in greater detail. The main characters in John F. Poole's *Ye Comedie of Errors*, written for Charley White's minstrel show and first performed in the 1860s, are black slaves who have escaped from the South on the underground railroad. Once in New York City, they look for work with the post office. The rustics spend their days working at white-washing jobs, avoiding imprisonment for debt on Blackwell's Island, and spending stretches of time in the Tombs for drunkenness. The tone of the play is set by topical references to New York's "dull preachers," its powerful Tammany Hall, its two-cent *Tribune* and P. T. Barnum, who threatens to inflict his memoirs on the general populace.

George W. H. Griffin's popular *Hamlet the Dainty*, which appeared in New York in the 1865–1866 season also made liberal use of topicality and comic incongruity to ridicule Shakespeare's upper-class characters. The members of Claudius' court are changed to "members of the alley" who frequent Fulton Street, gossip about Wall Street, and compare Claudius' palace to a Boston beanery. Horatio and Marcellus, in blackface, are particularly afraid of the white ghost because they suspect he's from the South. These characters box instead of fence and work by sweeping up floors. The ghost, hardly the dignified ex-king of Shakespeare's *Hamlet*, is found smoking a cigar and reading a newspaper. Furthermore, he is a "lush" who has been killed, not with poison, but with brandy mash, and who is presently tortured by being denied a drink. Griffin's *Othello* (1870) includes a Braban-

10. Violence in the Audience, Irreverence on the Stage

tio whose chief objection to his daughter's marriage is that he had intended to profit by her appearance as a fat lady in P. T. Barnum's establishment. As in many burlesques of *Othello*, Desdemona becomes a kitchen "Dinah," who busies herself with cooking and cleaning. In an 1874 *Othello* burlesque of Griffin's called *Desdemonum*, the characters lose their social status by becoming show people. Desdemonum admits that she is attracted to Othello because "burnt cork is in fashion." Even the judge in this play climbs down from his bench to dance a minstrel breakdown. And, in an anonymously printed burlesque called *The (Old Clothes) Merchant* (1870), Bassanio is a supernumerary in a theatre which requires his services to move scenery and furniture.

In the 1870s, *Julius Caesar* became a popular play to parody Tammany Hall politics. A series of these burlesques appeared, among them Addison Ryman's *Julius Sneezer* (1872), *Julius Seizer* (1872) and *Julius Snoozer* (1875). In the last play, the mighty Snoozer is a ward boss soliciting votes at a clambake. Charles Carrol Soule's *A Travesty Without a Pun* (1879) places *Hamlet* in an equally absurd setting — an American university. Hamlet and his friends are sophomore members of a fraternity and, although they anticipate having to enter military service, they spend their days avoiding expulsion from school, sweeping floors and singing fraternity songs:

> Oh alpha beta gamma delta
> With an epsilon zeta eta theta
> Eta Theta-eta theta

In the 1880s, John Kendrick Bangs, George M. Baker, and a group called The Larks continued to put Shakespeare's aristocrats in their place, or rather, a working-class American place which was sure to belittle them. One of the more effective burlesques is The Larks' *The Shakespeare Water-Cure* (1883). Here Shakespeare's better-known protagonists, having been stripped of their old places of privilege, gather at an American health resort. Romeo, no longer a member of the "FFV" (First Families of Venice), has lost everything but Juliet, whom he now supports by acting. Hamlet and Ophelia, also immigrants, squabble like other married couples until he apologizes by buying her a new dress from Macy's. Lord and Lady Macbeth, newly arrived Scottish royalty, are, meanwhile, out foxed by Shylock, an American street Jew who gives them collateral of "two dozen pawn tickets and one hundred shares of Brooklyn Bridge stock." Othello, as might be expected, is reduced to waiting on tables while Desdemona does the kitchen work.

In all of these burlesques the language of Shakespeare has vanished.

Church and Stage

Sometimes his names are given a ridiculous twist: Desdy, Oteller, Hamlet Senior, Andy Foolus, Dummy-O. The poetic dialogue is invariably replaced by street lingo as when, for example, the court in Edward Rice's 1811 play decides to depose Claudius: "Pitch Into Him! Dethrone Him! Punch His Head!" The most exaggerated minstrel dialogue and unlikely songs are put in the mouths of characters. The Larks' burlesque is a typical example:

> Otello, de military Moot
> A'waiting on de table
> At de Shakespear Water-Cure.
> Desdemona's in de kitchen
> Where de dishes she do clean.

Meanwhile the songs are sung to sprightly or folksy tunes, identified with the American scene: "Dixie," "Oh Suzannah," "Carry Me Back to Old Virginny," and "Roll Jordan Roll."

Although the ridiculing of the upper classes was obviously intended primarily for fun, to "fetch the Yankee Doodle boys," as John F. Poole writes in his burlesque, these plays were not without frequent political reference. The plays of the 1860s and 1870s, especially those by Addison Ryman, John F. Poole, John Brougham, and George Griffin, refer to the great wealth and subsequent corruption of Tammany Hall politicians. The characters in Poole's *Ye Comedie of Errors* sing of "riches too great" to the tune of "I Dreamt I Dwelt in Marble Halls":

> I Dreamt That I Dwelt in Tammany Hall
> Wid Sachems and such by my side;
> I thought that the place was prepared for a ball,
> And I had to let it all slide.

Unmistakable social as well as political comment is sprinkled throughout the burlesques. For example, the witches' cauldron in W. K. Northall's earlier *Macbeth Travestie* contained such abominations as "landlord's greed" and "lawyer's conscience." Macbeth himself is a despicable monarch not only because of the murders he has committed to gain his throne, but because under his rule many widows go poor and young boys are committed to workhouses. *The (Old Clothes) Merchant* shows how the poor go to Blackwell's Island for their debts while the wealthy, like Bassanio, can escape to Europe for "a change of creditors." A similar condemnation of the heartless manipulations by the rich is found in John Kendrick Bangs' burlesque

10. Violence in the Audience, Irreverence on the Stage

called *Katherine*, published in 1888. In this play businessmen are planning to:

> Work up a corner in grain and wheat
> And squeeze all the orphans you find in the street.

One of the most popular burlesques, John Brougham's *Much Ado About a Merchant of Venice* (1868), stresses the great inequities in society. There are the tycoons, like John Jacob Astor, who spent great sums in speculation, resulting in a peculiar linguistic situation: the word *stale* is no longer in fashion — "except in the dictionaries of the poor." His characters note that justice herself has flung off her blindfold, the more easily to distribute favors to those already in power, while the poor always feel the barbs of the courts. Shylock, usually the blood-thirsty villain, is here declared to be "victimized" and "persecuted." True justice is accomplished in this burlesque with the voluntary conversion of Lorenzo to Judaism rather than with the forced conversion of Shylock to Christianity.

The particular nature of the burlesque of Shakespeare was always directed at the patrician classes of England and America, those who were supported by the mainstream Protestant church of the United States. To make Othello a slave, to prepare to ship off Desdemona as the fat lady in P. T. Barnum's museum, to make Julius Caesar a petty New York politician or Kate a suffragette was to deflate a whole ensemble of uppity Englishmen and their admirers. To throw these Shakespearean characters onto the streets of New York or onto a Southern plantation was to portray them in a landscape where they were not supported by the past and its prerogatives.

The cultural superiority of the English was nowhere so painfully apparent as it was on the nineteenth-century American stage upon the occasion of a Shakespearean production. The relatively few American plays on the boards were embarrassingly poor by almost any standards and, in constant and frequent comparison with Shakespeare's plays, American efforts were excruciating failures. The public was repeatedly reminded by the English and Anglophiles that America had no literary tradition, no literary geniuses, and, seemingly, no prospects for developing respectability in any art form. Moreover, it was painfully apparent that American actors did not even speak the English of Shakespeare. For the patriotic democrat with high hopes that the common people's war of cultural independence could be won, the situation on the native stage was not only depressing, it was positively galling. One response was widespread ambivalence toward "our old home" and its foremost literary master, a kind of love-hate relationship on the part of a playgoing public which revered Shakespeare's plays and then, at the same time, burlesqued his characters with singular frequency. Certainly the cultural class war of the nineteenth century contributed to the importance of these burlesques, perhaps not in the foreground, but securely in the background of a conflict which many Americans considered to be a social necessity and branded the audiences that supported them as a contradiction of every religious Victorian value that insisted on respect for tradition, respect for one's betters, and acquiescence to one's lot in life.

11

The Winding Down of an Old War

An Actor's Church Alliance
— Aaron I. Abel

On any number of grounds, theatrical activity had failed, for most of the century, to fit into the grand, religiously defined economic, plan of America's industrial revolution. In its upside down world it had afforded authority to those who were usually denied it. It had reversed roles and countermanded values. After a century-long attack from the nineteenth-century progeny of American Puritans, by 1860 the theatre had long since come to accept as a way of life the religious public's displeasure. But even though there were still loud clerical objections in the last half of the century, a variety of elements served to improve relations between church and stage.

Several crucial events played into the changing reputation of the stage, surprising ironies in American cultural history — the death of a president and the death and burial of a respected actor. Concessions were made on both fronts which, at the turn of the twentieth century, brought a winding down of attacks against the stage from the church and a qualified victory for the comparatively poor, scorned, unorganized theatrical forces over their powerful adversary.

By the 1840s, it was obvious that despite numerous impediments the theatre had done more than merely endure; it had flourished, becoming established in every major city in the east, spreading throughout the Mississippi and Ohio Valleys and, by the 1850s, moving on to California, where even the most primitive mining camps often boasted traveling shows. Yet expansion came with considerable cost.

In the last three decades of the century, however, some improvements in the reputation of the stage were noted by the public, and as a result, pulpit personalities like Dwight L. Moody, Henry Ward Beecher, and DeWitt Talmage — the brightest clerical "stars" — stepped up their protestations against the theatre, proof that the war between the church and the stage continued in various degrees of intensity throughout the century.

The whole story of a beginning reconciliation is a multifaceted one of contradictions. The presentation of more moral dramas is often given as a reason for a lessening of antagonism from the church. But from the church's point of view, beginning in the 1860s the new realism made plays more offensive to Christians than they had ever been. The subjects of some of the most popular plays of the 1860s — plays that remained popular for the rest of the century — were scarcely designed to please the pulpits of America. *East Lynne*, a sympathetic treatment of a wife who leaves her husband and children to go away with her villainous lover, and *Camille*, a sympathetic portrait of a courtesan, were both sufficient to provide a month of ministerial tirades against theatrical immorality. In addition, as if the stage had not introduced enough of its abominations in one decade with these two plays, it also welcomed in the 1860s *The Black Crook* and, a few years later, Lydia Thompson and her British Blondes, each of which profited immensely from an unabashed display of the female figure. Both of these entertainments had long runs and many revivals, and both were the subjects of tracts against the theatre for the rest of the century.[1] Furthermore, the 1880s and 1890s also ushered into America Henrik Ibsen, that supreme questioner of family sanctity, who referred without shame to venereal disease, incest, and free love, not to mention the corrupt bases of popular morality. In 1891 the play *Margaret Fleming* was reviewed even in the *New York Times* as unpleasant, unhealthy, sordid, and mean.[2] David Belasco's 1899 adaptation from the French of a play called *Zaza* did not fare much better in pious circles. Then, when the theatrical syndicate came into power in the 1890s, further charges of immorality were leveled against the drama, this time not just by the clergy but also by supporters of the theatre. Theatre critics for the *Nation* and the *Commercial Advertiser* called the drama degenerate and deplorable. One professional reviewer even advocated throwing a few managers into the penitentiary for making money from the presentation of vice on stage.[3]

Still, despite the popularity of racy entertainments, there is testimony

11. The Winding Down of an Old War

from within the profession that the general tone of dramas had improved by the latter part of the century.[4] H. P. Phelps, long associated with the Albany Theatre, declared that in the 1880s the vulgarity of "most of the old-time comedians, would not be countenanced in an ordinary variety show ... the indelicacy which used to set the pit aroaring, has gone out and with it much of the profanity with which genteel comedy is interlarded." By 1880 Phelps found a growing secular antipathy to such plays as *The Black Crook* and the French farces.[5] More significantly, while there were more and more entertainments that were considered scandalous by both friends and foes of the theatre, there were also more plays of a type described as moral.

In almost every decade there seemed to be a special play regarded by observers of the day as historic because ministers and other religious people were drawn into the theatre for the first time to witness it. In the 1840s it was *The Drunkard*, the first of many temperance dramas that drew thousands of religious viewers and even earned some church support.[6] In the 1850s it was *Uncle Tom's Cabin*, the phenomenon of the century. This show attracted people from all denominations who had never darkened the door of a theatre—including, ironically, Harriet Beecher Stowe, who had for many years refused to condone its staging because it would attract religious people to the theatre to see this one play and then tempt them to return to see others not so harmless.[7] In the 1890s the play credited with bringing many religious people into the theatre for the first time was *Ben Hur*, by General Lew Wallace, an author who, like Stowe, had long delayed dramatizing his novel, holding out for ten years because of religious scruples and suspicion of the stage.[8]

By the 1860s there was some modification in the outlook of some clergymen: The theatre *could* be an agent for moral instruction. In the late seventies and early eighties, this emerging conviction, still radical for many of the clergy, was actually carried into action by the Mallory brothers, two ministers who established the Madison Square Theatre, run by Steele MacKaye, with "the avowed purpose ... to produce plays of a moral tendency."[9] McKaye's first production, *Hazel Kirke*, ran for a year in New York and was presented throughout the country by fourteen road companies sent from the Madison Square. In addition there were several pirate companies. According to Albert M. Palmer and Daniel Frohman, the Mallorys' influence was far-reaching. To Palmer, the Mallorys' theatre was "one of the most powerful agencies in breaking down the barriers between the theatre and religious people."[10] Frohman also sees the Mallory theatre as a turning point:

Within my memory, playgoing had been considered unethical not only by the clergy but by church goers, but the Brothers Mallory believed that a good play could preach a powerful sermon and other churchmen were beginning to agree with them.[11] By the early twentieth century, Charles M. Sheldon, author of the immensely popular *In His Steps*, publicly stated that a "Christian Theatre" should be established.[12] This was a phrase that many clergymen before 1865 would have considered oxymoronic.

In another critical area of controversy — the public's assessment of the character of actors — there was an even greater change. The earlier years had been characterized by blanket condemnations: actors were of necessity immoral; they were automatically corrupted by the profession. And in the last half of the century, many actors continued to lend credence to the old charge. There was, to mention just one case, Adah Isaacs Menken, a controversial star who in 1860 who was prominently accused in the press of being married to two men at the same time, of having had an illegitimate child, and, later, of flaunting her affairs with Alexander Dumas and, strangely enough, Algernon Swinburne.[13] By 1865, however, the public's kindly sympathy for and admiration of a few well-known actors was believed to have defused the general attack on all actors. The pre–Civil War career of Anna Cora Mowatt and the long reign of Charlotte Cushman were looked back upon with having disproved the charge that all actresses were degenerate.[14] The success and upper-class ancestry of both women further enhanced a general impression of respectability. Even performers from theatrical families, by living gentle and dignified lives, helped disprove the old generalization. To attack Joseph Jefferson, born in an acting family and reared on the stage, would surely have been tantamount to attacking the character he so often portrayed on the stage, old Rip Van Winkle himself.

That actors were shiftless vagabonds who made no contribution to society had also become an increasingly difficult argument to sustain. It had been supposed for centuries that actors were the dregs of society. They had no permanent homes; they moved around from place to place like hoboes. And even when they managed to make a few dollars from performances, it was argued, they could not hold onto their money — they squandered it or drank it away as fast as they made it. Such an argument could have been particularly effective in the last decades of the nineteenth century when some forms of social Darwinism were being popularized from many pulpits, in such works, for example, as Russell Conwell's *Acres of Diamonds,* a fabulous best seller, in which he insisted that good Christians make money and become wealthy, and that poverty is due to vice and lack

11. The Winding Down of an Old War

of character.[15] However, in light of the substantial fortunes being accumulated and very well managed by some actors, and with increasing public awareness of the philanthropy of a number of them, the more hostile clergy found the old arguments undermined; they were, in fact, turned upside down. Though Edwin Forrest was hardly a paragon of virtue, it could still be noted that he managed to accumulate a sufficiently impressive estate to found the Forrest Home for Actors in 1876. Charlotte Cushman, too, had contributed substantial sums for the benefit of Union soldiers and had left at her death an estate of six hundred thousand dollars. Lotta Crabtree, one of the wealthiest taxpayers in Boston in the 1890s, was well-known for her philanthropy to veterans and humane societies. Fortunes had been made by many actors, including Fanny Davenport, Maggie Mitchell, and Joseph Jefferson.[16]

Oddly enough, the developing star system in the early part of the century may also have improved the image of the actor. At its height in the 1840s and 1850s, the new system had certainly hurt the theatre as a whole, bleeding companies financially and seriously wounding the old stock system; but in the long run the star system, along with the star-supported combination shows that began to tour the country in the 1860s, helped dispel the notion that all actors were paupers of little consequence. The public could see rather plainly that many actors were individuals of some economic means and national importance. For whatever reasons, by the 1880s members of the profession were observing a change, at least in the public's attitude toward them.[17]

Two particularly notorious crises in this period brought the conflict between the church and members of the profession into the light for public scrutiny and self-appraisal. The first occurred with the assassination in 1865 of President Lincoln, by an actor, in a theatre. That tragedy was instrumental in bringing the whole profession under the blackest cloud of suspicion for a reason that was as much political as it was theological: That is, there was already a commonly held conviction that actors were secessionists. That John Wilkes Booth was no ordinary actor, but a member of a family whose very name in America was synonymous with acting, made the connections between the theatrical profession and Lincoln's assassination more pronounced. Even while the shot was still ringing in their ears, the audience's immediate reaction was to shift from the individual to general condemnation. As Booth leapt to the stage, brushing past the leading actress, Laura Keene, the shouts that reverberated through the hall were, "Burn the theatre! Kill the actors!"[18] Angry crowds gathered threateningly around the-

Church and Stage

atres in several cities throughout the country as news spread. As Eleanor Ruggles writes in *Prince of Players*:

> It was a sad time for actors. They were reminded once again that they were vagabonds. The martyred Lincoln's blood was on their heads.... The hue and cry sounded: "Arrest all actors!" Ugly-tempered crowds milled about the stage entrances. When a Washington store-keeper bravely defended the people of Ford's Theatre ... the mob threw a rope around his neck; he was barely saved from being lynched.[19]

Some of the members of Ford's Theatre were arrested in Washington, and other actors, including Laura Keene, who had continued on tour, were intercepted near Harrisburg by federal marshals and placed under arrest. Only some quick string-pulling by Keene's lover, a well-connected gambler named John Lutz, kept her from being jailed indefinitely.[20] Lloyd Lewis, in his study entitled *Myths After Lincoln*, even supposes that public sentiment was so violently antitheatrical that actors themselves called John Wilkes

In April of 1865, the assassination of President Abraham Lincoln in Ford's Theatre by an actor, John Wilkes Booth (a member of the most prominent theatre family in America), mobilized the religious public against the stage, which was suspected of being pro–Confederacy.

11. The Winding Down of an Old War

Laura Keene, another powerful American businesswoman in her role as theatrical manager, was onstage when Lincoln was shot. She immediately left town and was tracked down and brought back by the police who were then persuaded by her companion, a gambler, to release her.

Booth's sanity into question in order to put themselves in a better light. Word of Booth's lunacy, he writes, was "spread by his fellow actors to save themselves from the tar and feathers which raging mobs threatened to give the whole acting profession in the turmoil that arose after the assassination."[21]

Hostility toward actors as a whole, as a result of Lincoln's death, is certainly evident in the secular press. Some agreed with the *New York Times* that the profession "is not free from its taint of treason."[22] Much of the animosity appeared on the surface to have a political foundation. One example is a letter to the *Times* on April 21 that questioned the loyalty of actors:

> "Our native players have been for years (excepting, of course, the honorable few) the most offensive advocates and eulogists of 'the South'.... I *know* that three years ago there were not ten in one hundred of that profession who were not undisguised and outspoken friends of secession — in other words, latent traitors."[23]

Although a few newspapers like the *Chicago Times* and the *New York World* came to the defense of actors, the vindictiveness of much of the public prompted performers to go meekly on the defensive, not only closing down their theatres for over a week of mourning, but also offering a public resolution in support of the country and declaring their "detestation for that member of the profession who wrought so much mischief on the country."[24]

Public reaction to actors after the tragedy reinforced, and was reinforced by, the church's long-standing animosity. The pulpit now created a national myth in which the forces of evil, residing in the theatre, were pitted against the Kingdom of God. Just as the death of Lincoln inspired Whitman, so it inspired the nation's clergy. The event was poetry in action, an opportunity of immense typological richness: Lincoln was a savior; Booth a Judas, created from the haunt of Satan. The tragedy was cited without equivocation as God's clear warning against the theatre. Sermons against the theatre rolled like so much flaming lava from the pulpits of America and off the religious presses.[25] One of the earliest to take up the attack was the Reverend Phineas Gurley, pastor of the New York Avenue Presbyterian Church, one of Washington's most prestigious sanctuaries, attended regularly by Mrs. Lincoln and occasionally by the president himself. Note how Gurley's attack (his emphasis) is aimed at actors in particular:

> To whom is the dark and hellish work committed? *To a man schooled and trained in the theatre....* Just what we might expect from such a character, trained in such a place, maddened by disloyalty, heated with liquor, and *used to the exciting and tragic scenes of the theatre.*[26]

Controversy over the theatre's culpability in Lincoln's death continued in the press well into the fall as the fate of Ford's Theatre came under discussion: The *Times* wrote that the public "will never tolerate so gross an outrage upon propriety as the use of this building for the purpose for which

11. The Winding Down of an Old War

it was designed." Clergy, of course, agreed with the *Times* that Ford's Theatre should now be converted into a church—that any other use of the building would be a sacrilege.[27]

Even though the murder of Lincoln did reinforce many of the churches in their strong bias against actors, by January of 1866 much of the public, at least in New York City, was ready to forget the theatre's implication in the assassination: With an unexpectedly warm ovation, Edwin Booth was welcomed back to the stage in a gesture simultaneously personal and symbolic.[28] On that occasion many actors must have felt that the guilt they had been made to suffer nine months earlier through John Wilkes, as their representative, was now in some measure expiated through his brother Edwin.

Five years later, a second event that brought the clash between church and theatre into the open elicited very different reactions from both actors and clergymen. Noah Ludlow attributes the refusal of the Rev. W. T. Sabine to bury a beloved comedian, George Holland, from his church, with changing the public's view of actors.[29] The clergy's refusal to permit actors to be buried under the auspices of the church—they could not lie in holy ground—was an old grievance, going back for centuries. The pathetic account of the secretive, nighttime burial of Molière comes to mind. And it had not been unknown in America for a minister to refuse church burial for an actor or to use the occasion of an actor's funeral to deride the whole profession.[30] But in the case of Holland, friends of the theatre decided that enough was enough. Now, in 1870 as it had been in 1865, in the minds of theatre people and the public alike, one single actor

In 1870, the burial of George Holland, a beloved and highly respected comedian, created a backlash against the antitheatrical church when the Reverend W. T. Sabine refused to bury the actor from his church. From George C. D. Odell's 1927 *Annals of the New York Stage* (courtesy of the University of California-Berkeley).

became symbolic of the entire profession. Only in this case the humiliating incident became a cause célèbre that evoked the sympathy of much of the nation's clergy.

It was the widely popular, highly respected Joseph Jefferson who accompanied Holland's son to make funeral arrangements for Holland's father. Jefferson records the extraordinary incident in his memoirs:

> Upon the announcement of the death of George Holland, I called at the house of his family, and found them in great grief. The sister of Mrs. Holland informed me that they desired the funeral to take place from the church, as many of Mr. Holland's friends would like to make known their love and respect for him by their attendance, and that the house in which the family lived was too small to receive the large gathering of people that would be likely to assemble. The lady desired me to call upon the pastor of her own church, and request him to officiate at the service. I at once started in quest of the minister, taking one of the sons of Holland with me. On arriving at the house I explained to the reverend gentleman the nature of my visit, and the arrangements were made for the time and place at which the funeral was to be held. Something, I can scarcely say what, gave me the impression that I had better mention that Mr. Holland was an actor. I did so in a few words, and concluded by presuming that probably this fact would make no difference. I saw, however, by the restrained manner of the minister and an unmistakable change in the expression of his face that it would make, at least to him, a great deal of difference. After some hesitation he said that he would be compelled, if Mr. Holland had been an actor, to decline holding the service at the church.

Joseph Jefferson, a highly regarded character actor, went with Holland's son to seek burial for his friend and leaves the most thorough account of the episode.

11. The Winding Down of an Old War

While his refusal to perform the funeral rites for my old friend would have shocked under ordinary circumstances, the fact that it was made in the presence of the dead man's son was more painful than I can describe. I turned to look at the youth and saw that his eyes were filled with tears. He stood as one dazed with a blow just realized; as if he felt the terrible injustice of a reproach upon the kind and loving father who had often kissed him in his sleep, and had taken him on his knee when the boy was old enough to know the meaning of the words, and told him to grow up to be an honest man.... I paused at the door and said:

"Well, sire, in this dilemma is there no other church to which you can direct me from which my friend can be buried?"

He replied that "there was a little church around the corner" where I might get it done; to which I answered:

"Then, if this be so, God bless 'the little church around the corner':" and so I left the house.[31]

After the Reverend Sabine turned away George Holland's friends from his church, he suggested that they try "the little church around the corner," which has, ever since, been identified with the theatre.

Church and Stage

Without Jefferson's restraint, Noah Ludlow expressed the outrage that theatre people felt about Sabine, stressing the church's war on the theatre:

> The death of Mr. Holland was productive of a great excitement in New York, which soon extended to many of the States of this Union, and it occurred in this way: A well-known and popular comedian applied to the Rev. W. T. Sabine, rector of the Episcopal "Church of the Atonement," New York City, to perform the funeral services of his church over the remains of the deceased George Holland. He consented to do so, until he learned from the gentleman who had applied to him that the deceased man had been an actor. He then positively refused to comply with his previous promise, on the ground that he had always preached against theatres and actors, and that his officiating at the funeral of an actor would be inconsistent with his past private and public denouncements of the profession.
>
> Thus did this man avoid doing his duty as a clergyman, thus did he disgrace his calling and his Master, and thus did he endeavor to excuse an act of former injustice by committing a present offence against decency and every Christian principle. If such be *church* Christianity, I am content to be a Christian outside of the pale of the church. But I trust such conduct does not meet with approval from the Episcopal Church at large; in *fact, I* really believe, if their opinions could be ascertained, that a large majority of his own church condemned this act of their pastor. But, notwithstanding, I trust some good will arise from this apparently accidental occurrence. It has been found that, in the course of God's Providence, order and harmony have suddenly arisen out of confusion and discord. So may the error of this church official yet produce results totally at variance with his fanatical notions. This act of his has to a certain extent already broken down the barriers that have for ages existed between the church and the stage; it has caused candid minds to inquire into facts in regard to objections so long stereotyped against the stage, and they are finding that actors are not so bad, as a class, as they have been taught by the clergy to believe them to be. On the other side, it has been found that there are many more fair and liberal minds among church-members than the preaching of some pastors has caused actors to conceive.[32]

Even from the first report, the tone taken by the *Times* toward actors is strikingly different from its suspiciousness in 1865. When Jefferson and others made the incident public on December 29, the *Times* ran the story on page one. It also ran an editorial in the same issue:

> But Mr. Holland had committed an unpardonable sin, in the eyes of the Reverend William T. Sabine — he had earned his living by trying to please the public on the stage. For this offense, in the eyes of the Christian minister, he was fit only to be buried like a dog.[33]

11. The Winding Down of an Old War

Two more articles deriding Sabine appeared on December 30, and on the following day, the *Times* ran excerpts from editorials from all over the country expressing indignation at Sabine's refusal to bury Holland. On January 2, the reports of numerous New York sermons showed that the Sabine incident was receiving the same reaction in many pulpits that it had received from the public. Though there undoubtedly were clergymen who supported Sabine's actions, it is significant that all the clerical letters and sermons that reached the pages of the *Times* strongly condemned him as a bigot and a pharisee, dissociating the ministers who had written them and their churches from Sabine's opinions. From January 5 until January 20, there were numerous calls in the press for support of the massive testimonial for Holland — not just out of respect for the individual but "as a memorable tribute to the profession he followed."

Mark Twain was prompted to write an article called "A Live Parson is Worth More Than a Dead Actor," in which he labeled the Reverend Sabine a "crawling, slimy, sanctimonious, self-righteous reptile."[34] The testimonial to collect money for Holland's family was the largest cooperative effort of the sort in New York's theatrical memory. Eleven large theatres, numerous smaller places of entertainment in New York, and other theatres throughout the country devoted their day's proceeds to the Holland fund or contributed their profits to the newly christened Little-Church-Around-the-Corner. The *Times* reported a total of $15,554.35.[35] In 1871 other actors were presented as being like Holland himself: the lowly of the earth, especially beloved of God, through whose agency God himself had been betrayed at the hands of the pharisee.

Most evidence points to a considerable improvement in the reputation of actors in the eyes of the public and clergy. Fulminations against the stage were less likely to be founded on the bad character of one stage performer. The Reverend Lyman Abbott, for a time editor of Henry Ward Beecher's *The Christian Union*, wrote that the bitter hostility of the church toward the theatre was "much modified" by 1877.[36] Theatre people as well noticed a positive change in the religious public's attitude in the last decades of the century. Manager A. M. Palmer writes that from 1870:

> the unreasonable prejudice against the most enjoyable and least harmful of all forms of amusement has so materially lessened that it is estimated by good authority that not more than three-tenths of the people refuse to patronize the theatre as matters of principle.[37]

Church and Stage

Palmer and Abbott were supported in this judgment by Daniel Frohman, William Winter, and Clara Morris.[38] A change in outlook and a new toleration by at least a few very religious people is illustrated by the Reverend John Dyer, who protested that although he was not a theatregoer he found

> the wholesale denunciation of actors and actresses, and theatregoers, is no longer of such efficacy as it once was. It has the air of an attempt to supplement a weak case by authority or by what somebody calls "Godly bullying" and the day for that is gone by.[39]

Certainly by 1865 the most convincing of the clerical arguments against legitimate theatres was undermined — the one argument that many theatrical people had been unable to deny and unwilling to justify: More and more managers, following the lead of Noah Ludlow, P. T. Barnum, and others, were now beginning to operate successfully without the customary third tier. The practice seems to have been in a gradual decline from the 1850s, putting to rest the old charge that theatres could not be reformed because they could not survive without the third tier.

One striking change in the relationship between actors and clergymen is found in the creation of the Actors'-Church Alliance, an association formed in 1899 between members of the New York City Actors' Union and an interdenominational group of two hundred clergymen to "help the theatre to redeem its mission as one of the great ethical forces of society."[40] Eventually the church in the United States would consciously incorporate drama into its own activities.

Old objections had rested primarily on tangible evidence of vice in the audience, on the reputation of actors, and on the plays themselves, with a number of the clergy condemning all and any theatre because they thought that reform of abuses was impossible and that the very act of viewing any drama disordered character. By the end of the century, all these religious arguments had been undermined. The theatre had certainly redressed abuses in the audience and had gone a long way toward destroying stereotypes of the actor as shiftless and degenerate. Blame for moral corruption in the theatre now began to be laid not on the actor and theatre professional, but on the businessman who managed and financed the shows and, at the turn of the century, on the theatre syndicate. The theatre had, moreover, proven to many clergymen that some plays were not only harmless, but could even be "powerful sermons."

11. The Winding Down of an Old War

Not all the changes that affected the theatre's acceptance were made by the theatre. Changes also came about in the values the church held and in the church's standing as well. And to figure out who won the war is not a simple undertaking. The church and the economic structure it so strongly supported could claim at least some victory in that the clergy's prodding contributed to many of the modifications undertaken by the theatre. And at times the theatre scarcely seems the victor when one considers it had to bribe society with frequent productions of religious dramas and had to scramble for respectability on the church's religious and economic terms rather than its own artistic ones.

At the same time, the church had made too many tactical errors. Its many exaggerations and flights of fancy regarding the theatre had often been exposed, and this vulnerability had sometimes catalyzed a rare and embarrassing counterattack from the theatre as when, for example, critic William Winter was, for a period of a year, provoked to catalogue special crimes, gleaned from newspapers, committed by specific clergymen, whom he names.[40] Obvious divisions had also developed among the clerical troops, and secretive theatre attendance by some ministers left them open to charges of hypocrisy.

That the theatre had slowly begun to win acceptance among the religious public suggests that, after all the hurtful rhetoric, all the impediments, and all the humiliations, in the final tallying, at the close of the nineteenth century, the theatre could claim the greater victory.

Appendix 1: Cornelius Logan's Defense of the Stage

Solomon Smith ends his *Theatrical Memoirs* with a letter written by Cornelius A. Logan, a comedian, in which Logan outlines church objections to the theatre and counters with a defense of the stage. Editorial commentary appeared along with Logan's letter in The *New Orleans Republic* in 1844:

> Sol. Smith, Esq., the worthy manager of the St. Charles Theatre has kindly placed in our hands the following article for publication. Mr. Smith tells us it was written by Mr. Logan, the well-known comedian, in August last, which, we believe, was about the time his own most able and pungent letter to Dr. Beecher was published in the New York papers, and so extensively copied throughout the country. It will be remembered that the Tremont Theatre in Boston was last summer converted into a church, and at its consecration the reverend doctor preached a sermon, in which he assailed with great bitterness plays, players, and all things theatrical.

The following letter will explain why this "reply" was not published before:

> Mobile, February 9, 1844.
> To: Solomon Smith, ESQ. From C. A. Logan
> Dear Sir,
>
> I cheerfully comply with your flattering request to furnish you with a copy of my reply to Dr. Beecher's sermon, although it is with some reluc-

Appendix 1

tance I consent to its publication at this late day. I wrote the reply immediately after the sermon was delivered, and was about to publish it when your own letter to the reverend doctor met my eye. That letter, so admirably written, and so far superior to my humble effort, seemed to cover the whole ground, and leave nothing farther to be said on the subject.

Fully agreeing with you that when the Drama is assailed from so many quarters, all its friends should become its defenders, I respectfully submit the manuscript to your disposal.

Very respectfully.
Your obedient servant, C.A. Logan

We regret that we have not space for the whole of this reply. After an elaborate exordium the writer thus proceeds:

> The doctor's [Henry Ward Beecher] text is inappropriate — it means nothing in connection with his subject. He doubtless searched the Scriptures for a motto, and could find nothing nearer his subject-matter than "traitors, heady, high-minded lovers of pleasure more than lovers of God;" and yet he asserts that the Scriptures expressly forbid theatrical amusements. They do not. No sentence that can be tortured into such a prohibition is to be found in the sacred volume. He admits that the Drama is coeval with religion. If so, it must have been well known to the inspired writers, and yet, ... no human vice or folly escaped the strictures of these reverend characters, no word of censure, even in parable, was ever uttered against theatrical representations.
>
> The doctor enumerates as sinful pleasures "gladiatorial shows, bull-fights, excess of eating, inebriation, and groveling animalism," and says that "the theatre has in all time stood the temple of these Mammon worshipers." Here is a jumble of epithets from which no sense can be extracted. Surely no man ever saw a gladiatorial show, or a bull-fight, or excess of eating, or groveling animalism in a modern theatre. And how can it be called a temple of the worshipers of Mammon? The doctor says afterward that the amusement is too dear to be indulged in except by a few, and surely these few can not be worshipers of the sordid deity of gold, or they would not be there. He can not mean the actors, for if *they* worship gold, verily they bend the knee to an unknown God.

[Here Logan inserts the ancient history of the drama]

> This divine tells us that "the Drama has commenced its retreat, and will soon pass away." Nothing can be more evidently opposite to the truth than both the assertion and the prediction. At no period of the world were theatres and actors so numerous as now. In most of the civilized nations of Europe the Drama is under the special protection of the crown, and in

those countries where letters are most cultivated, and where refinement has attained its highest polish, the theatre *is* supported by the government. In this country, 'tis true, the recent commercial distress, pervading as it did all classes of the community, reached theatrical amusements, and prostrated several establishments whose capital was too slender to bear the shock. The Tremont House was one of these, and Dr. Beecher gloats over the fall of his imaginary foe in a strain of invective that falls harshly from the lips of a disciple of our meek and mild Redeemer.

The doctor next refers to his prediction — uttered, he says, at the building of the Tremont Theatre — "that he would live to preach in it." Let me record another prediction, uttered in my hearing at the same time. One day, while the workmen were shingling the roof of the theatre, I ascended to the cupola of the State-house in Boston, and, on reaching the platform, I found the Rev. Doctor — and two ladies enjoying the fine view of the city. Their eyes at length rested on this splendid temple of the Muses, and the doctor exclaimed, "So they're shingling the house of the devil! I prophesy that in less than *one year* God in his wrath will burn it up with fire!" This false prophet was a divine of no less reputation than Dr. Beecher, and I withhold his name only because, his prognostication baring failed, the disclosure might throw discredit on his future predictions.

The claims of the theatre to holiness will not be insisted on. No; the theatre lays as few claims to holiness as the Church does to comedy — each has its appropriate sphere. The Church is built upon the Rock of Ages, and the Drama is built upon the human heart: the divine truth of the one, and the sublime morality of the other, will find a living response to that heart as long as it beats with a single attribute of the Deity.

The doctor complains that ministers of religion are brought upon the stage to be ridiculed as "dolts, pedants, or dullards." The reply is that *there exist* ministers who *are* stupid, pedantic, and dull; and should these be exempt from censure or ridicule more than the rest of mankind? Should "such divinity hedge" *all* who wear the black robe that they should not be held amenable to the laws by which other men are governed? If there *are* reverend gentlemen who disgrace their holy calling by seduction, adultery, forgery, simony, or hypocrisy, should our awe of the cloth they pollute screen them from the punishment with which the law should visit their crimes, or the satire with which the stage should lash their vices?

"What school-houses, academies, or colleges has it (the theatre) built?" If the theatre added to its other important powers the building or endowing of educational institutions, it would surpass as an instrument of good all human inventions. But, unhappily, its ability is not equal to such attempts. Its means of doing good are crippled by the pulpit. The fulminations of clerical orators of all grades of intellect, from Dr. Beecher down to the poor mad ranter who desecrates the stillness of our Sabbath by his senseless bellowings in the highways and marketplaces of this city — all, all

Appendix 1

have a fling at their great rival, the theatre! Is this unchristian spirit imitated by the theatre? No. Not a sentence — not a syllable is ever heard from the stage that can be construed to swerve from that respect which the Drama ever pays to true religion.

"What streams of knowledge has it diffused? What science cultivated or explained?" Plays, for the most part, are founded on remarkable events in history, ancient and modern. Of the thirty-seven written by Shakespeare, twenty-four may for our present purpose be called poetical versions of well-authenticated historical passages. From no single historian can a tenth part of the truth of any event dramatized by Shakespeare be gathered. The immortal poet frequently drew his knowledge from sources which have not come down to our day. We can nowhere obtain so clear an insight into the characters, motives, passions, and politics of the men who fought the Wars of the Roses as in the plays of this author. Who ever *saw*, except their own contemporaries, the heroes of antiquity until Shakespeare introduced them to us face to face — the living, breathing, speaking inhabitants of Greece and Rome — their warriors, sages, orators, patriarchs, and plebeians? To the man who reads history only, Marius, Sylla, Nero, and Caligula have none of the features of humanity about them. The chief acts of their lives being exhibited unrelieved by a statement of the means by which their deeds were accomplished, they appear like the grotesque figures in a phantasmagoria — fearful from their indistinctness, horrible from their mysterious burlesque on human nature, and alike hideous whether we laugh or shudder at the monstrous chimera. Turn to the page of Shakespeare, or behold his swelling scene at the theatre, and these men — seen, arriving at natural ends by natural means— teach the eternal truth that the heart of man is the same in all ages, and that vice has produced misery and virtue happiness from the beginning of the world.

The doctor quotes Plato as adverse to the theatre. Every man who has not forgotten his schoolboy classics can quote passages in Plato which would make the doctor feel that he calculated too much on the ignorance of his hearers. And Aristotle, too, the divine drags into the argument. Why, every tyro knows that the only laws acknowledged even to this day for constructing comedies are those of this philosopher, who declares that "tragedy is intended to purge our passions by means of terror and pity." And "Tacitus says the German manners were guarded by having no playhouses among them." If that be true, the Germans have thought better on the subject since the time of Tacitus; for one of the modern writers of that nation (Zingerman) says, "We are greatly a dramatic people.... Nothing but good can result from the widest indulgence of this taste among us, unless it happen that the sedentary and imaginative student should, through his diseased appetite, draw poison from the stage, as the serpent distills venom from the nutritious things of nature."

The doctor next invokes Ovid to his aid. Surely nothing hut a design to frighten us with an array of classical names could induce the preacher to bolster his argument with the opinion of the most licentious poet of ancient or modern times. Ovid calling the theatre dissolute! and advising its suppression! Why, 'tis like Satan denouncing heaven from the burning lake, or like a pickpocket advising the suppression of the penal code.

Next we have a list of the formidable opinions of the early fathers of the Church, who were unanimous in their condemnation of the theatre. Doubtless. So they were in the condemnation and burning of martyrs and witches. However pious were many of them according to their unchristian and ferocious notions of piety, their sentiments on the subject of the Drama are not worth a moment's discussion.

The doctor here arrives at a point where the stage seems indeed vulnerable. He alludes to the bars for the sale of liquor, and to the third row.

In reply to the first, I would say, that if men will drink in despite of Temperance Societies, it matters but little where they get the liquor. If there were no bars within the house, the thirsty would most certainly find the stimulant out of doors. And yet bars are no more necessary to the theatre than to the pulpit. I am old enough to remember the time when men would assemble at the tavern nearest the church as soon as the service was over, and there discuss the merits of the sermon and of brandy and water at the same time. The Temperance movement, however, wrought wonders, and I believe the same men do not drink now — at least not until they reach home.

The other charge is a graver one — the third tier. This evil is no more essential to the Drama than the bars, nor is it "an inseparable concomitant of the theatre." The separation *has* taken place in many towns of this country. In Europe, and in the larger cities of this continent, the doors are thrown open to all who pay, and conform to certain regulations. No one has a right to say to his neighbor, "Stand aside, for I am holier than thou."

The third row is assigned to those who are without the pale of society, and the money of these, 'tis true, is often needful to a treasury impoverished by the absence of persons of enlightened piety, whom clerical denunciations deter from partaking of that elegant amusement, blended with wholesome instruction, which can be enjoyed nowhere but in a well-regulated theatre.

The "pants" and abbreviated garments of Fanny Ellsler next fall under the animadversions of the doctor. Of all the dancers that have appeared on the modern stage, this celebrated Terpsichorean is the most modest. In this lies her principal charm. Her dress, necessarily short, to permit the free use of her limbs, is managed with such graceful dexterity, that his imagination must be "as foul as Vulcan's smithy" who could conceive an impure thought while gazing on her ethereal movement or her classic repose; and what a libel on the ladies of Boston and other cities — the refined, the high, and the pure, who flocked in crowds, night after night, in thousands, to behold this fascinating artiste, to say that "her dancing

Appendix 1

might have made the devil blush, and female virtue, *had it been there*, burn with indignation, and hang her head in shame!"

No woman blushes to see the bold and slightly draped statuary of the great masters. The paintings of our first parents in Paradise suggest no indelicate ideas. Why is this? Because no taint of voluptuousness defiled the mind of the sculptor or the painter in the production of his work. His soul, filled only with sublime notions of the beautiful and the true, chisels or delineates humanity without its earthiness and passion — without its grossness. A rising young sculptor who was in New Orleans a year or two ago was desirous of studying the anatomical outline of the living subject. He made every exertion to induce a woman to sit for him — in vain. He sought out at length some of the abject and abandoned Quadroons, whose scanty meal was gained by the most loathsome infamy, and offered what to them must have been a large sum, to stand before *him* as a model for one hour. None could be found to do it. *The blush lay in the pollution of their own minds.*

Our young American, however, had but little right to complain. Two of the greatest masters of antiquity, Apelles the painter, and Praxiteles the sculptor, seemed to have had but one model between them for their respective works — Phryne of Boesia having been the original of the Venus in oil, as well as of the goddess in stone. Caroline, queen of Naples, sister to Napoleon and wife of Murat, stood as a model for Psyche at the Tribunal of Venus in Paris. The lady in the modern case may be condemned, but it went to show that in her lofty mind no impure thought could be connected with the Fine Arts.

Dr. Channing happened to remark two or three years ago that much of the *spirit* of the Drama — that is, its purer portions — divested of the necessary dross of bad acting (which seems to be only as shade in a picture), might be condensed into readings or "lectures": and, lo! a swarm of lecturers, numerous and noisy as the locusts of Egypt, devoured the land. Men of little education and less character committed to memory a few of the simplest truths of Natural Philosophy, Astronomy, Magnetism, Chemistry, and the laws of general Physics, and advertised, to instruct the public at a price for the course of lectures, half the amount of which would be sufficient to purchase at any book-store volumes; that contain not only the whole stock of the lecturer's knowledge, but more extended views of the subject than he himself, perhaps, ever read. This mania hurt the theatre a while, but the unnatural excitement was short-lived. The public has already turned from this paltry banquet, and seeks again the wholesome food spread before it by every well-conducted theatre.

Those periods in history in which the Drama declined are marked by bigotry, violence, and civil war. All the theatres in London were closed by order of Oliver Cromwell, and ten days afterward the head of Charles the First rolled from the block! Terror and gloom hung over the kingdom. The Drama was interdicted — the arts perished — the woof rotted in the loom — the plow rusted in the furrow, and men's hearts were strung to the ferocity of fanaticism. Fathers and sons shed each other's blood; and in the intervals of lust and murder, wild riot howled through the wasted land. Even if permitted by the laws, the theatre could not exist amid such horrors. But the actors were outlawed, and the bigoted Roundheads fixed that stigma upon the profession of a player which illiterate and narrow-minded people attach to it even to this day.

The pulpit too often depicts Virtue in austere and forbidding colors, and strips her of every attractive grace. The path of duty is made a rugged and toilsome way — narrow and steep; and the fainting pilgrim is sternly forbidden to turn aside his bleeding feet to tread, even for a moment, the soft and pleasant greensward of Sin, which smiles alluring on every side.

The stage paints Virtue in her holiday garments; and though storms sometimes gather round her radiant head, the countenance of the heavenly maid, resigned, serene, and meek, beams forth, after a season of patient suffering, with ineffable refulgence. Vice constantly wears his hideous features, and in the sure, inevitable punishment of the guilty we behold the type of that Eternal Justice before whose fiat the purest of us shall tremble when the curtain *falls* on the Great Drama of Life.

Appendix 2:
Cincinnati Daily Enquirer *on the Third Tier*

In *Before the Footlight and Behind the Scenes,* Olive Logan quotes from the *Cincinnati Daily Enquirer* on the problem of the third tier:

> "From the bills of this house," says the *Enquirer,* alluding to the old National theatre, "the public learn that its doors will be closed for the time being, for the purpose of redecoration, etc., and that it will again open, in a few days, with a powerful company. It is to be hoped that if its polluted doors are again to be opened to the public, the management will pursue a different course from the one which has characterized his conduct during the whole season, and give us dramatic entertainments worthy the patronage of the citizens and the public, not of the 'exclusiveness' which has been exhibited nightly on its boards, and which, was of such a 'powerful' character, in connection with the scenes enacted in 'third tier,' by drunken cyprians, as to drive the more respectable and order-loving portion of the lovers of drama from the house. The time was when a 'third tier' for prostitutes in a theatre was looked upon as a matter of necessity; and as long as these prostitutes were prevented from exhibiting themselves to those in the low tiers of boxes, it was thought nothing of. The parent saw no impropriety in taking his sons and daughters to the theatre. The precepts inculcated by the great bards, in the productions of the stage, were considered of a salutary character to the young mind. It made no difference to him how many cyprians were admitted to the third tier, so long as his children were not brought under their contaminating influence, and were not aware of the fact. But the times have changed. We are progressive, and have learned to the contrary. Many a parent has

Cincinnati Daily Enquirer *on the Third Tier*

learned from sad experience that he was in error when he permitted his children to visit places of amusement where free license was given to prostitutes of the most abandoned and degraded character, for we believe it is admitted on all sides that none but the most degraded of prostitutes visit the theatre, and they only to entrap and deceive the unwary. Some three months since, the press of this city in the most unqualified manner, denounced the National theatre as the vilest of 'assignation houses,' and advised their readers to discountenance the house unless the third tier was closed. The appeal to the people was too strong for the management to resist, and the third tier *was closed, with* a promise that it should not he opened again, — at least we were so advised by the stage manager. What *was* the result? It was announced in the bills and through the press, that the third tier would be *closed in future.* The better portion of our citizens took the manager at his word, and once more graced the theatre with the beauty and fashion of the city. The third tier being closed, everything was orderly and quiet; the ear of the wife and daughter was not shocked by the profanity of language and licentious actions that nightly before descended from that sink of iniquity, the 'assignation house' of the National. The warm season coming on, and the greater portion of our theatre-going public leaving the city on tours of pleasure, the attendance at the theatre necessarily diminished. The cause was natural, but the management thought not. They thought the people must be brought out; if they could not bring the respectable portion to the theatre when the thermometer stood at 95, the rabble must be induced to come; and to do this, the third tier was again opened, and an officer dispatched to the low dens of prostitution, to invite their inmates to revel once more within the luxurious bar-room of the assignation tier of the National. Reader, think for a moment on the idea of the management. Is it not horrible, revolting, and diabolical? He seeks to fill his theatre and put money in his pocket, by placing prostitutes in the third tier, that they may, by their temptations, allure the youth of our city from the paths of rectitude. It is nothing more, disguise it as you will, but opening an assignation house on a large scale, and in a public manner; for do not the abandoned women who visit there nightly do so for the purpose of carrying on a trade in the prostitution of their bodies and souls? Most assuredly they do. Our laws are stringent on this subject, and yet, although the police have been busy, within a few days past, in ferreting out houses of a lesser magnitude, the National theatre is permitted to continue on in its infamous career. Some one says the management has the police in his pay, and for fear that they may be deprived of the paltry pittance he pays them, they keep mum. It is, however, always the case in law, — the rich escape, no matter how guilty, and the poor, no matter how innocent, suffer. The rule is applicable to the National. The sovereigns — the people — are, however, becoming awakened to their great error in supporting a theatre whose only qualification lies in a desire to pander to vice and immorality, and are rapidly withdrawing

Appendix 2

their patronage from it. A case in point. Some six weeks since, the Italian Opera Troupe, under the management of M. De Fries, was, through motives which we do not propose here to discuss, induced to take the Lyceum theatre, an establishment which had been closed for some time on account of the disreputable character of the house, produced by a course of action similar to that being pursued by the management of the National. However, on that point our readers are perfectly conversant. Every lover of opera was pained to hear the announcement that the opera troupe were to play at the Lyceum, and the universal prediction was, their performances would be a failure. 'No one who has any respect for themselves or family will go to the Lyceum!' was a common remark, and the poor artists, with misgivings of their success, commenced their season with a comparatively small house. Everything passed off orderly and quietly; no prostitutes were admitted to the house, nor was the ear of the virtuous female insulted by the coarse ribaldry of the wanton. The next day the words passed rapidly from mouth to mouth, 'The opera troupe sing well, and deserve patronage. You can take your wife and daughter without fear of having their feelings shocked by indecencies.' What was the result? The next evening the Lyceum was crowded, and numbers were turned away, unable to gain admission, and so the attendance continued. The troupe left our *city* for Louisville, where they also played a most successful engagement. On returning to this city, the management of the National effected an engagement with the troupe, thinking that as they had crowded the Lyceum, under all disadvantageous circumstances, they would certainly crowd to overflowing the great National. But here they reckoned without their host. The opera troupe came, but the *people* did not follow them. The edict had gone forth, 'We will not patronize an institution that insults our wives and daughters by making a portion of its edifice a common assignation house, no matter how great the attraction. The man, who seeks to put money in his pocket by catering to the base passions of man, is no better than the most degraded cyprian.' The opera troupe, after playing to comparatively empty benches, left our city, we are informed, fully convinced of the unpopularity of the management of the National, and with the consciousness that the manager was one thousand dollars worse off in pocket than when they entered it. The people would not visit a house like the National after the exposition that had been made of the doings of its management by the Press of this *city,* no matter what the attraction. If the management of the National wish to make their theatre such as it should be, let them close their third tier, and put a good company on its stage. Unless they do this, we assure them all their efforts to draw respectable houses will be futile, and the result will be that they will have again to close their doors, at a heavy loss. The people will not countenance an attempt to play on the baser passions of man to fill their theatre. It is an insult to their good sense to cater to their amusement in a theatre by placing apart a portion of the house as a place of assignation."

Appendix 3: Mark Twain on the Reverend Sabine

Mark Twain's "Memoranda," in *The Galaxy*, February 1871

The Indignity Put Upon the Remains of George Holland by the Reverend Mr. Sabine.

What a ludicrous satire it was upon Christian charity! — even upon the vague, theoretical idea of it which doubtless this small saint mouths from his own pulpit every Sunday. Contemplate this freak of Nature, and think what a Cardiff giant of self-righteousness is crowded into his pigmy skin. If we probe, and dissect, and lay open this diseased, this cancerous piety of his, we are forced to the conviction that it is the production of an impression on his part that his guild do about all the good that is done in the earth, and hence are better than common clay — hence are competent to say to such as George Holland, "You are unworthy; you are a play actor, and consequently a sinner; I cannot take the responsibility of recommending you to the mercy of Heaven." ... This creature has violated the letter of the gospel and judged George Holland — not George Holland either — but his profession through him. Then it is in a measure fair that we judge this creature's guild through him. In effect he has said, "We are the salt of the earth; we do all the good work that is done; to learn how to be good and do good, men must come to us; actors and such are obstacles to moral progress."

[* REPORTER— What answer did you make, Mr. Sabine?

MR. SABINE— I said that I had a distaste for officiating at such a funeral, and that I did not care to be mixed up in it. I said to the gentleman that I

Appendix 3

was willing to bury the deceased from his house, but that I objected to having the funeral solemnized at a church.

REPORTER— Is it one of the laws of the Protestant Episcopal Church that a deceased theatrical performer shall not be buried from the church?

MR. SABINE— It is not; but I have always warned the professing members of my congregation to keep away from theatres and not to have anything to do with them. I don't think that they teach moral lessons.—*New York Times.*]

...And so I have said, and shall keep on saying, let us give the pulpit its full share of credit in elevating and ennobling the people; but when a pulpit takes to itself authority to pass judgment upon the work and the worth of just as legitimate an instrument of God as itself, who spent a long life preaching from the stage the self-same gospel with out the alteration of a single sentiment or a single axiom of right, it is fair and just that somebody who believes that actors were made for a high and good purpose, and that they accomplish the object of their creation and accomplish it well, to protest. And having protested, it is also fair and just — being driven to it, as it were — to whisper to the Sabine pattern of clergyman, under the breath, a simple, instructive truth, and say, "Ministers are not the only servants of God upon earth. Nor His most efficient ones either, by a very, very long distance!" Sensible ministers already know this, and it may do the other kind good to find it out.

But to cease teaching and go back to the beginning again, was it not pitiable, that spectacle? Honored and honorable old George Holland, whose theatrical ministry had for fifty years softened hard hearts, bred generosity in cold ones, kindled emotion in dead ones, uplifted base ones, broadened bigoted ones, and made many and many a stricken one glad and filled it brim full of gratitude, figuratively spit upon in his unoffending coffin by this crawling, slimy, sanctimonious, self-righteous reptile!

Chapter Notes

Introduction

1. Solomon Smith, *Theatrical Management in the West and South for Thirty Years*, p. 15 (hereafter *Theatrical Management*).
2. Herman Melville, "The Two Temples," in *Herman Melville*, pp. 1242–1256.
3. Tom Ford, *Theatrical Reminiscences*, p. 13.
4. Oscar G. Brockett, "Introduction: American Theatre History Scholarship," in *The American Stage*, p. 4.
5. David Grimsted, *Melodrama Unveiled*.
6. *Ibid.*, p. x.
7. Benjamin McArthur, *Actors and American Culture, 1880–1920*, pp. xi, xii (hereafter *Actors and American Culture*).

Chapter 1

1. Colin Rice, *Ungodly Delights*; Margot Heinemann, *Puritanism and Theatre*; Jonas Barish, *The Antitheatrical Prejudice*.
2. Jonas Barish, *The Antitheatrical Prejudice*, p. 80.
3. Philip Stubbes, *The Anatomy of Abuses*, pp. 201, 202.
4. Increase Mather, *Testimony Against Prophane Customes*, pp. 13, 14.
5. Henry Ward Beecher, *Lectures to Young Men*, p. 235 (hereafter *Lectures*).
6. Will Durant and Ariel Durant, *The Story of Civilization*, vol. 2, *The Life of Greece*, pp. 178, 189, 193, 200.
7. Tucker Brooke, "The Beginnings of the Drama," in *A Literary History of the Drama*, ed. Albert C. Baugh, pp. 273, 287.
8. Stephen Gossen, *Plays Confuted*, quoted in Colin Rice, p. 20.
9. Anthony Munday, quoted in Colin Rice, p. 45.
10. Colin Rice, *Ungodly Delights*, p. 115.
11. Arthur Freeman, "Introduction," in *Commonwealth Tracts*, p. 7.
12 "A Short Treatise Against Stage-Playes," quoted in Arthur Freeman, ed., *Commonwealth Tracts*, p. 12.
13. Quoted in Augustus Jones, *The Life and Work of Thomas Dudley*, p. 227.
14. William Bradford, *History of Plymouth Plantation, 1620–1647*, p. 29.
15. *Ibid.*, pp. 29, 30.
16. Nathaniel Hawthorne, "The May-Pole of Merrymount," in *Tales and Sketches*, p. 365.
17. *Colonial Laws of Massachusetts of 1672*, p. 57.
18. *Ibid.*
19. Samuel Sewall, *The Diary of Samuel Sewall, 1674–1729*, pp. 83, 88, 95–96, 118 (hereafter *Diary*).
20. Increase Mather, *Testimony Against Prophane Customes*, p. 3.
21. Samuel Sewall, *Diary*, p. 838.
22. Increase Mather, *An Arrow Against Profane and Promiscuous Dancing*, pp. 13–18.
23. Cotton Mather, *Manuductio ad Ministerium*, p.44.
24. Perry Miller and Thomas H. Johnson, *The Puritans*, p. 374.

25. Quoted in William W. Clapp, *Record of the Boston Stage*, pp. 2, 3 (hereafter *Record*).
26. Arthur Hornblow, *A History of the Theatre in America from Its Beginnings to the Present Time*, vol. 1, p. 93.
27. Quoted by Thomas E. Thomas in *The Theatre*, p. 12.
28. W. W. Clapp, *Record*, p. 13.
29. William Dunlap, *History of the American Theatre*, p. 272 (hereafter *History*).
30. W. W. Clapp, *Record*, p. 60.
31. John Hodgkinson, *A Narrative of His Connection with the Old America Company*, p. 27.
32. Thomas Wright, *The Passions of the Minde in General*, pp. 51, 52.
33. Richard Sibbes, *The Soul's Conflict and Victory over Itself*, p. 107.
34. Thomas Hooker, *The Application of Redemption*, p. 161.
35. William Perkins, The foundation of Christian religion gathered into six principles and it is to bee learned of ignorant people, that they may be fit to heare sermons with profit, and to receive the Lords Supper with comfort, p. 231.
36. Cotton Mather, *Manuductio ad Ministerium*, p. 43.
37. Owen Feltham, *Resolves*, p. 35.
38. Josiah Smith, *Solomon's Caution*, p. 3.
39. *The Colonial Laws of Massachusetts*, p. 66.
40. Samuel Willard, "The Christian Exercise," in *The Complete Body of Divinity*, pp. 162–165.
41. For books on the American Puritans' version of Calvinism, see James Truslow Adams, *The Founding of New England*; Robert Merrill Bartlett, *The Faith of the Pilgrims*; Sacvan Bercovitch, *The American Jeremiad*; Ezra Byington, *The Puritans in England and New England*; Stephen Foster, *Their Solitary Way* and *The Long Argument*; Philip J. Greven, *Four Generations*; David D. Hall, *The Antinomian Controversy*; Alan Heimert, *The Puritan in America*; Andrew Delbanco, *The Puritan Ordeal*; Perry Miller, *The New England Mind*; Miller and Johnson, *The Puritans*; Edmund S. Morgan, *The Founding of Massachusetts: Historians and the Sources* (1964), *Visible Saints: The History of a Puritan Idea* (1963), and *The Puritan Family: Religion & Domestic Relations in Seventeenth-Century New England* (1980); Richard Morris, *Government and Labor in Early America*; Keith Stavely, *Puritan Legacies*; Thomas Wertenbaker, *The First Americans*; and Larzer Ziff, *The Career of John Cotton: Puritanism and the American Experience*.

Chapter 2

1. Quoted in James E. Murdoch, *The Stage, or Recollections of Actors Acting*, p. 436.
2. Sidney E. Ahlstrom, *The Religious History of the American People*, p. 96.
3. Henry F. May, *Protestant Churches and Industrial America*, p. 4.
4. Alexis de Tocqueville, *Democracy in America*, pp. 305, 306.
5. Thomas Colley Grattan, *Civilized America*, p. 340.
6. Winthrop Hudson, *American Protestantism*, p. 96.
7. Frances Trollope, *Domestic Manners of the Americans*, p. 107 (hereafter *Domestic Manners*).
8. Ibid.
9. Hudson, *American Protestantism*, p. 100.
10. G. Lewis, *Impressions of America and American Churches*, p. 406.
11. Winthrop S. Hudson, *Religion in America*, pp. 109, 110.
12. Joseph N. Ireland, *Mrs. Duff*, pp. 122, 123.
13. Edward Westermarck, *The Origin and Development of the Moral Ideas*. See also L. P. Brockett. *Woman: Her Rights, Privileges, and Responsibilities* (hereafter *Woman*); Daniel Howe, "Victorian Culture in America," in *Victorian America*; Martha L. Rayne, *What Can a Woman Do?*; Alexander M. Gow, *Good Morals and Gentle Manners for Schools and Families;* Katherine Kish Sklar, *Catherine Beecher: A Study in American Domesticity*.
14. The following are clergymen whose works reflect their political leaning: John McVicker, a church leader and professor of

Notes—Chapter 3

Columbia University, who wrote *Outlines of Political Economy* (1825); Lyman Beecher, a Congregational minister and president of Lane Theological Seminary, who wrote *The Means of National Prosperity* (1820); Francis Wayland, a Baptist minister and president of Brown University, who wrote *Elements of Political Economy* (1837); Orville Dewey, a Unitarian minister, who wrote *Moral Views of Commerce, Society, and Politics* (1838); Calvin Colton, an Episcopalian minister and professor at Trinity College, who wrote *Economy for the United States* (1848); Beriah Green, a Congregational minister and professor of sacred theology at Western Reserve College, who wrote *The Divine Significance of Work* (1844) and *Success* (1843); and Horace Bushnell, a Congregational minister, who wrote *Prosperity Our Duty* (1847).

15. Elijah Parish, *Sermons, Practical and Doctrinal* (1826).
16. Lyman Beecher, *Works*, vol. 1, p. 139.
17. McArthur, *Actors and American Theatre*, p. 130.
18. Everts, "The Theatre," in *Problems of the City*, pp. 45–47.
19. Thomas, *The Theatre*, p. 16.
20. Josiah Leeds, *The Theatre*.
21. James Monroe Buckley, *Christians and the Theatre*, pp 16–18.
22. Herrick Johnson, *A Plain Talk About the Theatre*, p. 6.
23. John F. Ware, *Discourse: May I Go to the Theatre?*, p. 7.
24. William Wilberforce Newton, *Christianity and Popular Amusements*.
25. *Dictionary of American Religious Biography*, p. 40.
26. Ibid.

Chapter 3

1. Thomas, *The Theatre*, p. 30.
2. J. A. James, *The Young Man from Home*, p. 29.
3. H. W. Beecher, *Lectures*, p. 235.
4. DeWitt Talmage, *The Average Theatre*, p. 16.
5. Everts, "The Theatre," in *Problems of the City*, p. 10.
6. Ibid.
7. Ibid., p. 49.
8. Justin D. Fulton, *Theatres and Their Pernicious Influence*, p. 8.
9. Talmage, *The Average Theatre*, p. 17.
10. Ibid.
11. "A Letter to Respectable Ladies Who Frequent the Theater," pp. 415, 416.
12. Francis Wayland, *The Elements of Moral Science*, p. 309.
13. Robert Turnbull, *The Theater in Its Influence upon Literature, Morals and Religion*, p. 71 (hereafter *The Theater*).
14. Stephen Hill, *Theatrical Amusements*, p. 22.
15. Harvey Newcomb, *A Practical Director for Young Christian Females*, pp. 85, 86.
16. Quoted by Samuel G. Winchester, *The Theater*, p. 199.
17. Ibid., p. 365.
18. Fulton, *Theatres and Their Pernicious Influence*, pp. 16, 17.
19. Turnbull, *The Theater*, pp. 37–39.
20. Jeremiah Jeter, *A Discourse on the Immoral Tendencies of Theatrical Amusements*, p. 10.
21. Buckley, *Christians and the Theater*, p. 74.
22. Ibid., p. 75.
23. Ibid., p. 76.
24. Ibid., p. 75.
25. Turnbull, *The Theater*, p. 34.
26. Johnson, *A Plain Talk About the Theatre*, p. 34.
27. James, *The Young Man from Home*, p. 22.
28. Joseph W. Leeds, *The Theatre*, p. 30.
29. Timothy Dwight, *An Essay on the Stage*, p. 42.
30. James, *The Young Man from Home*, p. 23.
31. J. B. M'Ferrin, *The Pulpit and the Stage*, p. 65.
32. Everts, "The Theatre," in *Problems of the City*, p. 11.
33. Fulton, *Theatres and Their Pernicious Influence*, pp. 17, 18.
34. M'Ferrin, *The Pulpit and the Stage*, p. 42.
35. Thomas, *The Theatre*, p. 31.
36. Talmage, *The Average Theatre*, pp. 13, 14.
37. Ibid.

38. Everts, "The Theatre," in *Problems of the City*, p. 35.
39. Talmage, *The Average Theatre*, pp. 27, 28.
40. *Ibid.*, p. 11.
41. *Ibid.*, p. 12.
42. *Ibid.*
43. Dwight, *An Essay on the Stage*, p. 101.
44. *Ibid.*, pp. 101, 102.
45. Everts, "The Theatre," in *Problems of the City*, p. 36.
46. H. W. Beecher, *Lectures*, pp. 245, 246.
47. *Ibid.*, pp. 250, 251.
48. McArthur, *Actors and American Culture*, pp. 64–70.

Chapter 4

1. Some of the first and finest historians of the stage in context mistakenly dismiss the impact the church had on actors and the social ostracism they suffered as a result. David Grimsted, in *Melodrama Unveiled*, for instance, writes that the memoirs of William Wood, Noah Ludlow, and Solomon Smith give no suggestion of their feeling ostracized or belittled (p. 86). Both he and Benjamin McArthur, in *Actors and American Culture* (p. 125), cite the introduction to William Wood's memoir as showing that actors did not encounter active hostility. But Wood, in his introduction, actually complains that he and other actors were socially humiliated, and his memoirs and those of Smith and Ludlow show their extreme bitterness against the church and the religious public.
2. William Wood, *Personal Recollections of the Stage*, p. xvi (hereafter *Personal Recollections*).
3. *Ibid.*, p. 208.
4. McArthur, *Actors and American Culture*, p. 138.
5. Noah Ludlow, *Dramatic Life as I Found It*, p. 57 (hereafter *Dramatic Life*).
6. Francis C. Wemyss, *Twenty-six Years of the Life of an Actor and Manager*, p. 76 (hereafter *Twenty-six Years*).
7. Ludlow, *Dramatic Life*, p. 410.
8. Anna Cora Mowatt, *Autobiography of an Actress*, p. 214.
9. *Ibid.*, p. 445.
10. Clara Morris, *Stage Confidences*, pp, 12, 14.
11. *Ibid.*, p. 33.
12. *Ibid.*, p. 31.
13. James H. McVicker, *The Press, the Pulpit and the Stage*, p. 63.
14. Albert M. Palmer, "American Theatres," in *One Hundred Years of American Commerce*, vol. 1, p. 165.
15. Daniel Frohman, *Daniel Frohman Presents*, p. 44.
16. Ludlow, *Dramatic Life*, p. 347.
17. *Ibid.*, p. 383.
18. *Ibid.*, p. 351.
19. Maud Skinner and Otis Skinner, *One Man in His Time*, p. 152.
20. William Davidge, *Footlight Flashes*, p. 267.
21. *Ibid.*
22. Smith, *Theatrical Management*, p. 61.
23. *Ibid.*, p. 48.
24. *Ibid.*, p. 60.
25. *Ibid.*, p. 74.
26. *Ibid.*, p. 72.
27. *Ibid.*, p. 92.
28. Skinner and Skinner, *One Man in His Time*, p. 68.
29. *Ibid.*
30. Smith, *Theatrical Management*, p. 48.
31. Ludlow, *Dramatic Life*, p. 65.
32. *Ibid.*, p. 66.
33. James Herbert McVicker, *The Theatre: Its Early Days in Chicago*, pp. 17–23 (hereafter *The Theatre*).
34. Joseph Jefferson, *The Autobiography of Joseph Jefferson*, pp. 26, 27 (hereafter *The Autobiography*).
35. Smith, *Theatrical Management*, pp. 13–17.
36. Ludlow, *Dramatic Life*, pp. 175, 176.
37. McVicker, *The Theatre*, p. 42.
38. Ludlow, *Dramatic Life*, p. 86.
39. *Ibid.*, p. 105.
40. Smith, *Theatrical Management*, p. 39.
41. *Ibid.*, p. 52.
42. Ludlow, *Dramatic Life*, p. 57.
43. *Ibid.*, p. 556.
44. McVicker, *The Theatre*, p. 64.
45. Skinner and Skinner, *One Man in His Time*, p. 38.
46. *Ibid.*, p.47.
47. Ludlow, *Dramatic Life*, p. 176.

48. Quoted in Smith, *Theatrical Management*, p. 159.
49. *Ibid.*
50. *Ibid.*
51. Quoted in Smith, *Theatrical Management*, p. 159.
52. *Ibid.*
53. *Ibid.*, p. 175.
54. *Ibid.*, p. 177.
55. *Ibid.*, pp. 209, 210.
56. *Ibid.*, p. 210.
57. *Ibid.*, p. 239.

Chapter 5

1. Joseph Ireland, *Mrs. Duff.*
2. Ludlow, *Dramatic Life*, p. 466.
3. Joseph Ireland, *Mrs. Duff*, pp. 134–141.
4. Brockett, *Woman*, p. 127.
5. Trollope, *Domestic Manners*, p. 175.
6. *Ibid.*, p. 74.
7. J. S. Buckingham, *The Eastern and Western States of America*, vol. 2, p. 395.
8. Trollope, *Domestic Manners*, p. 75; Brockett, *Woman*, pp. 86, 87. See also Matilda Joslyn Gage, *Woman, Church and State* (1972).
9. Will Rossiter, *Temptations of the Stage*, p. 42.
10. Morris, *Stage Confidences*, pp. 192–196.
11. Turnbull, *The Theatre*, p. 92.
12. James, *Female Piety: A Young Woman's Friend and Guide*, p. 1.
13. *Ibid.*, p. 28.
14. R. W. Patterson, "Shall Women Preach?" *Chicago Pulpit*, p. 101.
15. Nathan Beman, *The Claims of Jesus Christ on Women*, p. 13.
16. Frances Power Cobb, *The Discussion of the Character, Education, Prerogatives, and Moral Influence of Women*, p. 121.
17. Justin D. Fulton, *The True Woman*, p. 68.
18. Mari Jo Buhle, Ann D. Gordon, and Nancy E. Schrom, *Women in American Society: A Historical Contribution*, p. 27. For an exhaustive study of women and work in the nineteenth-century British theatre, see Tracy C. Davis' *Actresses as Working Women* (1991).
19. Eliza Farrar, *The Young Lady's Friend*, p. 33.
20. Brockett, *Woman*, pp. 86, 87. Also see Gage, *Woman, Church and State*.
21. Andrew P. Peabody, *Manners: An Address*, pp. 6, 7.
22. John Y. Gholson, *Woman's Mission*, p. 11.
23. Mrs. A. J. Graves, *Women in America*, p. 147.
24. Gage, *Woman, Church and State*, p. 476.
25. Beth B. Gilchrist, *The Life of Mary Lyon*, p. 321.
26. Trollope, *Domestic Manners*, pp. 155–156.
27. Buckley, *Christians and the Theatre*, p. 476.
28. David H. Agnew, *Theatrical Amusements*, pp. 6, 7.
29. Eric Wollencott Barnes, *The Lady of Fashion*, p. 231.
30. Ludlow, *Dramatic Life*, p. 290.
31. Olive Logan, *Apropos of Women and the Theatre*, p. 8.
32. John Harold Wilson, *All the King's Ladies*, pp. 14, 19–25, 72.
33. Rossiter, *Temptations of the Stage*, p. 13.
34. W. W. Clapp, *Record*, p. 298.
35. Davidge, *The Drama Defended*, pp. 13, 14.
36. *Ibid.*, p. 36.
37. *Ibid.*
38. Mowatt, *Autobiography*, pp. 214, 313.
39. Morris, *Stage Confidences*, pp. 192–96.
40. Clara Morris, *Life on the Stage*, p. 41.
41. Margaret Armstrong, *Fanny Kemble: Passionate Victorian*, pp. 151, 153, 184; Fanny Kemble Wister, ed., *Fanny, the American Kemble: Her Journals and Unpublished Letters*, pp. 37, 92 (hereafter *Fanny, the American Kemble*).
42. Barnes, *The Lady of Fashion*, pp. 30, 76, 93, 94; Mowatt, *Autobiography*, pp. 37, 38, 14.

Chapter 6

1. McArthur, *Actors and American Culture*, p. 30.

Notes — Chapter 6

2. Elizabeth Dexter, *Career Women of America: 1776-1840*, p. 224.
3. Buhle, Gordon, and Schrom, *Women in American Society: A Historical Contribution*, p. 27.
4. Barbara Wertheimer, *We Were There*.
5. *Ibid.*, pp. 61-95.
6. *Ibid.*, p. 157.
7. Helen Campbell, *Women Wage Earners*, pp. 216-222.
8. Dunlap, *History.*, n.p.
9. See Richard Moody, *America Takes the Stage*; Alfred Bernheim, *The Business of the Theatre*; McArthur, *Actors and American Culture*; Garff Wilson, *A History of American Acting*.
10. John Bernard, *Retrospectives on America, 1797-1811*, pp. 259-263.
11. William Mammen, *The Old Stock Company Style of Acting*, p. 19 (hereafter *The Old Stock Company Style*).
12. Ludlow, *Dramatic Life*, pp. 470, 619, 715.
13. Joseph A. Hill, *Women in Gainful Occupations, 1870-1920*, p. 42.
14. Mammen, *The Old Stock Company Style*, p. 20.
15. Wood, *Personal Recollections*, p. 406.
16. J. J. Jennings, *Theatrical and Circus Life*, pp. 245-247.
17. Morris, *Life on the Stage*, pp. 58-60.
18. William Halliburton, *Effects of the Stage*, pp. 58-60.
19. Morris, *Stage Confidences*, pp. 134, 135.
20. Olive Logan, *Before the Footlights and Behind the Stage*, p. 173 (hereafter *Before the Footlights*).
21. *Ibid.*, pp. 152, 153.
22. Morris, *Stage Confidences*, pp. 136, 137.
23. Morris, *Life on the Stage*, p. 20.
24. "Miscellaneous Pamphlets," No. 12, in Helen L Sumner, *History of Women in Industry*, pp. 127, 128.
25. Barbara Wertheimer, *We Were There*, p. 60.
26. *Ibid.*
27. William Sanger, *The History of Prostitution*, pp. 452-473, 527-529.
28. "A Working Woman's Statement," *Nation*, p. 155.
29. "Women's Work and Wages," *Harper's*, December 1868, p. 667.
30. Gage, *Woman, Church and State*, pp. 459-460.
31. Horace Mann, "Eleventh Annual Report as Secretary of the Board of Education," *Cyclopedia of Education*, p. 509.
32. "A Working Woman's Statement," *Nation*, p. 155.
33. George C. D. Odell, *Annals of the New York Stage* (hereafter *Annals*); Logan, *Before the Footlights*; Davidge, *The Drama Defended*, pp. 175-266.
34. Mammen, *The Old Stock Company Style*, p. 38.
35. Jennings, *Theatrical and Circus Life*, pp. 241-247.
36. Dunlap, *History*, pp. 70, 120.
37. *Ibid*, p. 148.
38. Logan, *Before the Footlights*, p. 445.
39. Mammen, *The Old Stock Company Style*, p. 25.
40. George MacMinn, *Theatre of the Golden Era in California*, p. 31.
41. *Ibid.*
42. Ludlow, *Dramatic Life*, p. 431.
43. Morris, *Life on the Stage*, pp. 123-125.
44. Davidge, *The Drama Defended*, p. 185.
45. Mann, "Eleventh Annual Report as Secretary of the Board of Education," p. 509.
46. "A Working Woman's Statement," *Nation*, p. 156.
47. "Women's Work and Wages," *Harper's*, December 1868, p. 665.
48. Charles Elliott, "Women's Work and Wages," *North American Review* (August 1882), pp. 146-149.
49. Gage, *Woman, Church and State*, p. 442.
50. *Ibid.*
51. Vera Brittain and Elizabeth Dexter, *Lady into Woman*, p. 97.
52. *Ibid.*, p. 89.
53. Logan, *Apropos of Women and the Theatre*, pp. 15-17.
54. Dunlap, *History*, p. 120.
55. *Ibid.*, p. 148.
56. Mowatt, *Autobiography*, pp. 330-331.
57. Henry Austin Clapp, *Reminiscences of a Dramatic Critic*, pp. 52, 232.

58. T. Allston Brown, *A History of the New York Stage*, p. 112.
59. Morris, *Life on the Stage*, p. 152.
60. Moncure D. Conway, *The Theatre*, pp. 21–22.
61. Mowatt, *Autobiography*, p. 426.
62. Logan, *Before the Footlights*, p. 132.
63. Wister, *Fanny, the American Kemble*, p. 42.
64. Morris, *Stage Confidences*, p. 133.
65. Logan, *Before the Footlights*, p. 286.

Chapter 7

1. Fulton, *Theatres and Their Pernicious Influence*, pp. 10, 11.
2. Patterson, "Shall Women Preach?" *Chicago Pulpit*, p. 95.
3. Brockett, *Woman*, pp. 86, 87.
4. Joe Cowell, *Thirty Years Passed Among the Players*, p. 101.
5. MacMinn, *Theatre of the Golden Era in California*, pp. 70, 80; Constance Rourke, *Troupers of the Gold Coast*, pp. 35–37.
6. *Ibid.*, pp. 70, 80, 82.
7. *Ibid.*, pp. 3, 4.
8. MacMinn, *Theatre of the Golden Era of California*, pp. 91–94; Odell, *Annals*, vol. 6, pp. 450–550, and vol. 7, pp. 126–309.
9. Dewitt Bodeen, *Ladies of the Footlights*, p. 67.
10. John Creahan, *The Life of Laura Keene*; William Winter, *Vagrant Memories*, pp. 46–58.
11. Odell, *Annals*, vol. 6, p. 540.
12. *Ibid.*, vol. 7, p. 255.
13. Mrs. John Drew, *Autobiographical Sketch of Mrs. John Drew*.
14. Odell, *Annals*; Brown, *A History of the New York Stage*.
15. Ludlow, *Dramatic Life*, p. 463.
16. George Vandenhoff, *Leaves from an Actor's Note-Book*, p. 218.
17. *Ibid.*, p. 463.
18. Wood, *Personal Recollections*, p. 70.
19. Bernard Falk, *The Naked Lady*.
20. Odell, *Annals*; Brown, *History of the New York Stage*.
21. *Ibid.*
22. Drew, *Autobiographical Sketch of Mrs. John Drew*.
23. Falk, *The Naked Lady*.
24. Odell, *Annals*, vol. 7, p. 580.
25. *Ibid.*
26. James Willis Yeater, *Charlotte Cushman, American Actress*.
27. Jefferson, *The Autobiography*, pp. 154, 155.
28. Robert L. Sherman, *Drama Cyclopedia: A Bibliography of Plays and Players*.
29. Rossiter, *Temptations of the Stage*, p. 114.
30. Sue-Ellen Case, *Feminism and Theatre*, p. 44; Louise Mason, *The Fight to Be an American Playwright*.

Chapter 8

1. McArthur, *Actors and American Culture, 1880–1920*, pp. 13, 14.
2. Eric A. Shelman and Stephen Lazoritz, *The Mary Ellen Wilson Child Abuse Case and the Beginning of Children's Rights in 19th-Century America*.
3. "Little Infant Slaves of the Arena," *Harper's Weekly*, 19, p. 1009.
4. Fred Stone, *Rolling Stone*.
5. Jessie Bond, *The Life and Reminiscences of Jessie Bond*.
6. Josephine DeMott, *The Circus Lady*.
7. *The Penal Code of the State of New York*, Chapter 46, Section 292, p. 292.
8. Elbridge T. Gerry, *Manual of the New York Society for the Prevention of Cruelty to Children*, p. 53.
9. Elsie Janis, *So Far So Good! An Autobiography*, pp. 22, 23.
10. Leonard Benedict, *Waifs of the Slums*.
11. John Spargo, *Bitter Cry of the Children*, pp. 175–180. Also see Walter L. Trattner, *Crusade for the Children* (hereafter *Crusade*); Jeremy P. Felt, *Hostages of Fortune*; Charles Loring Brace, *The Dangerous Classes of New York*.
12. Trattner, *Crusade*, p. 32.
13. Felt, *Hostage of Fortune*, p. 1.
14. Edgar Murphy, *Problems of the Present South*, p. 135.
15. C. Vann Woodward, *Origins of the New South*, p. 416.
16. David Belasco. *The Theatre Through Its Stage Door*, p. 138.
17. Phyllis Dare, *From School to Stage*, p. 12.

Notes — Chapter 9

18. *Ibid.*, p. 130.
19. Fanny Davenport, "Stage Work of Children," *New York Times* (February 7, 1892), p. 13.
20. Eleanor Robeson, "Happy Experiences of the Child Who Acts and His Beneficent Influence on Grown-up Actors," *New York Times* (December 15, 1907) p. 1.
21. Dare, *From School to Stage*, p. 13.
22. "Employment of Children," *The Theatre* 1, no. 5 (August 1882), p. 4.
23. "Editorial," *New York Dramatic News* (July 19, 1883), p. 16.
24. "Youthful AntiGerryites," *New York Times* (February 7, 1893), p. 8; "To Protect Stage Children," *New York Times* (February 26, 1893), p. 4.
25. "The Society for the Prevention of Cruelty to Children," *New York Times* (December 5, 1881), p. 4.
26. "Editorial," *New York Dramatic News* (June 19, 1883), p. 16.
27. "Employment of Children," *The Theater* (August 5, 1882), p. 4.
28. "Mr. Gerry Says No," *New York Times* (August 27, 1889), p.8.
29. "Editorial," *New York Times* (February 15, 1890), p. 4.
30. "The Gerry Society," *New York Times* (November 23, 1907), p. 8.
31. Elbridge Gerry, "Cruelty to Children," *North American Review* (July 7, 1883), pp. 71–72.
32. "Called Mr. Gerry Whimsical," *New York Times* (June 4, 1895), p. 9.
33. *Ibid.*
34. Gerry, "Cruelty to Children," pp. 70–73.
35. "The Boy Pianist," *New York Times* (December 17, 1887), p. 9.
36. Gerry, "Letter to Col. E. H. Beck," *New York Dramatic News* (May 29, 1883), p. 6.
37. Gerry, "For the Protection of Children," *New York Times* (February 24, 1893), p. 3.
38. "The Society for the Prevention of Cruelty to Children," *New York Times* (December 5, 1881), p. 4.
39. Gerry, "Gerry's Letter," *New York Times* (December 6, 1881), p. 5.
40. "Little Corrine in Court," *New York Times* (December 8, 1881), p. 3; "Little Corrine Free at Last," *New York Times* (December 17, 1881), p. 17.
41. "Called Mr. Gerry Whimsical," *New York Times* (June 4, 1895), p. 9.
42. "Hofmann's Rival Stopped," *New York Times* (December 15, 1887), p. 6.
43. "Freddie May Sing," *New York Times* (August 27, 1889), p. 8.
44. "Mr. Gerry Says No," *New York Times* (January 17, 1890), p. 8.
45. Melville, "Bartleby the Scrivener," *Herman Melville*, p. 647.
46. Gerry, "Cruelty to Children," p. 72.
47. "Denounced by Mr. Gerry," *New York Times* (January 26, 1892), p. 2.
48. "Little Mildred Ewer's Case," *New York Times* (June 24, 1892), p. 7.

Chapter 9

1. See Claudia Durst Johnson, "That Guilty Third Tier: Prostitution in Nineteenth-Century American Theaters," *Victorian America*; Rosemarie Bank, *Theatre Culture in America, 1825–1860*; Rosemarie Bank, "Hustlers in the House," in *The American Stage*, pp. 47–64; Kirsten Pullen, *Actresses and Whores*.
2. Logan, *Before the Footlights*, p. 537.
3. *Ibid.*, pp. 33–35.
4. Dunlap, 407–412.
5. *Ibid.*
6. Moreau de Saint-Mercy, *Moreau de Saint-Mercy's American Journey*, p. 347.
7. Washington Irving, "Letter IV," *Complete Works of Washington Irving*, pp. 12–18.
8. Dunlap, *History*, pp. 407–412; John Murtagh and Sara Harris, *Cast the First Stone*, 1957, pp. 203–205.
9. Wemyss, *Twenty-six Years*, p. 73.
10. Ludlow, *Dramatic Life*, p. 477.
11. Smith, *Theatrical Management*, p. 209.
12. George G. Foster, *New York by Gas-Light*, p. 155.
13. Jennings, *Theatrical and Circus Life*, pp. 60–65; Meade Minnigerode, *The Fabulous Forties, 1840–1850: A Presentation of Private Life*, pp. 55, 151–156.
14. Turnbull, *The Theatre in Its Influence upon Literature, Morals, and Religion*, pp. 82–89.

Notes—Chapter 10

15. Jennings, *Theatrical and Circus Life*, pp. 60–65.
16. Murtagh and Harris, *Cast the First Stone*, pp. 203–205.
17. Ludlow, *Dramatic Life*, pp. 478, 479.
18. "Simpson's Attempt," *New York Herald*, p. 2, 8; Minnigerode, *The Fabulous Forties*, pp. 155–156.
19. "Editorial," *Spirit of the Times*, p. 8.
20. Agnew, *Theatrical Amusements*, pp. 8, 20.
21. Talmage, *The Average Theatre*, pp. 20, 22, 39, 232.
22. Logan, *Before the Footlights*, p. 542.
23. Dunlap, *History*, pp. 409–412.
24. Ludlow, *Dramatic Life*, p. 477.
25. Everts, "The Theatre," in *Problems of the City*, pp. 42, 43.
26. Foster, *New York by Gas-Light*, p. 154.
27. John N. Ireland, *Records of the New York Stage from 1750 to 1860*, vol. 1, p. 29.
28. Everts, "The Theatre," in *Problems of the City*, p. 81.
29. Ludlow, *Dramatic Life*, p. 477.
30. Logan, *Before the Footlights*, p. 510; Turnbull, *The Theatre*, p. 84.
31. Everts, "The Theatre," in *Problems of the City*, p. 81.
32. Logan, *Before the Footlights*, pp. 539, 541.
33. Everts, "The Theatre," in *Problems of the City*, p. 42.
34. H. W. Beecher, *Lectures*, p. 233; James, *The Young Man from Home*, p. 25.
35. Quoted in James, *The Young Man from Home*, p. 25.
36. Dunlap, *History*, pp. 407–412.
37. Logan, *Before the Footlights*, pp. 537–541.
38. Turnbull, *The Theatre*, pp. 82–87.
39. Ibid.
40. Robert M. Hatfield, *The Theatre*, pp. 3, 19–20.
41. Sanger, *The History of Prostitution*.
42. Foster, *New York by Gas-Light*, pp. 154, 155.
43. Quoted in Skinner and Skinner, *One Man in His Time*, p. 116.
44. Smith, *Theatrical Management*, p. 229.
45. Wemyss, *Twenty-six Years*, p. 121.
46. "Who Slew All These?" quoted in Wood, *Personal Recollections*, pp. 1–4.
47. Skinner and Skinner, *One Man in His Time*, pp. 99, 100.
48. Smith, *Theatrical Management*, p. 239.
49. Cornelius A. Logan, "A Defense of the Stage," quoted in Smith, *Theatrical Management*, p. 274.
50. Sean Wilentz, *Chants Democratic*, pp. 53, 54.

Chapter 10

1. Horace Bushnell, "Every Man's Life a Plan of God's," in *Sermons for the New Life*, pp. 18, 19.
2. Timothy Dwight, *An Essay on the Stage*, pp. 42, 101, 102.
3. Bruce A. McConachie, *Melodramatic Formations: American Theatre and Society*, pp. 119–156 (hereafter *Melodramatic Formations*); Tyler Anbinder, *Five Points*; Claudia Durst Johnson, *Gangs in Literature*, pp. 15–45.
4. William Knight Northall, *Before and Behind the Curtain*, p. 72.
5. Lester Wallack, *Memories of Fifty Years*, pp. 105, 106.
6. Irving, "Letter IV," *The Complete Works of Washington Irving*, pp. 12–18.
7. Odell, *Annals*; Charles H. Haswell, *Reminiscences of an Octogenarian of the City of New York*, p. 363.
8. Trollope, *Domestic Manners*, pp. 208, 209, 133, 243.
9. W. Stanley Hoole, *The Ante-Bellum Charleston Theater*, p. 14.
10. Maria Child, *Letters from New York*, p. 175.
11. David Brion Davis, ed., *The Fear of Conspiracy*; and Thomas Frazier, ed., *The Underside of American History*, especially David Grimsted's "Rioting in Its Jacksonian Setting."
12. Ralph Waldo Emerson, "The American Scholar," *The Heath Anthology of American Literature*, vol. 2, p. 1499.
13. Ludlow, *Dramatic Life*, pp. 251–252.
14. Ibid., p. 691.
15. Wood, *Personal Recollections*, pp. 146, 147.
16. Ibid., p. 147.
17. Ibid., p. 150.

18. W. W. Clapp, *Record*, pp. 180–193.
19. *Ibid.*, p. 233.
20. Wemyss, *Twenty-six Years*, p. 98.
21. *Ibid.*, p. 114.
22. *Ibid.*, p. 291.
23. *Ibid.*, p. 146.
24. *Ibid.*, p. 147.
25. *Ibid.*, pp. 200, 201.
26. McConachie, *Melodramatic Formations*, pp. 144–145; Sean Wilentz, *Chants Democratic*, pp. 265, 266.
27. William Leggett, *A Collection of the Political Writings of William Leggett*, pp. 207–208.
28. Walt Whitman, "Democratic Vistas," in *Prose Works*, vol. 2, p. 388; for a description of upper-class theatres and theatregoers, see Peter Buckley's dissertation, *To the Opera House: Culture and Society in New York City, 1820–1860*.
29. Elizabeth Cloudman Dunn, *Shakespeare in America*; Charles H. Shattuck, *Shakespeare on the American Stage*; Benjamin T. Spencer, *The Quest for Nationality*; Arthur Colby Sprague, *Shakespearean Players and Performances*.
30. See McConachie, "'The Theatre of the Mob': Apocalyptic Melodrama and Preindustrial Riots in Antebellum New York," in *Theatre for Working-Class Audiences in the United States, 1830–1980*, pp. 17–46; Meade Minnegerode, *The Fabulous Forties*; Laurence Hutton, *Curiosities of the American Stage*; Wallack, *Memories of Fifty Years*; Constance Rourke, *Troupers of the Gold Coast*; Carl Wittke, *Tambo and Bones*; Robert C. Toll, *Blacking Up*; Jules Tanger, "The Minstrel Show as Theatre of Misrule," *Quarterly Journal of Speech*, 60, pp. 33-38; David Rinear, "Blackface Comes to New York," *Nineteenth-Century Theatre Research*, 2, pp. 23, 24; George Kummer, "The Americanization of Burlesque," *Popular Literature in America*, pp. 146–153.
31. The scripts of the burlesques under discussion can be found in numerous collections, particularly those held by the Folger Shakespeare Library, the Library of Congress, and the university libraries of Yale, Harvard, Illinois, Texas, and Indiana. Also see Stanley Wells, *Nineteenth-Century Shakespeare Burlesques*, and an annotated bibliography which describes plays found in anthologies as well as separate acting editions of single plays: Henry E. Jacobs and Claudia D. Johnson, *An Annotated Bibliography of Shakespearean Burlesques, Parodies and Travesties*. The discussion of the content of nineteenth-century American burlesques of Shakespeare is based on the few extant scripts in the above collections. For accounts of various performances in their theatrical context, see Odell, *Annals*.
32. Odell, *Annals*, vol. 5, p. 44.
33. *Ibid.*, p. 211.
34. Richard Moody, *The Astor Place Riot*.
35. Odell, *Annals*, vol. 5, p. 457.
36. *Ibid.*, p. 471.
37. Quoted in McConachie, *Melodramatic Formations*, p. 68.
38. Richard Moody, *The Astor Place Riot*, p. 179.
39. Skinner and Skinner, *One Man in His Time*, p. 73.
40. William Charles Macready, *The Diaries of William Charles Macready*, pp. 424–428.
41. Skinner and Skinner, *One Man in His Time*, p. 74.
42. James Rees, *Life of Forrest*, pp. 332, 336.
43. Moody, *The Astor Place Riot*, p. 229; also see Alan S. Downer, *The Eminent Tragedian*.

Chapter 11

1. Odell, *Annals*.
2. Edward A. Dithmar, "Margaret Fleming," *New York Times* (December 10, 1891), p. 5.
3. "The Theatre and Public Morals," *The Nation* (February 9, 1899), p. 104; Henry Davies, "The Stage as a Moral Institution," *The Critic* (July 1903), pp. 24–28; "Muckraker in the Playhouse," *Current Literature* (May 1909), pp. 537–540.
4. Henry P. Phelps, "Editor's Easy Chair," *Harper's* (January 1889), pp. 316, 317.
5. Phelps, *Players of a Century*, pp. 408–410.
6. Claire McGlinchee, *The First Decade of the Boston Museum*, pp. 24, 25.
7. Moody, ed., *Dramas from the American Theatre, 1762–1909*, pp. 349–359.

Notes—Chapter 11

8. Ward Morehouse, *Matinee Tomorrow*, p. 13.
9. Albert Palmer "American Theatres," in *One Hundred Years of American Commerce*, p. 165.
10. Ibid.
11. Frohman, *Daniel Frohman Presents*, p. 44.
12. Charles M. Sheldon, "Christian Theatre—Is It Possible?," *The Independent* (1901), p. 616.
13. Allen Lesser, *The Naked Lady*.
14. Barnes, *The Lady of Fashion*; Emma Stebbins, *Charlotte Cushman*.
15. Russell Conwell, *Acres of Diamonds*.
16. Palmer, "American Theatres," p. 164; David K. Dempsey, *The Triumphs and Trials of Lotta Crabtree*.
17. Morris, *Life on the Stage*, p. 34.
18. Theodore Roscoe, *The Web of Conspiracy*, p. 132.
19. Eleanor Ruggles, *Prince of Players*, pp. 185–186.
20. Roscoe, *The Web of Conspiracy*, p. 324.
21. Lloyd Lewis, *Myths After Lincoln*, pp. 137, 156–157.
22. "The Theatres, Etc.," *New York Times* (April 21, 1866), p. 5.
23. "Theatrical Loyalty," *New York Times* (April 21, 1866), p. 5.
24. "The Theatres, Etc.," *New York Times* (April 21, 1866), p. 4.
25. Carl Sandburg, *Abraham Lincoln*, pp. 357–359.
26. Phineas Gurley, *The Voice of the Rod*, p. 15.
27. "Ford's Theatre," *New York Times* (June 21, 1865), p. 4.
28. William Winter, *The Life and Art of Edwin Booth*, p. 37.
29. Ludlow, *Dramatic Life*, p. 693.
30. Skinner and Skinner, *One Man in His Time*, pp. 38, 47.
31. Jefferson, *The Autobiography*, pp. 252, 253.
32. Ludlow, *Dramatic Life*, pp. 699, 700.
33. "A Sample of Priestly Intolerance," *New York Times* (December 29, 1871), p. 4.
34. Mark Twain, "A Live Parson Is Worth More Than a Dead Actor," *New York Times* (January 17, 1872), p. 9. See other notices and articles in the *Times* between December 29 and January 27, 1871.
35. "Total Receipts of Holland Testimonial," *New York Times* (January 20, 1871), p. 4.
36. Lyman Abbott, *Silhouettes of My Contemporaries*, p. 23.
37. Palmer, "American Theaters," in *One Hundred Years of American Commerce*, vol. 1, p. 157.
38. Frohman, *Daniel Frohman Presents*, p. 44; Winter, *The Life and Art of Edwin Booth*, p. 81.
39. John Dyer, "Church and Theatre," *Pennsylvania Monthly*, May 1879, p. 385.
40. Aaron I. Abell, "Actor's Church Alliance," *The Urban Impact on American Protestantism, 1865–1900*, p. 113.
41. Winter, *Wallet of Time*, pp. 631–648.

Bibliography

Primary Sources

Abbott, Lyman. *Silhouettes of My Contemporaries.* New York: Doubleday, Page and Co., 1922.
Agnew, David H. *Theatrical Amusements.* Philadelphia: W. S. Young, 1857.
Anonymous. *The Old Clothes Merchant.* New York: DeWitt's Acting Editions, 1870.
Baker, George M. *Capuletta.* Boston: C. H. Spencer, 1868. First performed in 1877.
Banges, John Kendrick. *Katherine.* New York: Gilliss Brothers and Turnure, 1888.
Beecher, Henry Ward. *Lectures to Young Men.* New York: J. P. Jewett, 1850.
Beecher, Lyman. *The Means of National Prosperity.* 3 vols. Hartford, CT: Printed by Lincoln and Stone, 1820.
———. *Works.* Boston: J. P. Jewitt, 1852.
Belasco, David. *The Theater Through Its Stage Door.* New York: n.p. 1969. First published 1919.
Beman, Nathan. *The Claims of Jesus Christ on Women.* Troy, NY: N. Tuttle, 1841.
Benedict, Leonard. *Waifs of the Slums.* New York: F. H. Revel, 1907.
Bernard, John. *Retrospections on America, 1797–1811.* New York: Harper and Brothers, 1887.
Bernheim, Alfred. *The Business of the Theater.* New York: Benjamin Blotn, 1932.
Bond, Jessie. *The Life and Reminiscences of Jessie Bond, the Old Savoyard.* London: John Lane, 1930.
Brace, Charles L. *The Dangerous Classes of New York and Twenty Years Work Among Them.* New York: Wynkoop and Hallenbeck, 1872.
Bradford, William. *Of Plymouth Plantation, 1620–1647.* New York: Knopf, 1996. First published c. 1650.
Brockett, L. P. *Woman: Her Rights, Privileges and Responsibilities.* Freeport, NY: Books for Libraries Press, 1970. First published 1869.
Brougham, John. *Much Ado About "A Merchant of Venice."* New York: Samuel French, 1868.
Buckingham, J. S. *The Eastern and Western States of America,* vol. 2. London: Fisher, Son and Company, 1842.
Buckley, James Monroe. *Christians and the Theatre.* New York: Nelson and Phillips, 1875.

Bibliography

Bushnell, Horace. "Every Man's Life a Plan of God." In *Sermons for the New Life*. New York: Scribner Armstrong and Co., 1858.
_____. *Horace Bushnell's Sermons*. Edited by Conrad Cherry. Mahwah, NJ: Paulist Press, 1985.
_____. *Prosperity Our Duty*. Hartford, CT: Case, Tiffany and Burnham, 1847.
Campbell, Helen. *Women Wage Earners*. Boston: Roberts Bro., 1893.
Carey, Matthew. *Miscellaneous Pamphlets*, no. 12. Cited in Helen L. Sumner's *History of Women in Industry*. Washington, D.C.: U.S. Government Printing Office, 1910.
Chestnut, Mary Boykin. *Diary from Dixie*. Edited by Ben Ames Williams. Boston: Houghton Mifflin Co., 1949.
Child, Maria. *Letters from New York*, 2nd Series. New York: C. S. Francis and Co., 1845.
Christian Examiner. "Existing Commercial Embarrassments," 22 (July 1837), 3rd series, 4:392–406.
Church as a Theatrical Manager. Boston: A. Williams and Co., 1878.
Clapp, Henry Austin. *Reminiscences of a Drama Critic*. Boston and New York: J. Monroe, 1902.
Clapp, William W. *Record of the Boston Stage*. Boston: J. Monroe, 1853.
Cobb, Francis Power. *The Discussion of the Character, Education, Prerogatives, and Moral Influence of Woman*. Boston: Charles Little, 1837.
Colonial Laws of Massachusetts of 1672. Boston: City Council of Boston, 1887. First published 1672.
Colton, Calvin. *Economy for the United States*. New York: A. S. Barnes, 1848.
_____. "Labor and Capital." In the *Junius Tracts*, no.7. New York: Greeley and McElrath, 1844.
_____. *The Rights of Labor*. New York: A. S. Barnes, 1847.
Conway, Moncure D. *The Theatre*. Cincinnati, OH: Truman and Spofford, 1857.
Conwell, Russell. *Acres of Diamonds*, with Conwell's life achievements by Robert Shakleton. New York: Harper and Bros., 1915.
Cowell, Joe. *Thirty Years Passed Among the Players*. New York: Harper and Brothers, 1844.
Dare, Phyllis. *From School to Stage*. London: Collier and Co., 1907.
Davenport, Fanny. "Stage Work of Children," *New York Times*, February 7, 1892.
Davidge, William. *The Drama Defended*. New York: Samuel French, 1859.
Davies, Henry. "The Stage as a Moral Institution," *The Critic* (July 1903): 24–28.
DeMott, Josephine. *The Circus Lady*. New York: Thomas Y. Crowell, 1926.
Depew, Chauncy. New York: D. O. Haynes and Co., 1895.
Dithmar, Edward A. "Margaret Fleming," *New York Times*, December 10, 1891.
DoMar, Alexander. *Othello*. London: T. L. Marks, 1850.
Drew, Mrs. John. *Autobiographical Sketch of Mrs. John Drew*. New York: Charles Scribner's Sons, 1899.
Dunlap, William. *The History of the American Theatre*. New York: J. and J. Harper, 1797.
Dwight, Timothy. *An Essay on the Stage*. Middletown, CT: Sharp, Jones and Co., 1824.
Dyer, John. "Church and Theater," *Pennsylvania Monthly* (May, 1879).
Egan, Maurice Francis. *The Theatre and Christian Parents*. New York: Benziger, 1885.
Elliott, Charles. "Women's Work and Wages," *North American Review* (August 1882).
Emerson, Ralph Waldo. "The American Scholar." In *The Heath Anthology of American Literature*, vol.1. Lexington, MA: D.C. Heath Company, 1990.
Everett, Charles Carroll. *Ethics for Young People*. Boston: Hun, 1892.
Everts, William. "The Theatre," *Problems of the City*, no. 1. Chicago: Church and Goodman, 1866.

Bibliography

Farrar, Eliza. *The Young Lady's Friend*. New York: Arno Press, 1974. First published 1836.
Feltham, Owen. *Resolves*. London: Pickering, 1628.
Ford, Thomas. *Peep Behind the Curtain*. Boston: Redding and Co., 1850.
Foster, George G. *New York by Gas-Light*. Berkeley: University of California Press, 1990. First published 1850.
Frohman, Daniel. *Daniel Frohman Presents*. New York: Kendall and W. Sharp, 1935.
Fulton, Justin D. *Theatres and Their Pernicious Influence*. Boston: Alfred Mudge, 1841.
_____. *The True Woman*. Boston: Lee and Shepard, 1869.
Gage, Matilda Joslyn. *Woman, Church and State*. New York: Arno Press, 1972. First published 1893.
Gerry, Elbridge T. "The Boy Pianist," *New York Times*, December 17, 1887.
_____. "Cruelty to Children," *North American Review*, 137 (July 1883): 71–72.
_____. "For the Protection of Children," *New York Times*, February 24, 1893.
_____. *Manual of the New York Society for the Prevention of Cruelty to Children*. New York: The Society, 1882.
Gholson, John Y. *Woman's Mission*. Philadelphia: McCalla and Stavely, 1883.
Gouley, George F. *The Legitimate Drama*. Washington, D.C.: W. H. Moore, 1857.
Gow, Alexander M. *Good Morals and Gentle Manners for Schools and Families*. New York: American Books, 1873.
Grattan, Thomas Colley. *Civilized America*, vol. 2. New York: Johnson Reprints, 1969. First published 1859.
Graves, Mrs. A. J. *Woman in America*. New York: Harper and Bros., 1841.
Green, Beriah. "The Divine Significance of Work." In *Sermons and Other Discourses*. New York: S.W. Green, 1861.
_____. *Success*. Utica, NY: Oneida Institute, 1843.
Griffin, George W. H. *Desdemonum*. New York: Happy Hours Co., 1874.
_____. *Hamlet the Dainty*. New York: Happy Hours Co., 1870.
_____. *Othello*. Clyde, OH: A. D. Ames, c. 1870.
_____. *Shylock*. New York: Happy Hours Co., c. 1874.
Gurley, Phineas D. *The Voice of the Rod*. Washington, D.C.: Ballantyne, 1865.
Halliburton, William. *Effects of the Stage*. Boston: Young and Etheridge, 1792.
Harper's. "Women's Work and Wages." December 1868.
Harper's Weekly. "Little Infant Slaves of the Arena." 19 (December 11, 1875).
Haswell, Charles Hayes. *Reminiscences of an Octogenarian of the City of New York, 1816–1860*. New York: Harper and Bros., 1896.
Hatfield, Robert M. *The Theater*. Chicago: Methodist Book Depository, 1866.
Hill, Stephen. *Theatrical Amusements*. Philadelphia: Baptist General Tract Society, 1830.
Hodgkinson, John. *A Narrative of His Connection with the Old America Company*. New York: J. Oram, 1797.
Hone, Philip. *The Diary of Philip Hone, 1828–1851*. Edited by Allan Nevins. New York: Dodd, Mead and Co., 1936.
Hooker, Thomas. *The Application of Redemption*. London: Peter Cole, 1659.
Hutton, Laurence. *Curiosities of the American Stage*. New York: Harper and Bros., 1891.
"The Incompatibility of Theatre-Going and Dancing with Membership in the Christian Church." Philadelphia: Leighton Publications, 1872.
Independent, The. "Approachment of Church and Theatre," December 31, 1903, pp. 31–37.
"Introduction," *Commonwealth Tracts, 1625–1650*. New York: Garland Publishing, 1974.
Ireland, John N. *Records of the New York Stage from 1750 to 1848*. New York: T.H. Morrell, 1866.

Bibliography

Ireland, Joseph N. *Mrs. Duff*. Boston: James R. Osgood and Co., 1882.
Irving, Washington. "Letter IV," First printed in *The Morning Chronicle*, December 4, 1802. In *The Complete Works of Washington Irving*, edited by T. T. Granger. Boston, 1977.
James, John Angell. *Female Piety: A Young Woman's Friend and Guide*. London: Hamilton Adams, 1860.
_____. *The Young Man from Home*. New York: American Tract Society, 1840.
Janis, Elsie. *So Far So Good! An Autobiography*. New York: E. P. Dutton, 1932.
Jefferson, Joseph. *The Autobiography of Joseph Jefferson*. New York: New Century Co., 1889.
Jennings, John J. *Theatrical and Circus Life*. St. Louis, MO: Sun Publishing Co., 1886.
Jeter, Jeremiah. *A Discourse on the Immoral Tendency of Theatrical Amusements*. Richmond, VA: W. MacFarland, 1838.
Johnson, Herrick. *A Plain Talk About the Theater*. Chicago: F. H. Revel, 1882.
Kellogg, Edward. "Labor and Capital" (New York, 1849). In *The Faith of Our Fathers: An Anthology Expressing the Aspirations of the American Common Man, 1790–1860*, edited by Irving Mark and Eugene Schwaab, pp. 388–391. New York: Alfred A. Knopf, 1952.
Larks, The. *The Shakespeare Water-Cure*. New York: Dick and Fitzgerald, 1897.
Lathrop, Joseph. *A View of the Doctrines and Duties of the Christian Religion*. Worchester, MA: Isaiah Thomas, 1810.
Leeds, Josiah. *The Theatre*. Philadelphia: Author, 1886.
Leggett, William. "The Inequality of the Human Condition" (1836). In *A Collection of the Political Writings of William Leggett*, 2 vols. New York: Arno, 1970.
_____. "The Right of Authors," an editorial from the *Plain Dealer*, February 11, 1837. In *A Collection of the Political Writings of William Leggett*. New York: Arno, 1970.
"A Letter to Respectable Ladies Who Frequent the Theatre." *Christian Spectator* (August 1827): 411–412. Vol. 1 New Haven: Howe and Spalding, 1827.
Lewis, G. *Impressions of America and the American Churches*. New York: Negro University Press, 1968. First published 1848.
Logan, Olive. *Apropos of Women and the Theatre*. New York: Carleton, 1869.
_____. *Before the Footlights and Behind the Stage*. Philadelphia: Parmelee and Co., 1870.
Lucas, Richard. *Rules Relating to Success in a Trade*. Boston: B. Mecom, 1780.
Ludlow, Noah M. *Dramatic Life as I Found It*. St. Louis, MO: G. I. Jones and Co., 1880.
Macready, William Charles. *The Diaries of William Charles Macready*, 2 vols. Edited by William Toynbee. New York: G. P. Putnam's Sons, 1912.
Mann, Horace. "Eleventh Annual Report as Secretary of the State Board of Education of Massachusetts, 1847." In *Cyclopedia of Education*, vol. 5, edited by Paul Monroe. New York: Macmillan and Co., 1926.
Manning, William. *The Key of Liberty* (1798). In *The Faith of Our Fathers: An Anthology Expressing the Aspirations of the American Common Man, 1790–1860*, edited by Irving Mark and Eugene Schwaab, pp. 358–361. New York: Alfred A. Knopf, 1952.
Martineau, Harriet. *Society in America*, vol. 2. New York: Sanders and Otley, 1962.
Mather, Cotton. *Manuductio ad Ministerium*. New York: Columbia University Press, 1938. First published 1726.
Mather, Increase. *Testimony Against Prophane Customes*. Charlottesville: University of Virginia Press, 1953. First published 1687.
McVicker, James Herbert. *The Theatre: Its Early Days in Chicago*. Chicago: Knight and Leonard Printers, 1884.

Bibliography

McVicker, John. *Outlines of Political Economy*. New York: Wilder and Campbell, 1825.

Melville Herman. "The Two Temples." In *Herman Melville*. New York: Literary Classics of the United States, 1984.

_____. "Bartleby the Scrivener." In *Herman Melville*. New York: Library Classics of the United States, 1984.

M'Ferrin, J. B. *The Pulpit and the Stage; or, the Two Itinerancies by One Who Knows*. Nashville, TN: Southern Methodist Publishing House, 1860.

Moody, Dwight L. *Moody's Latest Sermons*. Chicago: Fleming H. Revel, 1900.

Moorehead, Robert J. *Fighting the Devil's Triple Demons*. Philadelphia: National Publisher Co., 1911.

Morris, Clara. *Life on the Stage: My Personal Experiences and Recollections*. New York: McClure, Phillips and Co., 1901.

_____. *Stage Confidences*. Boston: Lothrop Publishing Co., 1902.

Mowatt, Anna Cora. *Autobiography of an Actress*. Boston: Ticknor, Reed, and Fields, 1854.

"Muckraker in the Playhouse." *Current Literature* (May 1909): 537–540.

Murdoch, James E. *The Stage, or Recollections of Actors Acting* from an Experience of Fifty Years. Philadelphia: J. M. Stoddart and Co., 1880.

Murphy, Edgar G. *Problems of the Present South*. New York: Macmillan and Co., 1904.

Nation. "The Theatre and Public Morals." February 9, 1899.

_____. "A Working Woman's Statement," February 21, 1867.

Newcomb, Harvey. *A Practical Director for Young Christian Females*. Boston: Sabbath School Society, 1850. First published 1832.

Newton, William Wilberforce. *Christianity and Popular Amusements*. Boston: Alfred Mudge and Sons, 1877.

New York Dramatic News. "Editorial," June 19, 1883.

New York Herald. "Simpson's Attempt." Nov. 1 and 2, 1842.

New York Times. "Called Mr. Gerry Whimsical," June 4, 1895.

_____. "Denounced by Mr. Gerry," January 26, 1892.

_____. "Editorial," February 15, 1890.

_____. "Editorial," April 16, 1865.

_____. "Ford's Theatre," June 21, 1865.

_____. "Freddie May Sing," August 27, 1889.

_____. "The Gerry Society," November 23, 1907.

_____. "Hofmann's Rival Stopped," December 15, 1887.

_____. "Little Corinne Free at Last," December 17, 1881.

_____. "Little Corinne in Court," December 8, 1881.

_____. "Little Mildred Ewer's Case," June 24, 1892.

_____. "Mr. Gerry Says No," August 27, 1889.

_____. "Mr. Gerry Says No," January 17, 1890.

_____. "A Sample of Priestly Intolerance," December 29, 1871.

_____. "The Society for the Prevention of Cruelty to Children," December 5, 1881.

_____. "Theatrical Loyalty," April 21, 1866.

_____. "The Theatres, Etc.," April 21, 1866.

_____. "To Protect Stage Children," February 26, 1893.

_____. "Total Receipts of Holland Testimonial," January 20, 1871.

_____. "Youthful AntiGerryites," February 7, 1893.

Northall, William Knight. *Before and Behind the Curtain*. New York: W. F. Burgess, 1851.

_____. *Macbeth Travesty*. New York: William Taylor Co., 1852.

Bibliography

Ossoli, Margaret Fuller. *Woman in the Nineteenth Century*. New York: Greenwood Press, 1968. First published 1847.
Palmer, Albert M. "American Theaters." In *Hundred Years of American Commerce*, vol. 1, edited by Chauncey M. Depew. New York: D. O. Haynes and Co., 1895.
Parish, Elijah. *Sermons, Practical and Doctrinal*. Boston: Crocker and Brewster, 1826.
Patterson, R. W. "Shall Women Preach?" *Chicago Pulpit* 1, no. 10 (March 2, 1872): 93–106.
Peabody, Andrew P. *Manners: An Address*. Boston: Sever, Francis, 1871.
Penal Code of the State of New York, Chapter 46, p. 292.
Perkins, William. *The foundation of Christian religion gathered into sixe principles and it is to bee learned of ignorant people, that they may be fit to heare sermons with profit, and to receive the Lords Supper with comfort*. Cambridge, 1642.
Phelps, H. P. "Editor's Easy Chair," *Harper's*, January 1889.
_____. *Players of a Century*. Albany, NY: J. McDonough, 1880.
Poole, John F. *Ye Comedy of Errors*. New York: Samuel French, n.d.
R. S. "To the Printer," *New York Journal*, January 28, 1768, no. 1308.
Rayne, Martha L. *What Can a Woman Do? or, Her Position in the Business and Literary World*. New York: Arno Press, 1974. First published 1893.
Rice, George Edward. *An Old Play in a New Garb*. New York: D. Longworth, 1811.
Robeson, Eleanor. "Happy Experiences of the Child Who Acts and His Beneficent Influence on Grown-Up Actors," *New York Times*, December 15, 1907, part 6, p. 1.
Rossiter, Will. *Temptations of the Stage*. New York: J. S. Ogilvie Publishing Co., 1903.
Ryman, Addison. *Julius Snoozer*. New York: Robert M. DeWitt, 1876.
Saint-Mercy, Moreau de. *Moreau de Saint-Mery's American Journey, 1793–98*. Translated by Kenneth and Anna M. Roberts. Garden City, NY: Doubleday and Co., 1947.
Sanger, William. *The History of Prostitution: Its Extent, Causes and Effects Throughout the World*. New York: Harper and Brothers, 1859.
Seccombe, Joseph. *Business and Diversion Inoffensive to God*. Boston: Printed for S. Kneeland and T. Green, 1743.
Sewall, Samuel. *The Diary of Samuel Sewall, 1674–1729*. Edited by M. Halsey Thomas. New York: Farrar, Straus and Giroux, 1973.
Sheldon, Charles M. "Christian Theatre — Is it Possible?" *Independent* (1901): 616.
"A Short Treatise Against Stage-Playes." In *Commonwealth Tracts, 1625–1650*, edited by Arthur Freeman. New York: Garland Publishing, 1974.
Sibbes, Richard. *The Soul's Conflict and Victory over Itself*. London: Printed for R. D., 1658.
Skinner, Maud, and Otis Skinner. *One Man in His Time: The Adventures of H. Watkins, Strolling Player, 1845–1863*. Philadelphia: University of Pennsylvania Press, 1938.
Smith, Josiah. *Solomon's Caution*. Boston: D. Henchman, 1730.
Smith, Solomon. *Theatrical Management in the West and South for Thirty Years*. New York: Benjamin Blom, 1868.
Soule, Charles Carroll. *A Travesty Without a Pun*. St. Louis, MO: G. I. Jones, 1879.
John Spargo. *The Bitter Cry of the Children*. New York: Garrett Press, 1907.
Spirit of the Times (July 18, 1846), p. 2.
Stebbins, Emma. *Charlotte Cushman: Her Life, Letters and Memories*. Boston: Houghton Osgood and Co., 1878.
Stone, Fred Andrew. *Rolling Stone*. New York and London, 1945.
Stubbes, Philip, *The Anatomy of Abuses*. Edited by Jane Kidnie. Tempe, AZ: Renaissance English Text Society, 2002.
Talmage, DeWitt. *The Average Theatre*. Edinburgh, Scotland: Andrew Elliot, 1875.

Bibliography

———. *Sports That Kill.* New York: Harper and Bros., 1875.
Theater: A Weekly Journal of the Stage. "Employment of Children," 1 (August 5, 1882), p. 4.
Thomas, Thomas E. *The Theatre.* Dayton, OH: Payne and Holden, 1855.
Tocqueville, Alexis de. *Democracy in America*, vol. 1. New York: Oxford University Press, 1951. First published 1853.
Todd, John. "Men of Business: Their Position, Influence, and Duties." In *The Man of Business Considered in His Various Relations*, vol. 2, pp. 1–54. New York: Anson D. F. Randolph, 1857.
Trollope, Frances. *Domestic Manners of the Americans.* New York: Alfred A. Knopf, 1949. First published 1832.
Turnbull, Robert. *The Theatre in Its Influence upon Literature, Morals and Religion.* Boston: Gould, Kendall, and Lincoln. 1839.
———. *The Theatre.* Hartford: Caufield and Robins, 1837.
Twain, Mark. "A Live Parson is Worth More Than a Dead Actor," *New York Times*, January 17, 1872.
Tyne, Stephen H. "Men of Business: Their Perplexities and Temptations." In *The Man of Business Considered in His Various Relations*, vol. 4, pp. 1–52. New York: Anson D. F. Randolph, 1857.
Vandenhoff, George. *Leaves from an Actor's Note-Book.* New York: D. Appleton and Co., 1860.
Walker, Alexander. *Woman, Psychologically Considered as to Mind, Morals, Marriage, Matrimonial Slavery, Infidelity, Divorce.* New York: Holland, 1842.
Wallack Lester. *Memories of Fifty Years.* New York: Charles Scribers' Sons, 1889.
Ware, John F. *Discourse: May I Go to the Theatre?* Baltimore: Sun Book and Printing Office, 1871.
Wayland, Francis. *The Elements of Moral Science.* Boston: Gould, Kendall, and Lincoln, 1846. First published 1835.
———. *Elements of Political Economy.* Boston: Gould, Kendall and Lincoln, 1837.
———. *Moral Law of Accumulation.* Boston: Gould, Kendall and Lincoln, 1837.
Wemyss, Francis C. *Twenty-Six Years of the Life of an Actor and Manager.* New York: Burgess, Stringer, and Co., 1847.
Westermarck, Edward. *The Origin and Development of the Moral Ideas.* New York: Macmillan and Co., 1906–1908.
Whitman. Walt. "Democratic Vistas." In *Prose Works, 1892*, Vol. 2, edited by Floyd Stovall. New York: New York University Press, 1964.
Willard, Samuel. *The Complete Body of Divinity.* Boston: B. Green, 1726.
Winchester, Samuel G. *The Theatre.* New York: W. S. Martin, 1840.
Winter, William. *The Life and Art of Edwin Booth.* New York: Macmillan and Co., 1893.
———. *Vagrant Memories.* New York: George H. Doran Co, 1915.
———. *Wallet of Time.* New York: Moffat, Yard and Co., 1913.
Wood, William. *Personal Recollections of the Stage.* Philadelphia: H. C. Laird, 1855; New York: A. Knopf, 1988.
Wright, Thomas. *The Passions of the Minde in General.* London: W. Burre, 1604

Secondary Sources

Abell, Aaron I. *The Urban Impact on American Protestantism, 1865–1900.* Cambridge, MA: H. Milford of Oxford University Press, 1943.

Bibliography

Adams, James Truslow. *The Founding of New England.* Boston: Little Brown, 1949.
Ahlstrom, Sidney E. *The Religious History of the American People.* New Haven, CT: Yale University Press, 1972.
Anbinder, Tyler. *Five Points.* New York: Penguin Putnam, 2001.
Appleby, Joyce. *Capitalism and a New Social Order.* New York: New York University Press, 1984.
Armstrong, Margaret. *Fanny Kemble: Passionate Victorian.* New York: Macmillan and Co., 1938.
Auster, Albert. *Actresses and Suffragists.* New York: Praeger, 1984.
Bank, Rosemarie. "Hustlers in the House: The Bowery Theatre as a Mode of Historical Information." In *The American Stage*, edited by Ron Engle and Tice Miller. Cambridge, UK: Cambridge University Press, 1992.
_____. *Theatre Culture in America, 1825–1860.* Cambridge, UK: Cambridge University Press, 1997.
Barish, Jonas. *The Antitheatrical Prejudice.* Berkeley: University of California Press, 1981.
Barlow, Judith E. *Plays by American Women: The Early Years.* New York: Avon Books, 1981.
Barnes, Eric Wollencott. *The Lady of Fashion.* New York: Charles Scribers' Sons, 1954.
Bartlett, Robert Merrill. *The Faith of the Pilgrims.* New York: United Church Press, 1978.
Bercovitch, Sacvan. *The American Jeremiad.* Madison: University of Wisconsin Press, 1978.
Bernheim, Alfred. *The Business of the Theater.* New York: Benjamin Blom, 1932.
Bodeen, DeWitt. *Ladies of the Footlights.* New York: Logan Press, 1937.
Boorstin, Daniel. *The Americans.* New York: Vintage Press, 1958.
Bowden, Henry Warner, ed. *Dictionary of American Religious Biography*, 2nd ed. Westport, CT: Greenwood Press, 1993
Brittain, Vera, and Elizabeth Dexter. *Lady into Woman: A History of Women from Victoria to Elizabeth II.* New York, 1853.
Brockett, Oscar. "Introduction: American Literary Scholarship." In *The American Stage*, eds. Ron Engle and Tice Miller. New York: Cambridge University Press, 1993.
Brook, Tucker. "The Beginnings of the Drama." In *A Literary History of England*, ed. A.C. Baugh, pp. 273–287. New York: Appleton-Century-Crofts, Inc, 1948.
Brown, T. Allston. *A History of the New York Stage, from the First Performance in 1732 to 1901*, vol. 1. New York: Dodd Mead and Company, 1903.
Browne, Gillian. *Domestic Individualism.* Berkeley: University of California Press, 1990.
Buckley, Peter. "To the Opera House: Culture and Society in New York City." PhD diss., SUNY–Stony Brook, 1984.
Buhle, Marl Jo, Ann D. Gordon, and Nancy E. Schrom. *Women in American Society: A Historical Contribution.* Andover, MA: Manuscript Modular Publications, 1973.
Byington, Ezra. *The Puritans in England and New England.* New York: B. Franklin, 1972.
Case, Sue-Ellen. *Feminism and Theatre.* London: Macmillan Publishers, 1988.
Children and Youth in America: A Documentary History. Cambridge, MA: Harvard University Press, 1971.
Chinoy, Helen Krich, and Linda Walsh Jenkins. *Women in the American Theatre.* New York: Theatre Communications Group, 1981.
Clark, Norman H. *Deliver Us from Evil: An Interpretation of Prohibition.* New York: W. W. Norton, 1976.
Clinton-Baddeley, V. C. *The Burlesque Tradition in the English Theatre After 1660.* New York: Benjamin Blom, 1971.

Bibliography

Cole, Charles. *The Social Ideas of the Northern Evangelists, 1826–1860.* New York: Columbia University Press, 1954.
Conway, Moncure. *The Theatre.* Cincinnati, OH: Truman and Spofford, 1857.
Creahan, John. *The Life of Laura Keene.* Philadelphia, PA: Rodgers Publishing Co., 1915.
Crowley, J. E. *This Sheba, Self: The Conceptualization of Economic Life in Eighteenth-Century America.* Baltimore, MD: Johns Hopkins University Press, 1974.
Davis, David Brian, ed. *The Fear of Conspiracy.* Ithaca, NY: Cornell University Press, 1971.
Davis, Tracy C. *Actresses as Working Women.* London: Routledge, 1991.
_____. "Questions for a Feminist Methodology in Theatre History." In *Interpreting the Theatrical Past,* edited by Thomas Postlewait and Bruce A. McConachie. Iowa City: University of Iowa Press, 1989.
Delbanco, Andrew. *The Puritan Ordeal.* Cambridge, MA: Harvard University Press, 1989.
Dempsey, David K. *The Triumphs and Trials of Lotta Crabtree.* New York: Morrow, 1968.
Dexter, Elizabeth. *Career Women of America: 1776–1840.* Francestown, NH: Marshall Jones, 1950.
Douglass, Ann. *The Feminization of American Culture.* New York: Knopf, 1977.
Downer, Alan S. *American Drama.* New York: Thomas Y. Crowell, 1960.
_____. *The Eminent Tragedian.* Cambridge, MA: Harvard University Press, 1966.
Dunn, Elizabeth Cloudman. *Shakespeare in America.* New York: Macmillan Company, 1939.
Durant, Will, and Ariel Durant. *The Story of Civilization: The Life of Greece.* New York: Simon and Schuster, 1939.
Engle, Ron, and Tice L. Miller, eds. *The American Stage.* New York: Cambridge University Press, 1993.
Falk, Bernard. *The Naked Lady, or Storm over Adah.* London: Hutchinson and Company, 1934.
Felt, Jeremy P. *Hostages of Fortune: Child Labor Reform in New York State.* Syracuse, NY: Syracuse University Press, 1965.
Foster, Stephen. *The Long Argument.* Chapel Hill: University of North Carolina Press, 1991.
_____. *The Puritan Social Ethic: Class and Calling in the First One Hundred Years of Settlement in New England.* New Haven, CT: Yale University Press, 1971.
_____. *Their Solitary Way.* New Haven: Yale University Press, 1971.
France, Rachel, ed. *A Century of Plans by American Women.* New York: Richards Rosen Press, 1978.
Freedman, Russell. *Kids at Work. Lewis Hine and the Crusade Against Child Labor.* New York: Clarion Books, 1994.
Fullerton, Kemper. "Calvinism and Capitalism." *Harvard Theological Review* 21 (1928): 163–191.
Furnas, J. C. *The Americans: A Social History of the United States.* New York: G. P. Putnam, 1969.
Gallegly, James. *Footlights on the Border.* The Hague, Netherlands: Mouton, 1962.
Gassner, John. *Best Plays of the Early American Theatre, from the Beginning to 1916.* New York: Crown Publishers, 1967.
Gaustad, Edwin S., ed. *A Documentary History of Religion in America, to the Civil War.* Grand Rapids: Eerdmans Publishing Co., 1982.
George, Charles H., and Katherine George. *The Protestant Mind of the English Reformation, 1570–1640.* Princeton, NJ: Princeton University Press, 1961.

Bibliography

Gilchrist, Beth B. *The Life of Mary Lyon.* Boston: Houghton-Mifflin, 1910.
Gilje, Paul. *The Road to Mobocracy.* Chapel Hill: University of North Carolina Press, 1987.
Greven, Philip J. *Four Generations.* Ithaca: Cornell University Press, 1970.
Grimsted, David. *Melodrama Unveiled.* Chicago: University of Chicago Press, 1968.
_____. "Rioting in Its Jacksonian Setting," *The Underside of American History*, edited by Thomas Frazier. New York: Harcourt, Brace, 1978.
Hall, Donald, ed. *The Antinomian Controversy.* Durham: Duke University Press, 1990.
Halline, Allan Gates. *American Plays.* New York: Arno Book Co., 1935.
Hawthorne, Nathaniel. "The May-Pole of Merrymount." In *Tales and Sketches.* New York: Library of America, 1972.
Heinemann, Margot. *Puritanism and Theatre: Thomas Middleton and Opposition Drama Under the Stuarts.* New York: Cambridge University Press, 1980.
Heimert, Alan, ed. *The Puritan in America.* Cambridge: Harvard University Press, 1985.
Henderson, Mary C. *The City and the Theater.* Clifton, NJ: James White Co., 1973.
Hertz, Karl. "Max Weber and American Puritanism." *Journal for the Scientific Study of Religion* 1 (1962): 189–197.
Hewitt, Barnard. *Theatre USA, 1667–1957.* New York: McGraw-Hill, 1959.
Hill, Joseph A. *Women in Gainful Occupations, 1870 to 1920.* Washington, D.C.: U.S. Government Printing Office, 1929.
Hobshawn, Eric. *The Age of Capital.* New York: New American Library, 1979.
Hoole, Stanley. *The Ante-Bellum Charleston Theatre.* Tuscaloosa: University of Alabama Press, 1946.
Hornblow, Arthur. *A History of the Theatre in America from Its Beginnings to the Present Time*, 2 vols. Philadelphia, PA: J. P. Lippincott, 1919.
Howe, Daniel. "Victorian Culture in America." In *Victorian America*, edited by Daniel Howe. Philadelphia: University of Pennsylvania Press, 1976.
Hudson, Winthrop S. *American Protestantism.* Chicago: University of Chicago Press, 1961.
Hunt, Gaillard. *Life in America.* New York: Harper and Bros., 1914.
Hupp, Sandra. "Chicago's Church-Theatre Controversy," *Players* (December–January 1970), pp. 60–64.
Jacobs, Henry E., and Claudia D. Johnson. *An Annotated Bibliography of Shakespearean Burlesques, Parodies and Travesties.* New York: Garland Publishers, 1976.
Johnson, Claudia D. *American Actress.* Chicago: Nelson-Hall, 1984.
_____. "That Guilty Third Tier: Prostitution in Nineteenth-Century American Theaters." In *Victorian America*, edited by Daniel Howe. Philadelphia: University of Pennsylvania Press, 1976.
Johnson, Claudia Durst. *Youth Gangs in Literature.* Westport, CT: Greenwood Press, 2004.
Jones, Augustus. *The Life and Work of Thomas Dudley.* Boston: Houghton-Mifflin, 1900.
Kummer, George. "The Americanization of Burlesque." In *Popular Literature in America*, edited by James C. Austin and Donald A. Koch. Bowling Green, OH: Bowling Green Popular Press, 1972.
Lenski, Gerhard E. *The Religious Factor: A Study of Religion's Impact on Politics, Economics, and Family Life.* Garden City, NY: Doubleday & Company, 1961.
Lerner, Ralph. "Commerce and Character: The Anglo American as New Model Man." *William and Mary Quarterly* 36 (1979).
Lesser, Allen. *The Naked Lady.* New York: Ruttle, Shaw and Wetherill, 1947.

Bibliography

Lewis, Lloyd. *Myths After Lincoln*. New York: Grosset and Dunlap, 1949.
MacMinn, George R. *Theatre of the Golden Era in California*. Caldwell, Idaho: Caxton Printers, 1941.
Mammen, William. *The Old Stock Company Style of Acting: A Study of the Boston Museum*. Boston: Trustees of the Boston Public Library, 1954.
Marshall, Gordon. *In Search of the Spirit of Capitalism*. London: Hutchinson and Co., 1982.
Martin, Marty E. *Righteous Empire: The Protestant Experience in America*. New York: The Dial Press, 1970.
Mather, Cotton. *An Arrow Against Profane and Promiscuous Dancing*. Boston: Samuel Green, 1684.
Mason, Louise. "The Fight to Be an American Playwright." PhD diss., University of California-Berkeley, 1983.
May, Henry F. *Protestant Churches and Industrial America*. New York: Harper and Row, 1949.
McArthur, Benjamin. *Actors and American Culture, 1880–1920*. Philadelphia, PA: Temple University, 1984.
McClosky, Robert Green, *American Conservatism in the Age of Enterprise, 1865–1910: A Study of W. G. Sumner, S. J. Field, and A. Carnegie*. Cambridge, MA: Harvard University Press, 1951.
McConachie, Bruce A. *Melodramatic Formations: American Theatre and Society*. Iowa City: University of Iowa Press, 1992.
―――. "'The Theatre of the Mob': Apocalyptic Melodrama and Preindustrial Riots in Antebellum New York." In *Theatre for Working-Class Audiences in the United States, 1830–1980*, edited by Bruce A. McConachie and Daniel Friedman, pp. 17–46. Westport, CT: Greenwood Press, 1985.
McConachie, Bruce A., and Daniel Friedman, eds. *Theatre for Working-Class Audiences in the United States, 1830–1980*. Westport, CT: Greenwood Press, 1985.
McGlinchee, Claire. *The First Decade of the Boston Museum*. Boston: Humphries, 1940.
McLean, Albert F., Jr. *American Vaudeville as Ritual*. Louisville, KY: University of Kentucky Press, 1965.
Michaelsen, Robert S. "Changes in the Puritan Concept of Calling or Vocation." *New England Quarterly* 26 (1953): 315–336.
Miller, Perry, and Thomas H. Johnson. *The Puritans*. 2 vols. New York: Harper Torchbooks, 1938.
Minnigerode, Meade. *The Fabulous Forties, 1840–1850: A Presentation of Private Life*. New York: G. P. Putnam's Sons, 1924.
Mintz, Steven. *A Prison of Expectation*. New York: New York University Press, 1983.
Moody, Richard. *America Takes the Stage: Romanticism in American Drama and Theatre*. Bloomington: University of Indiana Press, 1969.
―――. *The Astor Place Riot*. Bloomington: Indiana University Press, 1958.
―――, ed. *Dramas from the American Theater, 1762–1909*. Cleveland, OH: World Publishing, Co., 1966.
Moorehead, Robert J. *Fighting the Devil's Triple Demons*. Philadelphia, PA: National Publishing Co., 1911.
Morehouse, Ward. *Matinee Tomorrow*. New York: Whittlesey House, 1949.
Morgan, Edmund S., ed. *Founding of Massachusetts*. Philadelphia: Bobbs-Merrill, 1964.
―――. "The Puritan Ethic and the Coming of the American Revolution." In *Reinterpretations of the American Revolution, 1763–1789*, edited by Jack Greene. New York: Harper and Row, 1968.

Bibliography

———. *The Puritan Family*. Westport, Ct.: Greenwood Press, 1980.
———. *Visible Saints*. Ithaca: Cornell University Press, 1980.
Morris, Richard. *Government and Labor in Early America*. New York: Columbia University Press, 1946.
Moseley, James G. *A Cultural History of Religion in America*. Westport, CT: Greenwood Press, 1981.
Murtagh, John, and Sara Harris. *Cast of the First Stone*. New York: McGraw-Hill, 1957.
Odell, George C. D. *Annals of the New York Stage*. 15 vols. New York: Columbia University Press, 1931.
Pessen, Edward. *Jacksonian America: Society, Personality, and Politics*. Urbana: University of Illinois Press, 1985.
———. *New Perspectives on Jacksonian Parties and Politics*. Boston: Allyn and Bacon, 1969.
Poggi, Gianfranco. *Calvinism and the Calvinist Spirit*. London: Macmillan Press Ltd., 1983.
Poggi, Jack. *Theater in America: The Impact of Economic Forces*. Ithaca, NY: Cornell University Press, 1968.
Postlewait, Thomas, and Bruce McConachie. *Interpreting the Theatrical Past*. Iowa City: University of Iowa Press, 1989.
Pullen, Kirsten. *Actresses and Whores*. Cambridge: Cambridge University Press, 2005.
Rees, James. *Life of Forrest*. Philadelphia, PA: T. B. Peterson, 1874.
Rice, Colin. *Ungodly Delights*. Alessandria, Italy: Edizioni dell'Orso, 1997.
Rinear, David. "Blackface Comes to New York: William Mitchell's First Season at the Olympic." *Nineteenth-Century Theatre Research*, 2.
Robertson, H. M. *Aspects of the Rise of Economic Individualism: A Criticism of Max Weber and His School*. Cambridge, UK: Cambridge University Press, 1933.
Rorabaugh, William. *The Alcoholic Republic*. New York: Oxford University Press, 1979.
Roscoe, Theodore. *The Web of Conspiracy*. Englewood Cliffs, NJ: Prentice-Hall, 1959.
Rourke, Constance. *Troupers of the Gold Coast*. New York: Columbia University Press, 1950.
Ruggles, Eleanor. *Prince of Players: Edwin Booth*. New York: W. W. Norton Co., 1953.
Sandburg, Carl. *Abraham Lincoln: The War Years*. New York: Harcourt Brace and World, 1939.
Schorlin, Melvin H. *From Footlight to Candles*. Denver, CO: Old West Publishers, 1941.
Shattuck, Charles H. *Shakespeare on the American Stage*, 2 vols. Washington, D.C.: Folger Shakespeare Library, 1976.
Shelman, Eric A., and Stephen Lazoritz. *The Mary Ellen Wilson Child Abuse Case and the Beginning of Children's Rights in Nineteenth-Century America*. Jefferson, NC: McFarland, 2005.
Sherman, Robert L. *Drama Cyclopedia: A Bibliography of Plays and Players*. Typescript held in Boston Public Library.
Sklar, Katherine Kish. *Catherine Beecher: A Study in American Domesticity*. New Haven, CT: Yale University Press, 1973.
Smith, Page. *Daughters of the Promised Land*. Boston: Little, Brown, 1970.
Smith, Timothy. *Revivalism and Social Reform in Mid-Century America*. New York and Nashville, TN: Abingdon Press, 1957.
Spencer, Benjamin T. *The Quest for Nationality*. Syracuse, NY: Syracuse University Press, 1958.
Sprague, Arthur Colby. *Shakespearean Players and Performances*. Cambridge, MA: Harvard University Press, 1953.

Bibliography

Stavely, Keith. *Puritan Legacies*. Ithaca, N.Y.: Cornell University Press, 1987.
Stebbins, Emma. *Charlotte Cushman*. Boston: Houghton Osgood and Co., 1878.
Tawney, R. H. *Religion and the Rise of Capitalism*. New York: New American Library of World Literature, 1954.
Thomas, George M. *Revivalism and Cultural Change*. Chicago: University of Chicago Press, 1989.
Toll, Robert C. *Blacking Up*. New York: Oxford University Press, 1974.
Trattner, Walter L. *Crusade for the Children: A History of the National Child Labor Committee and Child Labor Reform in America*. Chicago: Quadrangle Books, 1970.
Troelsch, Ernst. *The Social Teaching of the Christian Churches*. New York: Macmillan and Co., 1931.
Thomas Frazier, ed. *The Underside of American History: Henry Ward Beecher, indisputably the most powerful minister in nineteenth-century America, with a gift, it was said, to reflect majority sentiment, was the pivotal figure in the Protestant Church's war on the stageside of Un-American Subversion from the Revolution to the Present*. New York: Harcourt Brace, 1978. First published in 1972.
Viner, Jacob. *Religious Thought and Economic Society*. Durham, NC: Duke University Press, 1978.
Weber, Max. *The Protestant Ethic and the Spirit of Capitalism*. New York: Charles Scribers' Sons, 1958.
_____. *The Sociology of Religion*. Translated by Ephriam Fischoff. Boston: Beacon Press, 1963.
Wells, Stanley. *Nineteenth-Century Shakespeare Burlesques*, 5 vols. London: Diploma Press Ltd, 1977.
Wertenbaker, Thomas. *The First Americans*. New York: Macmillan , 1927.
Wertheimer, Barbara. *We Were There*. New York: Pantheon Books, 1977.
Wilentz, Sean. *Chants Democratic*. New York: Oxford University Press, 1984.
Wilson, Garff. *A History of American Acting*. Bloomington: Indiana University Press, 1966.
Wilson, John Harold. *All the King's Ladies*. Chicago: University of Chicago Press, 1958.
Wister, Fanny Kemble, ed. *Fanny, the American Kemble: Her Journals and Unpublished Letters*. Tallahassee, FL: South Pass Press, 1972.
Wittke, Carl. *Tambo and Bones: A History of the American Minstrel Stage*. Durham, NC: Duke University Press, 1930.
Woodward, C. Vann. *Origins of the New South*. Baton Rouge: Louisiana University Press, 1951.
Yeater, James Willis. *Charlotte Cushman, American Actress*. Urbana: University of Illinois Press, 1959.
Zanger, Jules. "The Minstrel Show as Theatre of Misrule." *Quarterly Journal of Speech*, 60.
Zaretsky, Eli. *Capitalism, the Family, and Personal Life*. New York: Harper & Row, 1986.
Ziff, Larzer. *The Career of John Cotton*. Princeton, N.J.: Princeton University Press, 1962.

Index

Actors and Actor/Managers, attacks upon 28–65
Actors' Church Alliance 172
Actresses 66–102; wages 86–88
African-Americans 123, 144
Albany Theatre 161
Alcoholism 131–134
Arch Street Theatre 95–97
Astor Place Opera House 138, 150–154
Astor Place Riots 150–154
Audiences 135–158

Barnum, P.T. 129, 172
Bars in theatres 131–134, 179
Beecher, Henry Ward 1–4, 10, 11, 35, 36, 38, 39 46, 47, 63, 128, 160, 176, 177
Beecher, Lyman 33
Belasco, David 111, 160
Booth, Edwin 28, 167
Booth, John Wilkes 163–167
Booth, Junius Brutus 1, 132
Boston Museum 57, 58, 81
Boston Theatre 141
Bowery B'hoys 137, 147
Bowery Theatre 137, 144, 147
Bradford, William 17, 18
Breeches roles 97–99
Buckley, the Rev. James Monroe 35, 42, 43
Buntline, Ned 137, 151
Burton, William 146
Burton Theatre 137, 144
Bushnell, Horace 79, 136

Calvinist doctrine 27
Capitalism 32–35, 78–81, 103–104, 135–137
Catholicism 11, 12, 15, 54, 137
Channing, William Ellery 34
Chatham Theatre 137
Chestnut Street Theatre 121, 143
Child, Maria 138

Child labor 108–110
Child performers: Bond, Jessie 106; Dare, Phyllis, 111; Davenport, Fanny 111; DeMott, Josephine 106; Janis, Elsie 107–108; "Little Corrine" 115; Little Prince Leo 106; Robeson, Eleanor 191; Stone, Fred 106
Children 103–119
Church, effect on actors 49–65
Clapp, William W. 23, 74, 141, 142
Conwell, Russell 78–79, 162–163
Crabtree, Lotta 28, 93, 163
Cushman, Charlotte 28, 53, 78, 93, 97, 99, 162

Dancing 16–20; Euston, Edward 18, 19; Stepney, Francis 18, 19; and witchcraft 19
Davidge, William 54, 74, 75, 87
Drew, Mrs. John 95–97
The Drunkard 161
Dudley, Thomas 16
Duff, Mary Ann 31, 66, 67, 76
Dunlap, William 23, 81, 86, 121–122, 126, 129
Dwight, Timothy 34–36, 46, 136–137
Dyer, the Rev. John 172

Egan, Maurice Francis 37
Ellsler, Fanny 313
Emerson, Ralph Waldo 34, 139
Everett, Rev. C.C. 39
Everts, the Rev. William Wallace 34, 39, 128

Feltham, Owen 26
Ford, Tom 3
Ford's Theatre 163–164
Forrest, Edwin 28, 139–140, 146, 149–154, 163
Foster, George G. 123, 127, 131
Frohman, Daniel 51, 53, 161–162, 172
Fulton, the Rev. Justin D. 36, 38, 40, 42, 70

Gerry, Elbridge T. 103–119

213

Index

Gossen, the Rev. Stephen 12
Gurley, the Rev. Phinias 166

Hamblin, Thomas 144
Haswell, Judge Charles H. 138
Hatfield, the Rev. Robert 129, 130
Hawthorne, Nathaniel 18
History, theatre 5
Holland, George 167–171, 185, 186
Hooker, the Rev. Thomas 24

Ibsen, Henrik 160
Irish 137
Irving, Washington 122, 123, 138

James, the Rev. John Angell 38, 39, 43, 69, 128
Jefferson, Joseph 28, 112, 161–163, 167–171
Jennings, John J. 124
Jeter, the Rev. Jeremiah 42
Johnson, the Rev. Herrick 35

Kean, Charles 146, 148, 149
Kean, Edmund 144, 143
Keene, Laura 93–995, 101, 163–164
Kemble, Fanny 90
Kirby-Stark, Sarah 93, 94
Know-Nothing Party 137, 151

Labor unrest 135–158
Laws, antitheatrical 15, 16, 21–23, 26; Penal Code of the State of New York 106–107
Leeds, Joseph 43
Leggett, William 145
Lincoln, Abraham 7; assassination of 163–167
Little-Church-Around-the-Corner 169
Loco-foco party 137
Logan, Cornelius A. 4, 54, 133, 175–181
Logan, Olive 73, 83, 85, 88, 90, 91, 121
Ludlow, Noah 49, 51–54, 58–62, 67, 81, 123–125, 139, 140, 170, 172

Macready, William Charles 146, 149–154
Mallory Brothers 161, 162
Mather, the Rev Cotton 10, 11, 20, 21, 25
Mather, the Rev. Increase 10, 19, 20
Maypole 11, 16–20
McHenry Riot 143
McKenzie Riot 14, 141
McVicker, James H. 83, 93, 99
Medina, Louisa 101
Melville, Herman 3, 5, 116
Menken, Adah Isaacs 73, 93, 98, 101, 162
Merry, Mrs. 88
Merry Mounters 17, 18
M'Ferrin, the Rev. John Berry 36, 37, 44
Miller, Father William 261

Minstrels 154–158
Mitchell, William 137, 148, 149
Moody, the Rev. Dwight L. 150
Morgan, Martha 101
Morris, Clara 52, 68, 75–77, 82, 83, 85, 89, 90, 93, 172
Morton, Thomas 17, 18
Mose 137
Mowatt, Anna Cora 52, 53, 72, 73, 75, 76, 78, 89, 90, 162

National Theatre 182–184
Nationalism 137–154
Native American Democratic Association 137
Native American Party 137
Newton, the Rev. William Wilberforce 35
Niblo's Theatre 123

Olympic Theatre 137, 146, 148

Palmer, Albert 51, 53, 161, 171, 172
Pankhurst, the Rev. Charles H. 130
Parish, the Rev. Elijah 33
Park Theatre 123, 125, 138
Patterson, the Rev. R.W. 69, 70, 92
Peabody, the Rev. R.W. 70, 71
Perkins, the Rev. William 25
Phelps, H. P. 161
Prostitution 120–134
Protestants: and capitalism 32–35, 78–81, 103, 104, 135–137; observers of 29–30; power of 28–37; values 28–37; views of women 66–72
Puritans, English 9–15; New England 16–27; satires of 11–15

Riots in theatres 249–272
Rossiter, Will 68

Sabbatarianism 11, 12
Sabine, the Rev. W. T. 167–171, 185, 186
St.Clair, Sallie 89
Shakespeare, William 12, 42; disapproval of 144, 145; burlesques of 146–158
Sibbes, the Rev. Richard 24
Simpson, Edmond 125, 126
Sinclair, Catherine 93, 94
Skinner, Maud 54, 132, 133
Skinner, Otis 54, 132, 133
Smith, Solomon 49, 51, 54–65, 81, 123, 133, 175, 176
Society for the Elevation and Purity of the Stage 35
Society for the Prevention of Cruelty to Animals 104
Society for the Prevention of Cruelty to Children 105

Index

Society to Protect Stage Children 122
Standish, Myles 17
Stowe, Harriet Beecher 10, 161
Stubbes, the Rev. Philip 10–12

Talmage, the Rev. DeWitt 37, 39, 40, 44–46, 160
Third Tier 120–134, 172, 179, 182–84
Thomas, the Rev. Ebenezer 35, 38, 44
Tocqueville, Alexis de 29, 30
Tremont Temple 1–3, 40
Tremont Theatre 1–4, 36, 128, 177
Trollope, Frances 30, 31, 67, 68, 138
Turnbull, the Rev. Robert 41, 42, 68, 69, 124, 129
Twain, Mark 55, 171, 185, 186

Uncle Tom's Cabin 161

Violence in theatres 135–154

Wallace, General Lew 161

Wallack, Lester 81, 87
Wallack's Theatre 81, 87
Walnut Street riot 144
Walnut Street Theatre 144
Ware, John F. 35
Watkins, Harry 54, 57, 62, 132, 133, 152
Wayland, the Rev. Frances 41
Weymss, Francis 51, 52, 123, 132, 142, 143
Whitman, Walt 145
Willard, the Rev. Samuel 27
Winter, William 172, 173
Witchcraft 19
Woman's place 66–72
Women and capitalism 77–81
Women and the clergy 56–68
Women and work 77–91; salaries 85–86
Women managers 92–97
Women playwrights 99–102
Wood, William 49–51, 132, 139, 140, 143
Working Classes and class conflict 33, 34, 78–81, 135–158

www.ingramcontent.com/pod-product-compliance
Lightning Source LLC
Chambersburg PA
CBHW032055300426
44116CB00007B/747